Write for
Mathematics

Second Edition

Write for
Mathematics

Second Edition

Andrew Rothstein

Evelyn Rothstein

Gerald Lauber

CORWIN PRESS
A SAGE Publications Company
Thousand Oaks, California

For information:

Corwin Press, Inc.
A Sage Publications Company
2455 Teller Road
Thousand Oaks, California 91320
www.corwinpress.com

Sage Publications Ltd.
1 Oliver's Yard
55 City Road
London EC1Y 1SP
United Kingdom

Sage Publications India Pvt. Ltd.
B-42, Panchsheel Enclave
Post Box 4109
New Delhi 110 017 India

Printed in the United States of America.

This book is printed on acid-free paper.

Library of Congress Cataloging-in-Publication Data

Rothstein, Andrew, Ph. D.
Write for mathematics.– 2nd ed. / Andrew Rothstein, Evelyn Rothstein, Gerald Lauber.
       p. cm.
Evelyn Rothstein's name appears first on the previous ed.
Includes bibliographical references and index.
ISBN 1-4129-3993-3 or 978-1-4129-3993-5 (cloth : acid-free paper) — ISBN 1-4129-3994-1 or 978-1-4129-3994-2 (pbk. : acid-free paper)
   1. Mathematics—Study and teaching (Elementary) 2. Mathematics—Study and teaching (Middle school) 3. Technical writing. I. Rothstein, Evelyn. II. Lauber, Gerald. III. Title.
QA135.6.R67 2007
372.7—dc22   2006007321

06   07   08   09   10   10 9 8 7 6 5 4 3 2 1

Acquisitions Editor:	Cathy Hernandez
Editorial Assistant:	Charline Wu
Production Editor:	Kate Peterson
Copy Editor:	Diana Breti
Typesetter:	C&M Digitals (P) Ltd.
Indexer:	Kathy Paparchontis
Cover Designer:	Lisa Miller

Contents

Preface

In 2003, when *Write for Mathematics* was first published, the relationship between school mathematics and writing was just emerging. Research on whether students' explanations of mathematical problems enhanced mathematical understanding was only a few years old, and state standards on communicating in mathematics were just finding their way into the curriculum. Today, there is little doubt that writing and mathematics are inextricably linked. The issue now is how teachers who are focusing on teaching mathematics also instruct their students on writing for mathematics.

Prior to writing this book, we veered towards the language side of the curriculum, developing and presenting strategies that would help teachers actively teach students to write. Our work with schools in implementing *Write for Mathematics* led us to reorganize sections of this book to make the linkage between writing and mathematical content more balanced. In our workshops for teachers and in our classroom demonstration lessons, we emphasized the importance of words and their meanings in the context of mathematics. We believed, and still do, that knowing the vocabulary of the subject is the first layer of fluency. To be fluent in a subject is to know how to "talk about" it or express your ideas.

A second and concurrent aspect of fluency is organization. Organization includes putting the words into context, sentences, paragraphs, and essays. Organization includes understanding the typical organizational structures of genres in which mathematical thinking appears. It also entails making the writing clear and appropriate for the audience. We condensed this thinking into a formula: Writing = Organization + Fluency.

The first edition of this book was well received, and we are pleased that teachers across the country are now applying the strategies. In preparation for the second edition, a substantial peer review of the first edition was conducted. The group of experts both validated the approach and offered excellent suggestions for this new edition. We have taken their guidance and advice to make modifications that we believe have made this edition even more focused and practical. We have also responded to ideas that emerged as a result our own work in the field with teachers and students across the country.

If this is your first copy of *Write for Mathematics*, we hope you will find it useful and beneficial for your students. For those of you buying your second copy, we thank you for your continued interest in integrating writing and mathematics. We believe you will find new ideas here that will further expand your repertoire.

Publisher's Acknowledgments

Corwin Press gratefully acknowledges the contributions of the following reviewers:

Deidre Austen, Fourth-Grade Teacher
Lutherville Laboratory for Science, Mathematics, and Communications
Lutherville, MD

Dawn Brailsford, Middle School Mathematics Teacher
Murray Middle School
St. Augustine, FL

Marilyn Brown, Eighth- and Ninth-Grade Mathematics Teacher
Northwest Junior High School
Meridian, MS

Dewey Gottlieb, Mathematics Resource Teacher
Pearl City High School
Pearl City, HI

Christina Hunter, Instructional Coach
Sara Collins Elementary
Greenville, SC

Faith Kline, Curriculum Coordinator
Wailupe Valley Elementary School
Honolulu, HI

Vicky L. Kouba, Professor of Educational Theory and Practice
The University at Albany, State University of New York

Sarah Lamb, Eighth-Grade Mathematics Teacher
Owensboro Middle School
Owensboro, KY

About the Authors

 **Andrew Rothstein** has had a distinguished career as a teacher, administrator, and researcher. His diverse and enriching experiences in international schools, special education, public schools, and consulting have given him a broad perspective of the contexts in which children learn. As an author and presenter, he has achieved wide acclaim for his work in improving school performance by focusing on improving instruction and its supervision. His work in integrating many subject areas through writing has been highly effective in improving test scores in districts across the country. Dr. Rothstein earned a master's degree in special education from the University of North Carolina at Chapel Hill and a doctorate in educational administration from New York University. As principal, Dr. Rothstein led site-based improvements that resulted in strong increases in student academic performance. While superintendent of a regional school serving children with severe physical disabilities and health impairments, Dr. Rothstein reorganized staff development, created new curricula, and integrated technology into the instructional program for children from pre-kindergarten through high school. Dr. Rothstein has been an adjunct professor at Southern Connecticut State University and Touro College. In his current position as Curriculum Manager for the National Academy Foundation, Dr. Rothstein oversees the development of the national curriculum for the academy.

 **Evelyn Rothstein** has been an educational consultant specializing in teaching writing across the curriculum for the past 20 years. With a background in classroom teaching and a specialization in linguistics and language development, she has trained teachers and implemented her strategy-based Writing as Learning and Write for Mathematics programs in hundreds of schools and school districts throughout the United States. Dr. Rothstein is a graduate of the City University of New York and Teachers College, Columbia University, with degrees in education, speech, reading, and psycholinguistics. She is the author of numerous books and articles, including *Teaching Writing, Staying at the Top, Creative Writes,* and *Easy Writer.* She is currently working on her next book, *Grammar That Works,* as co-author with her son Andrew Rothstein, as well as a series of children's books.

 **Gerald Lauber**, currently Chief Operating Officer of the National Urban Alliance, previously served as superintendent in three New York State school districts, where he initiated programs to meet the needs of diverse student populations while stabilizing long-range fiscal plans. Under his administration, state-of-the-art computer-assisted instructional programs, as well as innovative writing and mathematics programs, were put into place. As president and CEO of Purewater Sciences and Melric Technologies, he developed a corporate perspective on what schools must provide to prepare children for success in the workplace and the world in which they live. Dr. Lauber's writings have appeared in *Electronic School*, *THE Journal*, *American School Boards Journal*, *New York Slate Education*, *Viewpoints*, *Newsday*, and other publications. Dr. Lauber co-authored *Writing as Learning* and *Write for Mathematics* and makes numerous presentations for school districts across the country. Dr. Lauber has an MA and MEd in school administration from Teachers College and an EdD in systems administration from New York University.

1

Writing and Mathematics

An Introduction

"Would you tell me please, which way I ought to go from here?" asked Alice.

"That depends a good deal on where you want to get to," said the Cat.

—*Alice's Adventures in Wonderland*
(Carroll, 1965a, p. 71)

Instructional programs from prekindergarten through grade 12 should enable all students to

- organize and consolidate their mathematical thinking through communication;
- communicate their mathematical thinking coherently and clearly to peers, teachers, and others;
- analyze and evaluate the mathematical thinking and strategies of others;
- use the language of mathematics to express mathematical ideas precisely. (National Council of Teachers of Mathematics [NCTM], 2000, p. 159)

> Imagine a classroom, a school, or a school district where all the students have access to high-quality, engaging mathematics instruction. . . . Alone or in groups and with access to technology, they work productively and reflectively, with the skilled guidance of their teachers. Orally *and in writing* [italics added], students communicate their ideas and results effectively. (NCTM, 2000, p. 3)

THE PURPOSE OF THIS BOOK

The primary purpose of *Write for Mathematics* is to help you *teach* your students how to communicate in mathematics and with mathematics so that they develop the deepest possible understanding and application of this essential subject.

We have written this book for elementary and secondary school teachers who are being asked to integrate what were once assumed to be two different and even disparate subjects—mathematics and writing—and who may find themselves unprepared for this daunting task. We focus primarily on teaching students how to write for mathematics and about mathematics, an idea that has captured educators' interest over the past 20 years or so (Meier & Rishel, 1998) and is now included as part of mathematics assessment throughout the nation (NCTM, 2004).

WHY WRITE IN MATHEMATICS?

The benefits of linking writing with mathematics are cited in numerous books and periodicals. McLoughlin (1998) explains that teachers who ask their students to write about mathematics are able to

- gain insight into their students' mathematical thinking,
- diagnose their students' misconceptions,
- assess students' study habits and attitudes, and
- evaluate their own teaching techniques.

Among the principles for school mathematics cited in *Principles and Standards for School Mathematics* (NCTM, 2000) are learning and assessment. Learning means "understanding" and assessment must "furnish useful information to both teachers and students" (p. 11). It is through writing, as well as through algorithms, that students can gain and show their understanding and provide others with "useful information."

Yet many teachers worry that if they teach writing during mathematics time, they may take away instructional time from mathematics itself. Teachers of mathematics worry about "correcting" writing and spending time going over students' papers. They are concerned (understandably) about taking the role of the language arts or English teachers and thinking about grammar and punctuation and format. However, research by Gopen and Smith (1990) indicates that teachers can cover "the [mathematics] material" and "incorporate writing assignments . . . with significant success and without unduly burdensome effort" (p. 18). This research has also been corroborated by Reeves (2002) and Burns (1992). However, teachers also need to have an understanding of the tools or strategies of writing (see Rothstein & Lauber, 2000). Mathematics, after all, is a written language and mathematicians write about mathematics. Miller (1991) focuses on the advantages of teaming mathematics with writing and points out that "because writing leads people to think, improved mastery of mathematics concepts and skills is possible if students are asked to write about their understanding" (p. 520). Writing about a topic requires students to internalize important concepts as well as analyze, compare facts, and synthesize information (Kennedy, 1980). Studies by Freeman and Murphy (1992), Johnson (1983), and Rishel (1991, 1993) indicate that the integration of writing with mathematics fosters greater student interest and higher student achievement levels in mathematics.

By systematically merging writing with mathematics in every grade, students learn to think mathematically as well as express their mathematical ideas and concepts. Now that schools have declared that writing and mathematics are a "team," teachers need to have a wide range of writing strategies that are *specifically suited* to mathematics and that clearly integrate what needs to be taught in mathematics with the writing activities. We believe that this book will provide you with many of these strategies.

Concerns of Mathematics Teachers

Only a few years ago, school administrators felt they had to apologize to mathematics teachers who were required to attend writing workshops. Today, however, "students at all levels are being asked to write in their mathematics classes" and future mathematics teachers studying in universities across the country are required to pass writing assignments that are over 400 words in length (Brewster, Fleron, Giuliano, Hoagland, & Rothermel, 2000). Less than a generation ago, writing (and its handmaidens—spelling, grammar, word usage, and punctuation) was the domain of English or language arts teachers and possibly a minor concern of social studies teachers. Mathematics teachers (or those who taught mathematics within the total curriculum) had enough to do when teaching students to solve word problems without asking them to construct word problems. These teachers asked, How important is it for students to write about mathematics if they have difficulty understanding the basics of mathematics? Even those mathematics teachers who recognized the value of writing in mathematics asked, Is it my responsibility to correct, grade, and comment on my students' compositions? Above all, with so much difficult material to cover and with so much drill and skill required, how much time could—or should—be set aside for writing in mathematics? How is it possible for teachers to meet state curriculum standards that require students to "become mathematically confident by communicating and reasoning mathematically, by applying mathematics in real world settings, by solving problems through the integrated study of number systems, geometry, algebra, data analysis, probability, and trigonometry" or to "apply technological knowledge and skills to design, construct, use, and evaluate products and systems to satisfy human and environmental needs" (Barker et al., 1996, p. 1)?

Standards such as those listed above seem overwhelming, especially when mathematics is only one part of an already demanding curriculum. Even more overwhelming is the requirement that students must now "write" for mathematics with clarity and comprehension, using appropriate syntax and written conventions. This demand is an extra heavy burden since most teachers—both elementary and secondary—have seen themselves as either teaching mathematics or teaching language. Rarely can teachers recall their English teachers explaining how to write statements in algebra or geometry or their mathematics teachers helping them write a comparative essay on the mathematical efficacy of Roman numerals versus Arabic numerals.

THINKING AND MATHEMATICS

No one doubts that mathematics requires thinking, yet the relationship of thinking to mathematics is not always spelled out either to the teacher or the students. Strong, Silver, and Perini (2001) denote five key areas of thinking: knowledge acquisition, inquiry, problem solving, communication, and reflection. They then apply these areas to mathematics. Figure 1.1 shows the five key areas applied to a student learning multiplication.

Hirsch (1996) emphasizes the reciprocal relationship between automatic mastery of repeated lower-level activities and higher-order thinking skills mediated by "particular vocabulary meanings" (p. 151). In mathematics, "the repeated grammar-like operations [are] rules, and the more vocabulary-like, content-area [are] schemas" (p. 151). According to Hirsch, "the development of math skills with the . . . development of communication/learning skills suggests . . . a general structure for real-world problem solving and critical thinking skills" (p. 151). Combining writing with mathematics is a natural partnership for achieving the high-level standards of learning and thinking that schools are seeking.

MATHEMATICS AND STANDARDS

As states began implementing performance standards in all subjects, they looked more closely at what students need to know and be able to do in a complex, technological society. In *Promises to Keep* (Wurtz & Malcolm, 1993) and *Performance Standards* (National Center on Education and the Economy [NCEE], 1995), performance standards are described as a "social compact" with students. This compact promises students a quality education and the means to apply what they have learned in school to their careers and other aspects of their lives. In mathematics, this application (termed "applied learning" in the above documents) focuses on "helping students to be productive members of society, as individuals who apply the knowledge gained in school . . . to analyze problems and propose solutions, to *communicate effectively* [italics added] and coordinate action with others, and to use the tools of the information age workplace" (Rizzo et al., 1998, p. 5). In *Principles and Standards*, the first principle is "equity," which is defined as "high expectations and strong support for all students" (NCTM, 2000, p. 11).

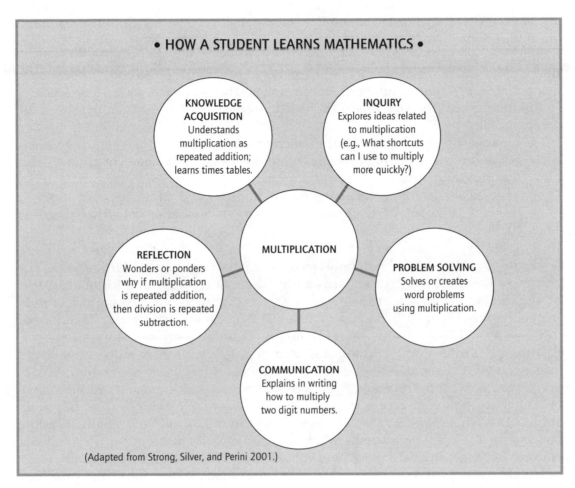

Figure 1.1

The National Council of Teachers of Mathematics (NCTM, 2000), the leading educational organization representing mathematics teachers, also explains the societal needs for mathematics:

- mathematical literacy for everyday life,
- cultural literacy (understanding the historical/cultural significance of mathematics),
- mathematical literacy for the workplace, and
- mathematical literacy for scientific and technical careers (pp. 3–4).

In addition, the NCTM (2000) makes the following comments that relate to writing in mathematics:

- As students learn mathematics, they will develop an increasing repertoire of problem-solving skills, a wide range of mathematical "habits of the mind," and increasing sophistication in mathematical argument.
- Also students should become proficient in expressing themselves mathematically, both orally and in writing, gaining fluency in the language of mathematics and being able to make connections within mathematics and from mathematics to other disciplines. (p. 1)

The NCTM (2000) created 10 standards for mathematics instruction. The standards are divided into two categories: content standards and process standards. In organizing *Write for Mathematics,* we drew particularly from the eighth standard because this standard requires mathematics instructional programs to use communication to foster a deeper understanding of mathematics. This standard states that students from kindergarten through grade 12 should be able to

- organize and consolidate their mathematical thinking through communication;
- communicate their mathematical thinking coherently and clearly to peers, teachers, and others;
- analyze and evaluate the mathematical thinking and strategies of others;
- use the language of mathematics to express mathematical ideas precisely. (p. 59)

Write for Mathematics not only focuses on the eighth standard, but it also addresses the other NCTM standards within the context of writing for mathematics by organizing these standards into 10 strategies that incorporate a variety of writing genres (see Figure 1.2: Planning Wheel). The first seven strategies—Taxonomies; Composing With Keywords; Metacognition; Defining Format; Morphology and Etymology; Profiles and Frames; and Reasons, Procedures, Results—specifically target the NCTM standards. The first four strategies focus largely on terminology and vocabulary; the Profiles and Frames and Reasons, Procedures, Results focus on different types or genres of mathematical writing products. The last three strategies—Who's Who in Mathematics, Where in the World, and Personifications and Interactions—guide students in relating mathematics to everyday life, students' cultural heritage, the workplace, and the scientific and technical community (cited in NCTM, 2000, p. 4). When these strategies are systematically taught and practiced, students will become mathematically literate. Chapters 2 through 11 address and expand upon each of these 10 strategies.

WRITING STRATEGIES RELATED TO THE TEACHING OF MATHEMATICS

In our earlier book, *Writing as Learning* (Rothstein & Lauber, 2000), we explained that learning to write requires fluency plus organization. Simply stated, a writer must know the language of the subject or topic and must know the different types of organizational schema (also called genres) that are appropriate for specific subject-area writing. In social studies, for example, students studying the pilgrims need to know the vocabulary related to the pilgrims: England, religious freedom, colony, compact, native population, and so forth. If students do not understand this specialized vocabulary, they will view the story of the pilgrims as merely an American legend repeated each fall. To further understand the story, the students must express their knowledge in a variety of writing forms: explanation, narrative, biography, personal, poetic, and more. In mathematics, "developing fluency requires a balance and connection between conceptual understanding and computational proficiency" (NCTM, 2000, p. 35). The organization schema in mathematics relates to representational ways that computation understanding is presented.

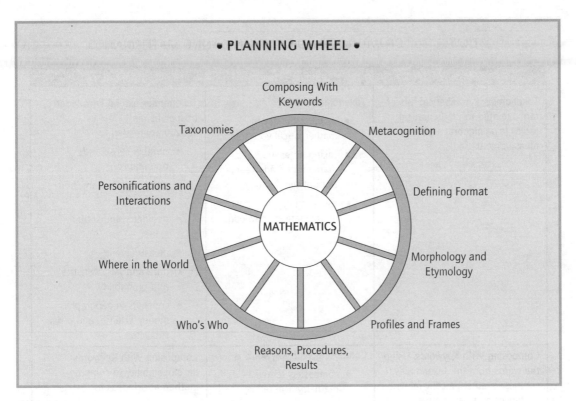

Figure 1.2

The concept of fluency-plus-organization in mathematics can be more readily understood through the writings of Howard Gardner who, in his work on multiple intelligences, defines intelligence as "the ability to solve problems or fashion products that are of consequence in a particular cultural setting or community" (1993, p. 15). Gardner speaks of intelligences (plural) rather than intelligence (singular) to denote problem-solving ability in specific domains, such as verbal/linguistic, musical/rhythmic, logical/mathematical, and others. He stresses the importance of focusing on both "the content of instruction and the means or medium for communicating that content" (p. 32). The content of mathematical instruction is well known; all of us remember our years of "math"—memorizing multiplication tables, measuring with rulers and yardsticks, drawing graphs, constructing triangles, and taking weekly math tests so that we could get a grade for the report card. What we may not remember (or didn't learn) are the different means of communicating mathematical content other than through tests or occasional projects.

The 10 writing strategies (Figure 1.2), when implemented systemically from primary grades through high school in every subject area, including mathematics, teach students not merely the content but the means of communicating that content. Each of these strategies has a place on the Planning Wheel and is a way of visualizing the order of the strategies and their relationship to each other. Since this book is about writing for mathematics, MATHEMATICS is placed in the center of the wheel with the idea that content will be delivered through these various strategies. Figure 1.3 defines each strategy and shows related learning extensions and applications for each strategy.

STRATEGIES FOR WRITING AND COMMUNICATING MATHEMATICS

Strategy	Learning Extension	Applications
Taxonomies: Alphabetical lists of terms related to mathematical topics (e.g., algebra, numbers, measurement)	**Taxonomies** are for • building fluency in mathematical vocabulary; • taking notes in mathematics and keeping track of terminology; • assessing pre- and post-mathematical knowledge.	**Taxonomies** extend knowledge of specific mathematical vocabulary related to • number sense and operations; • patterns, functions, and algebra; • geometry and spatial sense; • measurement; • data analysis, statistics, and probability; • concepts in geography, money, science, and other subjects.
Composing With Keywords: Using the words from the Taxonomies to compose mathematically related sentences and paragraphs	**Composing With Keywords** is for • composing sentences using mathematical terms; • writing paragraphs for mathematics; • focusing on a mathematical topic or concept.	**Composing With Keywords** develops ability to compose mathematical ideas in • response logs; • journals; • proofs.
Metacognition: Self-awareness of mathematical knowledge (e.g., using statements such as, I know that I know something about a polygon)	**Metacognition** guides students in • questioning mathematical ideas; • searching and researching for mathematics around us; • responding in writing to prior and new mathematics-related knowledge.	**Metacognition** enhances questioning skills: • How is what I already know in mathematics connected to what I need to know? • What else must I know in mathematics? • How can I best learn what I need to know mathematically?
Defining Format: A three-part format to define a mathematical term (e.g., number) that consists of the question, the category, and the characteristics	**Defining Format** provides a template for • asking questions related to mathematical terms; • categorizing mathematical terms; • adding details to expand mathematical knowledge; • writing clear mathematical statements.	**Defining Format** promotes learning how to • write accurate mathematical definitions; • categorize mathematical terms accurately; • compare mathematical concepts; • support mathematical ideas; • state mathematical facts.

Figure 1.3

STRATEGIES FOR WRITING AND COMMUNICATING MATHEMATICS

Strategy	Learning Extension	Applications
Morphology and Etymology: The study of the formation and history of words related to mathematics (e.g., number, numeral,numerical, enumerate, numeration, numeracy)	**Morphology and Etymology** focuses on • understanding the meaning of related mathematical terms; • clarifying mathematical terms that have multiple meanings; • learning mathematical idioms.	**Morphology and Etymology** helps students • create mathematical word stories; • relate mathematics to the world of mythology and legends; • write mathematical alliterations, poetry, puns, jokes, and do other mathematical word play.
Profiles and Frames: Templates for outlining information in all mathematical subcategories (e.g., arithmetic, geometry, algebra)	**Frames and Profiles** provide additional templates for • organizing research of mathematical topics; • paraphrasing and restating mathematical ideas and concepts.	**Frames and Profiles** help students • make oral presentations; • report on mathematics-related topics; • create mathematical reports.
Reasons, Procedures, Results: An organizational essay format for detailing reasons, procedures, and results related to mathematical ideas and concepts	**Reasons, Procedures, Results** provide organizational essay formats for • focusing on the mathematical topic; • adding supporting details; • writing paragraphs or reports.	**Reasons, Procedures, Results** are for • solving mathematical problems; • explaining mathematical ideas; • persuading others of mathematical concepts or beliefs; • reasoning, proving, and refuting mathematical statements; • creating personal essays related to mathematics.
Who's Who in Mathematics: Formats for researching and writing about accomplished mathematicians and their contributions to mathematics	**Who's Who in Mathematics** is for • biographic research related to mathematicians; • relating mathematics to other subject areas; • learning advanced mathematical ideas developed by renowned mathematicians.	**Who's Who in Mathematics** helps students in • making connections to the mathematical community; • understanding mathematical minds; • considering careers that use mathematics or need mathematicians.

(Continued on page 10)

STRATEGIES FOR WRITING AND COMMUNICATING MATHEMATICS

Strategy	Learning Extension	Applications
Where in the World: Strategies for relating mathematics and mathematical ideas to geography, culture, and mathematical ideas (e.g., Greeks, Arabs, Mayans, maps)	**Where in the World** shows the • relationship of geography to mathematics; • mathematical aspects of charts, graphs, maps, globes; • related vocabulary of mathematics and geography.	**Where in the World** builds awareness of • social issues and mathematics; • exploration and mathematics; • demographics and mathematics; • history of mathematics.
Personifications and Interactions: Strategy in which the writer assumes the persona of a mathematical term or concept and writes to another mathematical persona (e.g., a square writing to a circle)	**Personifications and Interactions** is another way to • write mathematical research; • direct writing to an audience; • express mathematical ideas in an informal or imaginative voice.	**Personifications and Interactions** • add humor to mathematics; • bring reality and fantasy to mathematical ideas; • foster in-depth understanding of concepts by assuming the persona of the concept.

Figure 1.3 *(Continued from page 9)*

By combining the 10 writing strategies illustrated in the Planning Wheel (Figure 1.2) with the 10 NCTM standards, you will have an expanded way of teaching students how to learn mathematics, how to think mathematically, and how to appreciate the remarkable invention of mathematics given to all humanity by teachers, philosophers, traders, and many others who needed to find a way to solve problems and fashion products.

HOW TO USE THIS BOOK FOR WRITING IN MATHEMATICS

The purpose of this book is to give you the tools that will help make your students mathematically literate. By juxtaposing mathematics with literacy, you will focus on uniting two intelligences—logical/mathematical with verbal/linguistic—a powerful partnership that Gardner (1993) points out is the principal basis of IQ and SAT tests (p. 20). The book is arranged so that you can develop many of your mathematical lessons within the framework of this partnership regardless of what skill or topic you are presenting. No matter which grade you teach, you will be able to enhance your students' knowledge and communication ability by incorporating the writing strategies in this book with your mathematical instruction.

Introduce each strategy slowly and thoroughly. Keep in mind that one strategy builds upon the other, no differently than in traditional mathematics instruction. Begin by teaching the strategies consecutively and *within the context of the mathematics you are teaching.* The activities presented cover a wide range of topics and grade levels as exemplars, so they will often have to be adapted to your own students' levels and abilities. However, every strategy can be effectively used with all students.

When students have mastered the strategies, you may use them in any order to maximize learning and understanding. For example, in the middle of the year your students might use Defining Format, add to their Taxonomy, create a Profile, and end with a Personification. You will find that the strategies will guide your students in applying their knowledge; they will gain proficiency in solving word problems, state reasons with proof, make connections between two mathematical ideas or concepts, and explain clearly and cogently their mathematical representations.

Chapters 2 through 11 each contain a section called **Mathematics the Write Way.** You can use the activities in this section as they are presented, or you may modify them to meet your students' needs or your district's curriculum. In every chapter, the sample activities focus on six mathematical areas: number and operations, algebra, geometry, measurement, data and analysis, and money. The first five areas are derived from the NCTM (2000) content standards. We added the sixth content area—money—because it has its own specialized vocabulary and approach.

Chapters 2 through 11 also include a section called **Internet Links.** This section will help you find activities and ideas for expanding your students' mathematical knowledge. These activities and ideas can be integrated with the specific strategy students are learning.

An issue for many teachers is time. How much time to spend on each strategy is a reasonable and essential question. One answer comes from *Principles and Standards,* which states that "school mathematics programs should not address every topic every year" and that "instructional programs . . . focus on important mathematical areas" (NCTM, 2000, p. 7). We would like to add that building mathematical understanding and communication does take time and, when given the time, results in the enhancement of the intelligence that allows us, as Gardner (1993) so cogently says, to solve problems and fashion products.

Below is a summary of each chapter that describes the writing strategy and its relationship to specific aspects of mathematics. Notice that every strategy is listed with a slogan that focuses on the major idea or purpose of that strategy, followed by the strategy name, as in "Words Are Free!—Taxonomies for Mathematics." Share these slogans with the students and post them in your classrooms. (If you would like to see how all the strategies fit together after you have taught them, go to Chapter 12.)

Chapter 2: **Words Are Free!—Taxonomies for Mathematics** introduces the concept of Taxonomies—organized lists of words pertaining to mathematical areas and topics for the purpose of building fluency and a personal thesaurus. These Taxonomies include words that refer to the following:

- number and operations (e.g., odd, digit, positive)
- algebra (e.g., same, similar, equivalent, attributes)
- geometry (e.g., scalene, congruent, polyhedron)
- measurement (e.g., metric, weight, time)
- data analysis and probability (e.g., sample, predict, compare, analyze)
- problem solving with money (e.g., penny, quarter, value, worth)

Chapter 3: **Have Words, Can Write—Composing With Keywords** shows the students how to use the mathematical words from Taxonomies to create sentences that state mathematical ideas in all strands of the mathematics curriculum. Composing with keywords provides students with ongoing, continuous practice in writing for mathematics.

Chapter 4: **Know What You Know—Metacognition for Mathematical Thinking** gives the students templates for expressing their prior knowledge and their developing knowledge as they learn more complex mathematical concepts. Metacognition statements help students "put in writing" what they know or think about a mathematical term or concept (e.g., triangle) before they receive instruction and what they know or think after they receive instruction.

Chapter 5: **Write to a Martian—Defining Format** brings the words from the Taxonomies into full focus and requires the writer (student) to explain the word (or concept) to a distant audience, a.k.a. The Martian. By focusing on a distant or unknowing audience, the student must clearly define significant mathematical terms (What is a rectangle? What is a rational number? What is addition?). Defining format requires the student to categorize terms and list their essential characteristics, placing the student in the position of instructor to an audience seeking information.

Chapter 6: **Every Word Has a Story—Morphology and Etymology** helps students expand their mathematical vocabulary through the study of various forms of the terms they use and linguistic origins of these terms. Students learn that the language of mathematics is both specific to mathematics and part of our everyday life.

Chapter 7: **Frame Your Writing—Profiles and Frames** provides students with templates for gathering information and structural formats for organizing writing and enhancing communicative abilities. Profiles and Frames are two types of detailed outlines that give the student the organizational schema needed for different mathematical genres (e.g., problem solving, reasoning and proof, representation).

Chapter 8: **Think in Threes—Reasons, Procedures, Results** shows students how to compose problem-solving statements, give reasons and proofs, use persuasion related to mathematics, state results, and explain methodology. This extensive strategy provides students with the essential essay formats commonly used in mathematical writing and on standardized tests.

Chapter 9: **Meet a Mathematician—Who's Who in Mathematics** introduces students to accomplished mathematicians and their contributions to our mathematical knowledge. Students are exposed to mathematicians from different backgrounds and cultures and gain an understanding of the history of mathematics through human endeavor and knowledge. The strategy also shows students, through biographies, different careers related to mathematics.

Chapter 10: **Mathematics Takes You Places—Where in the World** relates the world of geography to the world of mathematics. From measuring distances in our neighborhood to understanding light years, there is an integral relationship between our world and the world of mathematics. Where in the World combines strategies to make students aware that mathematics is worldwide and universal and that mathematics can be used to understand where we have been, where we are now, and where we might be going.

Chapter 11: **Know Thyself—Personifications and Interactions** asks students to personify mathematical terms and concepts so that they can write about these terms and concepts in vivid and in-depth ways, focusing on significant details and accuracy of information. Through "interactions" with mathematical "personae," students become knowledgeable about the mathematical terms they are personifying and see mathematics from different perspectives, including humor.

Chapter 12: **Mathematically Literate—The Way to Go** summarizes how the 10 strategies can be used together to teach the mathematics and the communication skills students need to meet the standards for mathematics. The Planning Wheel has been completed.

Resources: At the request of many teachers, we have added rubrics and templates related to the strategies. Use them as appropriate for your own students and feel comfortable to create your own.

By following these strategies, you will help your students become good mathematical writers and better learners of mathematics. Before you begin instruction, use the Prologue (Figure 1.4) to explain to students what they will learn by becoming mathematicians of accomplishment.

Prologue for Students

Be a mathematician so that you will know

- words of mathematics,

- numerous symbols and signs,

- various types of numbers,

- careers and subjects that use mathematics,

- problems that mathematics can solve in your own life and in the world,

- tools used by mathematicians,

- mathematicians who have contributed to our knowledge,

- creative ideas that come from mathematicians and mathematics,

- games and lively activities that use mathematics.

Figure 1.4

2

Taxonomies

The Words and Symbols of Mathematics

"Let's travel by miles," advised the Humbug;

"it's shorter."

"Let's travel by half inches," suggested Milo;

"it's quicker."

—The Phantom Tollbooth (Juster, 1964, p. 171)

Words are tools with which we think, and thinking is the central concern of mathematics teaching. (Countryman, 1992, p. 54)

THE IMPORTANCE OF WORDS IN MATHEMATICS

Mathematics, like all fields, has a specialized vocabulary. It also relies upon common definitions of key terms, even if such terms might have various meanings or uses beyond mathematics. Vocabulary is as critical to understanding mathematics as numbers and symbols. In *Principles and Standards for School Mathematics*, the NCTM states that "mathematical language builds on the existing structure and logic of common language" but then points out an important difference between mathematical and "ordinary" languages (NCTM, 2000, p. 5). One difference is that ordinary language can be imprecise. For example, in ordinary discourse we may use the word *factor* this way: We have to consider all the factors when making a decision. Or we may use the word *area*, as follows: We covered a broad area of topics. A gap exists between how we use mathematical words in everyday language and how we use them in mathematics. Therefore, teachers must assume the responsibility to help students connect the meanings of words they may already know and use in their speech to the specialized meanings of the same words in mathematics. It is essential that students in all grade levels develop a clear understanding of how words are used in mathematics and how they may be differentiated from the same words used in non-mathematical situations.

This book approaches the teaching of mathematical vocabulary with specific strategies based on a point of view that "words have a story"—meaning that every word belongs to a category, conveys meaning or definition, can have expanded meanings, and has a history. Many students, unfortunately, have experienced the random teaching of vocabulary. By "random" teaching, we mean the process of teaching vocabulary as words come along, rather than organized and put into context. Recent research strongly indicates that learning (in any subject) is facilitated when there is an organizational system that is apparent to the students (Bomer, 1995; Jensen, 1998; Martin, 1996). In line with this research, we have organized vocabulary instruction in mathematics around these four aspects that constitute the "story" of any word:

- Category (Chapters 2, 5, 6)
- Definition (Chapters 3, 4, 5)
- Expansion of Meaning (Chapters 3, 4, 5, 6)
- History and Expansion of Meaning (Chapter 6)

For each of these aspects of words, we have included a strategy as indicated in the Planning Wheel (Figure 1.2). These strategies are interrelated and should be used as appropriate to your students' levels and needs. When students are aware that "words have a story," they become interested in the story and curious to know more. Furthermore, knowing the "story" enables students to have a system for acquiring an extensive mathematical vocabulary and linking this vocabulary to other subjects. We begin with Taxonomies.

WHAT ARE TAXONOMIES?

A Taxonomy is a classification system that organizes information on a specific topic or concept. In this book, we use the term Taxonomy to refer to an alphabetic list of words related to a specific mathematics topic. As in *Writing as Learning*

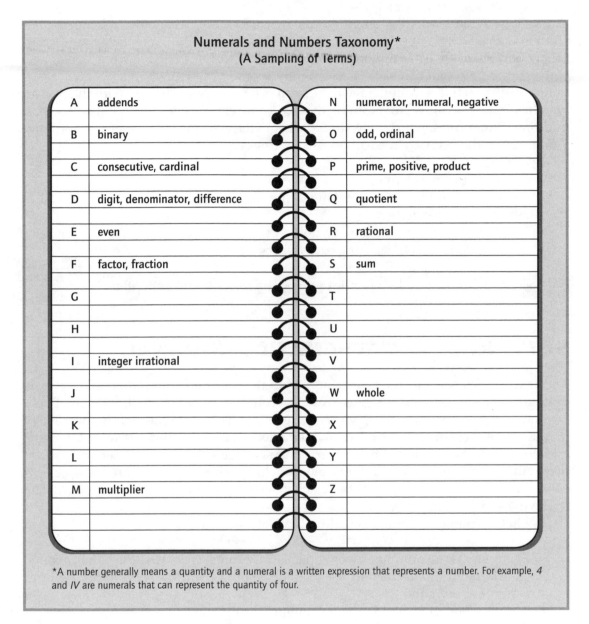

A	addends		N	numerator, numeral, negative	
B	binary		O	odd, ordinal	
C	consecutive, cardinal		P	prime, positive, product	
D	digit, denominator, difference		Q	quotient	
E	even		R	rational	
F	factor, fraction		S	sum	
G			T		
H			U		
I	integer irrational		V		
J			W	whole	
K			X		
L			Y		
M	multiplier		Z		

Numerals and Numbers Taxonomy*
(A Sampling of Terms)

*A number generally means a quantity and a numeral is a written expression that represents a number. For example, *4* and *IV* are numerals that can represent the quantity of four.

Figure 2.1

(Rothstein & Lauber, 2000), we begin with the premise that students must accumulate and keep track of their ever-growing mathematical vocabulary. By keeping track, students build a "personal thesaurus" in mathematics—a thesaurus that they continuously add to and use for study, review, and clarification of meaning. See Figure 2.1 for a "Numerals and Numbers" Taxonomy.

BUILDING MATHEMATICAL VOCABULARY WITH TAXONOMIES

Because of the importance of words in mathematics, the first six strategies in the Planning Wheel emphasize knowing mathematical words and using them as precisely as possible. What is exciting about words is that they are *free*. Being free means that students can have access to all the words in their language; they can "take them" from others and share their own words freely. They are freely available from books and conversation. No one can say, "You took my word" because when someone "takes your word" you not only still have it, but you can now communicate with the person who has "taken" your word! Nothing that we know emphasizes this point better than building Taxonomies, which help students begin the essential system of categorizing, a first step in the "story." In addition, Taxonomies can be used to

- assess prior knowledge,
- serve as a continuous note-taking system,
- assess new knowledge,
- build mathematical vocabulary, and
- develop cooperative learning experiences.

Each of these uses of Taxonomies will be discussed in this chapter.

SETTING UP A MATHEMATICS JOURNAL

The Taxonomies serve as the representation of the hundreds of mathematical words that your students need to grasp in order to understand mathematics. These Taxonomies become, in effect, your students' personal thesaurus. To physically maintain the thesaurus (plus other mathematical material), students from Grades 2 and up need to keep track of their words and subsequent entries in a separate spiral or composition notebook. Kindergarten and first-grade teachers can set up a flip chart to serve as a journal, with the teacher writing material on the flip chart. The following setup works very well.

Begin by asking students to create a Table of Contents.

- Have students number several pages at a time. The first right-hand page should be numbered 1 and the students should continue by numbering both sides of every page.
- Tell students to write "Table of Contents" at the top of page 1.
- Ask students to make a table, as shown in Figure 2.2, using the following headings: Date, Mathematics Topic and Strategy, and Page.
- Begin the first entry on page 6 so that there will be room on the previous pages for the many topics you will be introducing and teaching.

Explain that students will add to their Table of Contents each time they learn a new concept or strategy.

> Journals (or notebooks) are nontraditional workbooks. They are, in a sense, a portfolio of students' math experiences. Students use their journals as references for learning and are encouraged to return to past activities . . . to assist them in new learning. (Tangretti & Liptak, 1995, p. 7)

INTRODUCING MATHEMATICAL TAXONOMIES

Students of all ages will benefit from Taxonomies because Taxonomies serve as the "holder" of terms and represent what one already knows or is getting to know. For primary students, Taxonomies are particularly valuable as retrieval systems during writing or discussion time. For older students, they indicate accumulated knowledge and provide the core for building new information. They represent a growing body of knowledge that students can constantly update and use. Until your students can create their own Taxonomies, we suggest the following procedure:

- Write letters alphabetically down the left-hand side of a piece of chart paper.
- Write the title or topic at the top of the page (e.g., Our Mathematical Words).
- Tell the students that they are going to keep a list of the words (called a Taxonomy) they already know and will get to know on the subject of mathematics (sometimes shortened to math).
- Point out that by knowing the meaning of these words, they will be able to count, calculate, measure, tell time, and do many more wonderful activities. They will become members of a group of people called mathematicians.
- Give the students an example of a mathematical word and write it next to its corresponding letter (e.g., write "number" next to N).
- Ask students to suggest words that they think belong on this Taxonomy. If a word doesn't seem to belong, ask the student why she or he has suggested that word. Accept any reasonable answer.

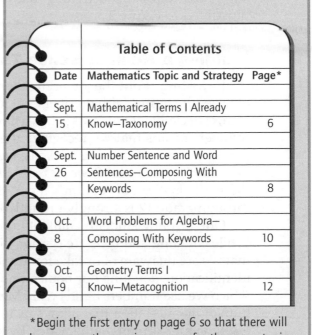

Table of Contents		
Date	Mathematics Topic and Strategy	Page*
Sept. 15	Mathematical Terms I Already Know—Taxonomy	6
Sept. 26	Number Sentence and Word Sentences—Composing With Keywords	8
Oct. 8	Word Problems for Algebra— Composing With Keywords	10
Oct. 19	Geometry Terms I Know—Metacognition	12

*Begin the first entry on page 6 so that there will be room on the previous pages for the many topics you will be introducing and teaching.

Figure 2.2

Use the word **mathematics** as much as possible, rather than **math. Mathematics** leads students to become **mathematicians** and enters students into the **mathematical** world of numbers, geometry, algebra, and so forth.

Begin by completing a general Taxonomy that includes any words the students suggest that relate to mathematics. Then, guide the students into creating separate Taxonomies for specific aspects or areas they are learning (e.g., number and operations; patterns, functions, and algebra; geometry and spatial sense; measurement; data analysis, statistics, and probability). It usually takes two to three class periods to introduce Taxonomies to young children; older children will grasp the strategy more quickly. As students become familiar with the process, they quickly learn to set up their template and independently follow the procedures they have been taught. The following section gives the rationale for creating a Taxonomy of numbers with suggested follow-up activities that are subsequently explained. The Taxonomy is illustrated in Figure 2.3.

Building a Number Sense Through Taxonomies

In writing about the joy of numbers, Wells (1995) states that students should "be on 'friendly terms' with numbers," at least those "from 1 to 100" (p. 30). What a lovely idea, especially for students just starting out in the number world. Being friendly with numbers means that we recognize them all around us, that we see their many purposes, and that, according to Wells, we do not "panic and start sweating at the sight of a sum" (p. 30). In *Principles and Standards*, "number has been a cornerstone of the mathematics curriculum" and "all mathematics proposed for pre-kindergarten through grade 12 is strongly grounded in number" (NCTM, 2000, p. 32).

Often, young students think of numbers only as a way of counting or doing facts. While counting and facts are certainly important, we use numbers in numerous ways that we are unaware of or take for granted—for sequence, chronology, approximation, identification, denoting our homes, and so forth. Becoming aware of the many ways in which we use numbers builds what Menninger (1992) calls a "number sense," an early human manifestation that allows us to comprehend what is around us. This sense is essential for learning mathematics. By building a strong number sense in students, we develop not only their operational abilities but "the numerical core of mathematical intelligence," which "seems to be honored universally" (Gardner, 1983, p. 163).

Discussing and listing the various ways to use numbers alert your students to the amazing benefits of numbers in our lives and how these numbers are always with us. To begin this development of number sense, we suggest that you and your students create a Taxonomy called "The Many Ways We Use Numbers." Ask students to think of the many uses of numbers and add them to the Taxonomy. Your classroom and school undoubtedly have many examples of numbers that the students can observe. Students can take a "field trip" around the school looking for uses of numbers; they can interview people who work in the school to find out how they use numbers, and they can ask family or community members how they use numbers. Each room is likely to have a number, some schools have a number, and the calendar has numbers.

Post the Taxonomy on the wall and ask students to collect as many ways to use numbers as they can, adding to the Taxonomy each time they think of another example. The Taxonomy in Figure 2.3 illustrates items collected by a multiage first- and second-grade class.

As you and your students develop this Taxonomy, ask the students to use the words in sentences that demonstrate their understanding of the multiple uses of numbers. One way to do this is to initiate a daily activity in which the students write sentences for each word in the Taxonomy. Following are sentences written by students in Grades 1 and 2 using the words from the Taxonomy in Figure 2.3:

- **Age** tells how old you are in years. I am eight years old. My mother told me that if we counted age by months I would be 96 months old. That sounds really old.
- A **calendar** shows months and days and weeks. There are 12 months in a calendar. Some months have 30 days. Some months have 31 days. February has 28 days. A week has 7 days.
- My **telephone** number has ten numbers. They are 248 555 1212. I think it has ten numbers because ten is easy to remember.

To further enhance number sense, ask students to illustrate their sentences, making sure that the keywords are represented. For example, a student who writes, "My telephone number is 248 555 1212" could draw a telephone that shows the numbers and letters on the dial pad. Illustrating both the numbers and letters demonstrates the relationship of alphabetic symbols with numerical symbols. A drawing of a street with house numbers can show ordination, while numbers on a stove can illustrate temperature and time.

INTRODUCING TAXONOMIES FOR ASSESSING PRIOR AND COLLECTIVE KNOWLEDGE

Creating Taxonomies allows students to develop flexibility in learning by working solo, collaborating in small groups, or "cross-pollinating" ideas in whole-class discussions. Each approach, as shown in Figure 2.4, builds different learning and participation skills and allows for differentiated abilities and learning styles. Each aspect of building Taxonomies gives you the opportunity to assess your students' prior knowledge as well as their collective knowledge, so that you have advance organizers for planning and pacing.

Below is the suggested procedure for introducing your students to using solo, collaborative, and cross-pollination strategies for creating Taxonomies. In this example, the teacher is assessing how many mathematical terms the students know at the beginning of fourth grade.

The Many Ways We Use Numbers

Here are words that describe ways that we use numbers. Add other words using numbers that you discover as you look around your home, school, and neighborhood.

A	age, amount, attendance
B	budgets
C	counting, calendar, clock, computer, credit card, cafeteria
D	date, distance, depth
E	expenses
F	field trips
G	games
H	height, house numbers
I	
J	
K	
L	length, lunch
M	measuring, microwave, money
N	number lines
O	
P	pages
Q	
R	room numbers, ruler
S	street numbers, school numbers, stove, shoe size, speedometer
T	time, telephone, temperature, team numbers, TV, tape measure, taxi, train
U	
V	
W	weight, width, watch
X	
Y	years
Z	

Figure 2.3

Solo

Begin by having the students write the Taxonomy topic (e.g., Mathematical Terms I Already Know) and the page number on the Table of Contents in their mathematics notebook (see Figure 2.2). Tell the students that they will first work solo (alone). Ask the students to write three to five words on the Taxonomy that they associate with mathematics. Give an example (e.g., fraction) and place the word next to the appropriate letter. Instruct students to work silently and not discuss their ideas with their neighbors. Give students about two minutes to work. Walk around the room and observe whether the students are fluent in the topic. Notice students who have many words (fluency) and those who seem to have few.

We are frequently asked whether spelling should count. Our response is, "Yes, but not yet. You can check your spelling later." The purpose of this initial gathering of words is the check for vocabulary. Since you are using the Taxonomy as a pre-assessment tool, you will also discover what spelling instruction your students might need!

Collaborate

Ask students to form groups of three or four. Tell students to share the words from their Taxonomies with their groups. As students share their words, group members should add these words to their Taxonomies. When students finish sharing in their groups, lead a whole-class discussion. Ask groups how many words they have and why collaborating can be helpful in learning. Take time to introduce the slogan "Words are free!" Explain that words represent knowledge and that we learn from each other's words. You might also want to add that we can share all our words, yet still have them for ourselves. Tell the students that as they think of other words related to the topic, they can add them and share them.

Cross-Pollinate

By this point, each student likely has at least 10 words on the Taxonomy. However, they probably still know more words than they have recorded. Motivate students to find other words by giving these instructions:

- Look at your Taxonomy and find a letter for which you have no term.
- Raise your hand and say to the whole group, "I need a mathematical term for the letter ___."
- If someone has a term for this letter, raise your hand and say, "I have a mathematical term for the letter ___ and it is___."

You might have your students walk around the room and find words from other students' Taxonomies that they can add to their own list. We suggest three rules for this activity, if necessary: no running, no touching, no negative comments. By using this sequence of working solo, collaborating, and cross-pollinating, all of the students are participating and learning from each other.

Continuous Note Taking

The Taxonomy continues as a work in progress. As you discuss the topic, students should add to their Taxonomy. New information can come from your presentation, class discussion, textbook reading, and Internet "surfing." Using the Taxonomy for note taking encourages the students to listen and read interactively. An important advantage is that students can recognize their own growth and expanded knowledge of the topic as they add to the Taxonomy.

Post-Assessment

After students have studied a mathematical topic, ask them to create a new Taxonomy in which they list (from memory) all the terms that relate to the topic. Tell them to put an asterisk (or other marker) next to words that they understand and a question mark (or other marker) next to words that they need to study or learn more about. Or they can color code the words on the basis of "know a lot," "know something," and "know just a little." This post-assessment process gives students an opportunity to build the important learning skills of self-assessment (see Chapter 4 on Metacognition) and defining terms (see Chapter 5 on Defining Format).

Instructions to Students for Creating Taxonomies

Note: These instructions are for students in Grades 2 and up.

A good way to learn the meanings of mathematical words is to keep track of them and use them in writing. One way to begin a Taxonomy in mathematics is to think of all the words you know related to mathematics and write these words next to the letter with which the word begins. For example, the word **geometry** should be written next to the letter G. Start by working by yourself, which is also called working **solo.**

Next, **collaborate** with a partner or a group. Add each other's words to the Taxonomy. You will find that you "own" many mathematical words—more than you imagined. Owning words means you possess knowledge; for each word that you own, you possess the **potential** for meaning.

After you collaborate with a partner or group, collect more words from other groups or teams. By doing this activity, we **cross-pollinate** and get ideas from everyone.

A Mathematics Taxonomy by Fourth Graders

A	addition, abacus
B	base
C	calculator, commutation, circle, count
D	divide, division, difference,
	denominator
E	equal, even
F	fraction
G	graph, geometry, greater than
H	half
I	inch
J	join
K	kilometer, kilogram
L	line, less than
M	multiplication, multiply, measure,
	meter, minus
N	number, number sentence, numerator
O	one, odd
P	product, plus sign
Q	quotient
R	ruler, rectangle, rhombus
S	sum, square, sphere
T	temperature, time, total, triangle, take
	away
U	underline bar, unit
V	vertex
W	weight, whole number
X	x-axis
Y	y-axis, yardstick
Z	zero

Figure 2.4

TAXONOMIES FOR STANDARDS: NUMBER AND OPERATIONS, ALGEBRA, GEOMETRY, MEASUREMENT, DATA ANALYSIS AND PROBABILITY, AND MONEY

The inclusion of Taxonomies in your mathematics program helps your students integrate their number sense with language sense. It brings about what Piaget calls the development of formal mental operations that allow the child to "link words with symbols" and eventually move on to the higher levels of formulating reasons, hypotheses, and logical thought (cited in Gardner, 1983, p. 132). According to Kline (1985), "reasoning about numbers . . . requires the mastery of two faculties, vocabulary and technique, or . . . vocabulary and grammar" (p. 94).

We strongly recommend that you ask students to create Taxonomies for each mathematical content area, even though words for different areas will overlap. As students create these Taxonomies, they learn the specific vocabulary for each mathematical area and they recognize how these vocabularies are connected.

Following are examples of Taxonomies for each content standard (number and operations, algebra, geometry, measurement, and data analysis and probability)—and money—that should be developed throughout the grades (Figures 2.5 through 2.10). These Taxonomies are not necessarily complete but serve as starting points for you and your students.

Our examples throughout the book focus on six mathematical areas: number and operations, algebra, geometry, measurement, data and analysis, and money. The first five areas are derived from the NCTM (2000) content standards. We added the sixth content area—money—because it has its own specialized vocabulary and can be included with the problem-solving standard.

Taxonomies that the students build in the lower grades in the major areas of mathematics should be continued into the upper grades and, hopefully, in a systemic curriculum, through high school. For example, the Taxonomy on Data Analysis and Probability started in the elementary grades (Figure 2.9) could be expanded in the higher grades as shown in Figure 2.11 (see boldfaced words).

Number and Operations

• TAXONOMY •

A	add, addition, addend
B	backward
C	count, calculate, cardinal
D	divide, difference, digit, double
E	even, equal
F	forward, factor
G	greater than
H	half, hundreds
I	integer
J	
K	
L	less than
M	more, money, minus
N	number, number line
O	odd, ordinal, ones
P	plus, place value, product
Q	quantity, quotient
R	regroup
S	same, sum
T	take away, tens, tallies
U	
V	value
W	what, when, why, where
X	
Y	
Z	zero

Figure 2.5

Algebra

• TAXONOMY •

A	arithmetic, attributes, arrays
B	binomial
C	coefficient
D	distributive laws
E	equal, even
F	factor, formula
G	grid
H	
I	intervals, integers
J	
K	
L	linear
M	minus, multiplier, monomial
N	numbers, number line
O	order, odd, operator
P	plus, positive, negative points, polynomials, parentheses
Q	quadratic
R	rules
S	sequence, same, symbols, sum, solution
T	
U	units
V	
W	
X	x
Y	y
Z	zero

Figure 2.6

Geometry

• TAXONOMY •

A	area, angle, acute
B	base
C	circle, cube, circumference, coordinates
D	dimensions, diameter
E	equilateral
F	face, figure
G	geodesic, graphing
H	horizontal, hypotenuse
I	incline, inner
J	join
K	
L	length, line segment, linear
M	
N	narrow
O	outer, octagon, obtuse
P	perimeter, plane, polygon, pyramid, prism, parallelogram
Q	quadrilateral
R	rectangle
S	shape, square, solid, sides, semi-circle, surface area, scalene
T	triangle, trapezoid, theorem
U	
V	vertical, vertex, vertices, volume
W	wide
X	
Y	
Z	

Figure 2.7

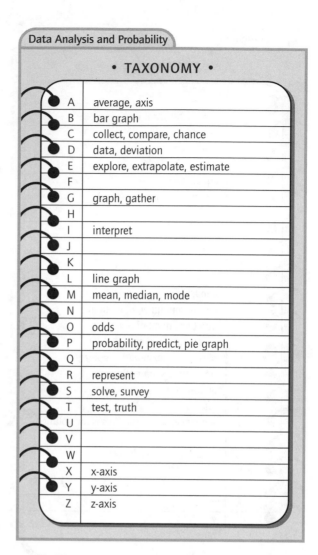

Figure 2.9

Measurement

• TAXONOMY •

A	age, analog
B	bushel
C	centimeter, clock
D	day, digital
E	estimation, estimate
F	foot, feet
G	gram, gallon
H	heavy, hour, height
I	inch
J	
K	kilometer, kilogram
L	light, long, liter
M	miles, meter, millimeter, meter stick, minute, month
N	nano
O	ounce
P	pound, pint
Q	quart
R	ruler
S	short, second, scale
T	tall, thin, time, ton, tape measure, thermometer, temperature
U	unit
V	
W	week, weight, weigh
X	
Y	year, yard
Z	

Figure 2.8

Money

• TAXONOMY •

A	amount
B	bill, barter, borrow
C	coin, cents, cents sign, change, currency, credit
D	dollar, dollar sign, dime, debt
E	exchange
F	five-dollar bill, finance
G	gold (standard)
H	half dollar
I	interest
J	
K	
L	lend
M	mortgage
N	notes
O	one-dollar bill
P	penny, percent, peso, peseta, pound
Q	quarter
R	return
S	symbols
T	ten-dollar bill
U	unit
V	value
W	worth
X	
Y	yen, yuan
Z	zloty

Figure 2.10

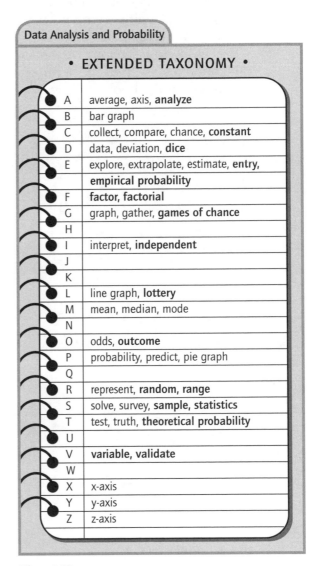

Data Analysis and Probability

• EXTENDED TAXONOMY •

A	average, axis, **analyze**
B	bar graph
C	collect, compare, chance, **constant**
D	data, deviation, **dice**
E	explore, extrapolate, estimate, **entry**, **empirical probability**
F	**factor, factorial**
G	graph, gather, **games of chance**
H	
I	interpret, **independent**
J	
K	
L	line graph, **lottery**
M	mean, median, mode
N	
O	odds, **outcome**
P	probability, predict, pie graph
Q	
R	represent, **random, range**
S	solve, survey, **sample, statistics**
T	test, truth, **theoretical probability**
U	
V	**variable, validate**
W	
X	x-axis
Y	y-axis
Z	z-axis

Figure 2.11

INTEGRATING TAXONOMIES WITH WRITING ACTIVITIES

Taxonomies serve as a student's personal thesaurus. Because of this important function, students need to create Taxonomies for all aspects of mathematics they are learning, as well as for subject areas that require mathematical knowledge (e.g., geography, health, sports). These Taxonomies serve as the foundation of mathematical writing lessons because they provide fluency and an easy retrieval system. The following section, Mathematics the Write Way, gives suggestions for using Taxonomies as part of writing activities, with subsequent activities following throughout the book.

Mathematics the Write Way

■ ACTIVITY 1
Mathematicians Try Geometry

One of the first activities you might try with your students is to ask them for suggestions for using a Taxonomy to create a variety of writing products. Suppose your students have created a Taxonomy of Geometric Terms, as in Figure 2.12. The collection of terms represents a broad range of collective knowledge that the students can use for a variety of writing activities. (Note that as you and your students go through the Planning Wheel, writing activities will be integrated continuously with Taxonomies.)

With your students, brainstorm a list of writing activities, as in the following examples.

Suggestions for Writing in Geometry

- Write a definition for the words.
- Use the words in sentences.
- Write a story using as many of the words in the Taxonomy as you can.
- Explain how to construct a geometric form using words from the Taxonomy.
- Compare one geometric form with another geometric form.
- Research the "history" of a geometric concept or idea (e.g., measuring the circumference) and include words from the Taxonomy.
- Construct a geometric city using words from the Taxonomy as a guide.

Geometry	
• TAXONOMY •	
A	arc, angle, angular axis, alternate interior angles
B	bisect
C	cylinder, cylindrical, circle, circular, circumference, cone, conical, cube, chord
D	degree, diameter
E	equilateral, ellipse, equiangular, exterior angles
F	focus, foci
G	geodome, geometric
H	hypotenuse, hemisphere
I	isosceles, intersection
J	join, joint
K	
L	line
M	midpoint
N	node
O	obtuse
P	pit, parallel, parallelogram, pyramid, prism, perpendicular
Q	quarter, quadrant, quadrilateral
R	radius, rectangle, rectangular, right angle
S	scalene, square, sphere, spherical, sector
T	triangle, triangular, trapezoid, trapezoidal, tangent
U	unit
V	vector, vertex, vertices, vertical angles
W	wide, width
X	x-axis
Y	y-axis
Z	z-axis

Figure 2.12

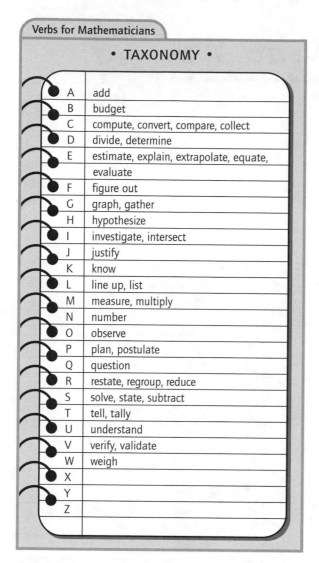

Figure 2.13

Build a Geometric City

Since you are familiar with many geometry terms, try to draw or construct a city using as many of the geometrical shapes or terms as possible. Then write a description of your city identifying the geometric shapes you have used. To help you write your description, we are going to create a Taxonomy of Verbs for Mathematicians (Figure 2.13). We can easily build a Mathematical Verb Taxonomy by using the starting word "Mathematicians . . ." Then construct a phrase with a verb, such as "Mathematicians estimate" or "Mathematicians weigh" or "Mathematicians observe."

■ ACTIVITY 2
Mathematics as Symbols

So far we have been writing about mathematics as "words." Yet we all know that mathematics is mainly written in symbols and that these symbols generally define what mathematics is. Throughout the grades, students learn new symbols for the different aspects of mathematics, from operations to probability. Keeping a running Taxonomy of these symbols will help your students remember them and use them as needed. The origins and purposes of these symbols are both interesting and informative. Figure 2.14 is a Taxonomy of the symbols that each student can add to his or her personal thesaurus. Remember to have the students enter this activity into their Table of Contents.

Mathematical Symbols

Figure 2.14 shows many of the symbols used by mathematicians to write about mathematics. Add any other symbols you know. Then write a story using mathematical symbols in place of words wherever you can. For example, you might write

"You are > any 1 I know. You are a + in my life. You give me 100% joy."

Symbols and Signs of Mathematics

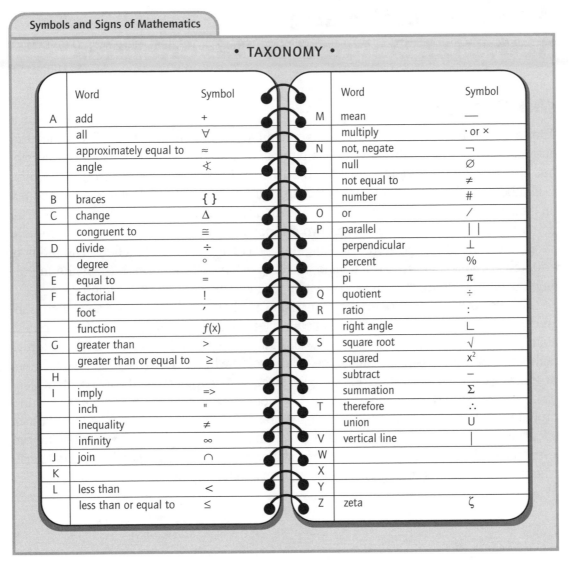

• TAXONOMY •

	Word	Symbol		Word	Symbol
A	add	+	M	mean	—
	all	∀		multiply	· or ×
	approximately equal to	≈	N	not, negate	¬
	angle	∡		null	∅
				not equal to	≠
B	braces	{ }		number	#
C	change	Δ	O	or	/
	congruent to	≅	P	parallel	| |
D	divide	÷		perpendicular	⊥
	degree	°		percent	%
E	equal to	=		pi	π
F	factorial	!	Q	quotient	÷
	foot	′	R	ratio	:
	function	$f(x)$		right angle	∟
G	greater than	>	S	square root	√
	greater than or equal to	≥		squared	x^2
H				subtract	−
I	imply	=>		summation	Σ
	inch	″	T	therefore	∴
	inequality	≠		union	U
	infinity	∞	V	vertical line	|
J	join	∩	W		
K			X		
L	less than	<	Y		
	less than or equal to	≤	Z	zeta	ζ

Figure 2.14

Additional Writing Activities Related to Taxonomies

(All Grades)

After students have created a Taxonomy related to a mathematical topic (e.g., numbers and numerals, or the many ways to use numbers), they should write sentences and stories about the topic. Students should also do the reverse—they should change the words to numbers and mathematical symbols. Composing with words from a Taxonomy is based on the premise that the students know something about the meaning of these words. The ability to make connections between two symbolic systems—words and numbers—is a strong indicator of student understanding. Jensen (1998), in a chapter titled "The Brain as a Meaning Maker," refers to "meaning as complex" (p. 92) and emphasizes the importance of interdisciplinary models to create relevance and context for learning.

Chapter 3 presents models for composing mathematical sentences and word sentences. Having students write mathematical sentences and word sentences that are equivalent in meaning helps them not only to distinguish between the two but allows them to compare their similarities and differences and discuss why one form may be more efficient or effective than another form. The examples in the next chapter cover the five content standards—number and operations, algebra, geometry, measurement, and data analysis and probability—and money. These examples represent a wide range of grade-level knowledge and are illustrative of the potential for writing. They also show opportunities for differentiation within a classroom where some students can show emerging knowledge while others can express more complex ideas on the same topic (Tomlinson, 1999).

INTERNET RESOURCES RELATED TO TAXONOMIES

One of the exciting tools available to students to apply and learn about mathematics is the Internet, a vast source of information that allows students to go far beyond the textbooks. Furthermore, the material on the Internet can be a source for differentiating instruction to meet students' personal interests and abilities.

Information on the Internet is constantly evolving and changing, so we cannot provide a comprehensive list of appropriate sites for all mathematical topics. However, we have selected sites that integrate mathematics with the writing strategies in this book. We hope these sites will provoke challenging discussions and investigations by students. The following sites particularly relate to building Taxonomies and mathematical vocabulary.

INTERNET LINKS

Glossary of Mathematical Terms

http://www.cut-the-knot.com/glossary/atop.html

Harcourt Brace Math Glossary (Grades K–6)

http://www.hbschool.com/glossary/math/

Improving Achievement in Mathematics and Science

http://www.sedl.org

3

Composing
With Keywords

Mathematical Word Play

> As I was going to St. Ives,
> I met a crowd of seven wives.
> Every wife had seven sacks,
> Every sack had seven cats,
> Every cat had seven kits.
> Kits, cats, sacks, and wives,
> How many were going to St. Ives?
>
> —Traditional Nursery Rhyme (modified)

Instructional programs from prekindergarten through grade 12 should enable all students to communicate their mathematical thinking coherently and clearly to peers, teachers, and others. (NCTM, 2000, p. 60)

WHAT IS COMPOSING WITH KEYWORDS?

Countryman (1992) states that "attending to words will help students learn mathematics better," and for further emphasis adds that "although we might disagree about the nature of mathematics, even that argument will take place in the context of language" (p. 55). In the previous chapter we made the case for creating Taxonomies as a system for "having words." With words, students have something to say, and what they can say is what they know or are getting to know. This chapter offers activities and suggestions for Composing With Keywords, a strategy that will help your students develop fluency in composing so that they may better understand the mathematical ideas you are trying to teach. If one accepts Countryman's premise that we learn better when we pay attention to words, then we must give students frequent and continuous opportunities to express mathematical ideas in both symbols and words. For example, when students begin to learn the words *addition, subtraction, multiplication,* and *division,* they are likely to do dozens of worksheets practicing the operations ($3 \times 4 = 12$). Yet they spend much less time (if any) on writing about (composing) what they are doing or learning what the operational words actually mean.

In the Composing With Keywords strategy, students are asked to select words from a Taxonomy and write sentences that relate to the Taxonomy topic. For example, a student might select the words *hexagon, perimeter,* and *angle* from the geometry Taxonomy. She would then write a sentence: A hexagon is a shape with six angles that like any other shape also has a perimeter. To compose this sentence, a student might first relate the word *hexagon* to the word *angle.* But now the student must also think of how the word *perimeter* is related and how that word can be incorporated into the statement on hexagons.

Composing With Keywords helps students reflect on the meanings of mathematical words (or terms), clarify their understanding of these words through the process of association, and incorporate the words into a statement that shows how each word relates to the other mathematical words. Through Composing With Keywords, the student is engaged in the processes of reflecting, clarifying, understanding, and incorporating, all of which represent what Costa and Kallick (2000) define as "thinking and communicating with clarity and precision" (p. 31).

Motz and Weaver (1991), who are mathematicians and writers, give excellent examples of how words can explain mathematical ideas:

> $5 \times 9 = 9 \times 5$ means that we add five groups of nine steps each or nine groups of five steps; we therefore also speak of the products as five times nine or nine times five. Starting from 0 we move nine steps to the right to point 9 and then nine more to the point 18, and so on. (p. 12)

If we look closely at this statement, we can pick out the keywords that a student needs to know in order to understand the commutative concept. For example, why *five times nine* will yield the same product as *nine times five* (an idea that escaped one of these authors all through her elementary school years). Understanding the keywords—product, times, equal—is essential for the student to be able to explain why $5 \times 9 = 9 \times 5$.

INTRODUCING COMPOSING WITH KEYWORDS

Every time you teach mathematics, you use words. This means that you and your students are constantly building Taxonomies, which serve as the foundation for composing mathematical statements and offer the students choices of what to say. In addition, your students are practicing mathematics through algorithms, an explicit set of rules for solving a mathematical problem. These algorithms are "written" as symbols, but stated in "words," as in 3 (three) + (plus) 4 (four) = (equal) 7 (seven). Presented below are examples of Composing With Keywords that can be developed from Taxonomies and from algorithms representative of different grade levels and aspects of mathematics.

These examples are models that you can use "as is" if appropriate to your students or modify for your own mathematics levels or curriculum. These models lend themselves to differentiated learning because they are *open-ended*, meaning that students can express themselves in a variety of ways, stating the same idea differently or stating the same idea with different levels of understanding. By using or adapting these models, you will receive specific information about your individual student's mathematical knowledge and his or her ability to communicate that knowledge. This information will enable you to provide your students with specific feedback, which, according to Marzano, Pickering, and Pollock (2001), plays an important role in student achievement.

COMPOSING WITH KEYWORDS ACTIVITIES RELATED TO TAXONOMIES AND ALGORITHMS (ALL GRADES)

After students have created a Taxonomy related to a mathematical topic (e.g., numbers and numerals, or the many ways to use numbers), they should write sentences and stories about the topic. Students should also do the reverse—they should change the words to numbers and mathematical symbols. Composing with words from a Taxonomy is based on the premise that the students know something about the meaning of these words. The ability to make connections between two symbolic systems—words and numbers—is a strong indicator of student understanding. Jensen (1998), in a chapter titled "The Brain as a Meaning Maker," refers to "meaning as complex" (p. 92) and emphasizes the importance of interdisciplinary models to create relevance and context for learning.

The following steps will help your students learn to compose with keywords.

- Ask your students to select three words from a Taxonomy that the class has created (e.g., number, sign, even).
- Model a sentence for the students using all three of these words (e.g., When we put a plus sign between two even numbers, we can add them and get an even number as an answer).
- Ask students to compose a different sentence using all three of the same words.

- Encourage students to read their sentences aloud using the following method:

  These are my words: number, plus sign, even.

  This is my sentence: I put a plus sign between two even numbers.

  This is how it looked: 4 + 6.

- Give your students the slogan "Have Words, Can Write" and post it on the wall.

In the beginning, some students may have difficulty combining several words into one sentence that has meaning, but with frequent practice they will gain the skills they need to do so. It is essential that the students learn to compose with three words (in contrast to one word or even two) in order to create statements that build concepts. Notice that after the students have composed their sentences, they can elaborate on what their sentence "shows" when they use numbers and symbols. The templates shown in Figures 3.1 to 3.15 represent a range of possible responses, from simple to fairly sophisticated.

Following are several models for composing mathematical sentences and word sentences. Having students write mathematical sentences and word sentences that are equivalent in meaning helps them not only to distinguish between the two, but to compare their similarities and differences and discuss why one form may be more efficient or effective than another form. The examples cover the five content standards—number and operations, algebra, geometry, measurement, and data analysis and probability—plus money. These examples represent a wide range of grade-level knowledge, both basic and advanced, and are illustrative of the potential for writing. They also show opportunities for differentiation within a classroom where some students can show emerging knowledge while others can express more complex ideas on the same topic (Tomlinson, 1999).

COMPOSING WITH KEYWORDS TO BUILD MATHEMATICAL VOCABULARY

Menninger (1992) emphasizes that "numbers seek form as words and as symbols," further pointing out "that every culture began by expressing its numbers as words" (p. 262). Yet most students learn to believe (in school) that mathematics is "about numbers" and writing is "about words," a belief that is reinforced when students change from "math time" to "language arts time" or "reading time" or "writing time." However, we only have to look at simple mathematical word problems to see the importance of words for solving these problems. Here is an example taken from Crowe's *Strategies for Success in Mathematics* (2000):

Find a number between 20 and 80. The sum of its digits is 12. The number is a multiple of 8. What is the number? (p. 38)

This problem is designed for intermediate-grade students and requires a very basic knowledge of adding and multiplication. But if students do not understand the meaning of the words *number, digit,* and *multiple,* they cannot solve this problem.

Sentences for Number and Operations

Task: Write as many word sentences as you can about the number sentence 4 + 4 = 8.

Number Sentence	Word Sentence
4 + 4 = 8	<ul><li>Four plus four equals eight.</li><li>Two even numbers have been added.</li><li>The sum is an even number.</li><li>This problem contains the same addend twice and is doubled.</li><li>This problem is written horizontally.</li><li>It can also be written vertically. $$\begin{array}{r} 4 \\ + 4 \\ \hline 8 \end{array}$$</li></ul>

Task: Change these word sentences to number sentences.

Word Sentence	Number Sentence
Two plus two equals four	2 + 2 = 4
One half of fourteen is the same amount as twenty-one divided by three.	$1/2 \times 14 = 21 \div 3$
One thousand four hundred seventy is greater than one thousand four hundred twenty-one.	1470 > 1421

Figure 3.1

Sentences for Algebra*

Algebra Sentences	Word Sentences
a + b = b + a	a plus b equals b plus a
ax + bx = (a + b)x	a times x plus b times x is equal to adding a plus b times x.
3(2x + 3y) = 6x + 9y	The multiplier three makes two x become six x and three y become nine y. The equal signs show that both sides of the equation represent the same amount.

Word Sentence	Algebra Sentence
x times the sum of x plus y plus z equals x squared plus xy plus xz	$x(x + y + z) = x2 + xy + xz$

Figure 3.2

*An excellent resource for helping students understand and compose algebraic sentences is the Southwest Educational Development Laboratory Web site (www.sedl.org), especially the article "It's Elementary: Introducing Algebraic Thinking Before High School" (*SEDL Letter, XV*(1), December, 2003).

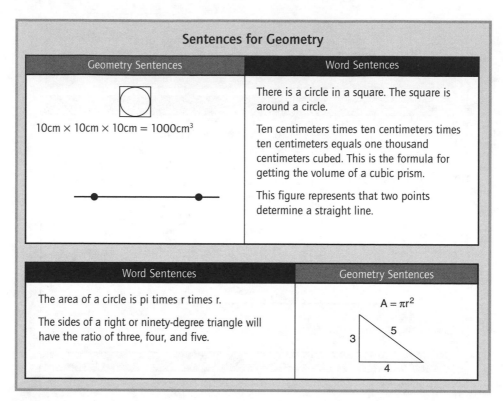

Figure 3.3

Sentences for Measurement

Measurement Sentences	Word Sentences
$2' = 12'' + 12''$	Two feet equals twelve inches plus twelve inches.
$1\ m = 100\ cm = 1000\ mm$	One meter equals one hundred centimeters, which equals one thousand millimeters.
$A = 14 \times 12 = 168$ square units	The area of a rectangle (or parallelogram) is found by multiplying the length, which here is fourteen linear units, times the width, which is twelve linear units. The answer is one hundred sixty-eight square units.

Word Sentences	Measurement Sentences
To know how much a quarter of a mile is, you have to know that a mile is five thousand two hundred eighty feet. Then we multiply one quarter times five thousand two hundred eighty feet to get the answer one thousand three hundred twenty feet.	$1/4\ mile = 1/4 \times 5{,}280\ feet = 1{,}320\ feet$
To know how many miles you can go per gallon, you divide the number of gallons by the mileage you have gone. If you go three hundred miles and use ten gallons, you are getting thirty miles per gallon.	$300\ miles \div 10\ gal. = 30\ m.p.g.$

Figure 3.4

Sentences for Data Analysis and Probability

Data Statement	Word Statement
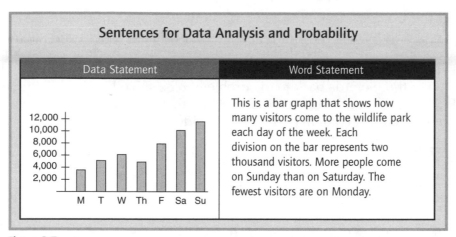	This is a bar graph that shows how many visitors come to the wildlife park each day of the week. Each division on the bar represents two thousand visitors. More people come on Sunday than on Saturday. The fewest visitors are on Monday.

Figure 3.5

Sentences for Money

Money Sentences	Word Sentences
4¢ + 10¢ + $1.00 = $1.14	Four cents plus ten cents plus one dollar equals one dollar and fourteen cents.
$1.00 − $.25 − $.08 − $.43 − $.15 = $.09	Example: I had a dollar to spend. I spent twenty-five cents for an orange, eight cents for a small cookie, forty-three cents for two bananas, and fifteen cents for a peach. I got back nine cents in change.

Word Sentences	Money Sentences
I sold ten cups of lemonade for ten cents each to earn one dollar.	$.10 × 10 = $1.00
I earn twenty five hundred dollars a month. Twenty-five percent of this amount is for rent. My rent is six hundred twenty-five dollars a month.	25% × $2,500.00 = $625.00
My mother lent me one thousand dollars for school. She asked me to pay her six percent simple interest for four years. She also said I could pay her the total amount of one thousand two hundred forty dollars at one time.	.06 × $1,000 = $60(4) + $1,000 = $1,240

Figure 3.6

Using the Composing With Keywords strategy, a student would first compose a sentence that shows the relationship of the words *number, digit,* and *multiple,* apart from the problem to be solved. For example, he might write, "Every digit is a number that can be counted and has one or more multiples." He would then take his knowledge of these words back to the problem to be solved and solve the problem.

Following is another mathematical question that contains no numbers:
Which figure must contain perpendicular sides?

    a. parallelogram
    b. trapezoid
    c. rectangle
    d. octagon (Crowe, 2000, p. 115)

Clearly, the student needs to know the meanings of seven words to solve this problem: figure, perpendicular, sides, parallelogram, trapezoid, rectangle, and octagon. If a student uses the Composing With Keywords strategy, she might write, "Parallelograms, trapezoids, rectangles, and octagons all have sides, but only the rectangle has sides that form a right angle and therefore it is a figure that contains perpendicular sides."

By composing with keywords frequently, your students will build up the fluency they need to respond to problems such as those illustrated above as well as to the many other problems they need to solve.

Think of Composing With Keywords as a warm-up activity that allows the students to create mathematically correct as well as "imaginative" statements that might be challenged. Obviously, "correct" statements are necessary for understanding mathematical concepts, but why might you allow the students to write imaginative or "non-correct" statements? One answer to this question comes from Wells (1995), in his discussion of mathematics games in which he compares mathematics with chess. In thinking of mathematics as a game, he points out that "it takes imagination and insight to discover the best moves, at chess or mathematics, and the more difficult the position, the harder they are to find" (p. 83). He goes on to explain that

> the player must explore the game by playing it, thinking about it, and analyzing it. For the chess player and the mathematician, this process is scientific: you test ideas, experiment with new possibilities, develop the ones that work and discard the ones that fail. (p. 83)

So while accuracy is important, mathematical word play gives the students an opportunity to play the "game" of mathematics, to explore both real and fantasy ideas.

The activities in Mathematics the Write Way further illustrate how to use this strategy.

Mathematics the Write Way

■ ACTIVITY 1

Composing With Keywords Using Taxonomies

The following activity helps students move from creating Taxonomies into Composing With Keywords.

Now that you have created Taxonomies of mathematical words, you have a lot of words for composing mathematical sentences.

1. Select three words from one of your mathematical Taxonomies.
2. *Use all three words* to compose *one* mathematically correct or accurate sentence. You may change the form of the words to make your sentence work grammatically. See the example in Figure 3.7.

You can also expand the templates, as in Figures 3.8 to 3.13. The following activities use keywords from each of the content areas—number and operations, algebra, geometry, measurement, data analysis and probability—and money. The main goal is to have students create their own word problems or statements based on keywords. The word problems and statements shown here are examples that you can use as a model for your own students.

KEYWORDS	
Words	**Sentence**
Fraction Triangle Measure	Mathematicians try to measure triangles as accurately as possible so as to not be wrong by even a fraction.

Figure 3.7

Composing With Keywords—Number and Operations

Create at least three different word problems by using the same three mathematical words in each problem. You can change the forms of the words. For example, you can change the word *ten* to *tens* or *tenth,* or you can change the word *add* to *adds, added, adding,* or *addition.* The examples in Figure 3.8 are models of what to do.

KEYWORDS

Concept	Keywords	Word Problems or Statements
Number and Operations	six, ten, add	1. I had six toys. My mother bought me ten more. I added them together. How many toys do I have? 2. I have six sixes and ten tens. If I add these numbers, how much do I have? If I have ten sixes and six tens and add them up, how much do I have? If I add six and ten, will the sum be odd or even. Why? 3. There are sixty students in the fifth grade. Every day one-sixth of them go to band practice, one-tenth go to soccer practice, and the rest stay in their classrooms. Add the total number of students who go out. Tell how many stay in the room.
Number and Operations	multiply, divide, four	1. My teacher bought four storybooks for each student. There are twenty-five students in the class. She then multiplied the number of books times the number of students. How many books did she buy? She then divided the class into five groups and gave each group the same number of books. How many books did she give each group? 2. If you multiply four times four, what divisor do you need to get the answer two? 3. If I divide a hundred by minus four and multiply the answer by minus forty-four, what is the final answer?

Figure 3.8

Composing With Keywords—Algebra

Choose three words related to algebra and compose statements using the words. You can change the forms of the words. For example, you can change the word *number* to *numerator* or *enumerate,* or you can change the word *multiply* to *multiplication.* The examples in Figure 3.9 are models of what to do.

Composing With Keywords—Geometry

Choose three words related to geometry and compose statements using the words. You can change the forms of the words. For example, you can change the word *rectangle* to *rectangular,* or you can change the word *circle* to *circular.* The examples in Figure 3.10 are models of what to do.

Composing With Keywords—Measurement

Choose three words related to measurement and compose statements using the words. You can change the forms of the words. For example, you can make the words plural. The examples in Figure 3.11 are models of what to do.

Algebra

KEYWORDS

Concept	Keywords	Word Problems or Statements
Algebra	coefficient, sum, number	The number that stands in front of x (or other symbol) is called the coefficient. I can get the sum of the coefficients by placing the numbers within the parentheses. The algebraic statement will look like this: $2x + 6x + 8x = (2 + 6 + 8)x = 16x$.
Algebra	multiply, quantities, dot	When we multiply two quantities, for example x and y, we use a dot rather than an x because an x in algebra stands for an unknown quantity. The multiplication problem looks like this: $x \bullet y$.

Figure 3.9

Geometry

KEYWORDS

Concept	Keywords	Word Problems or Statements
Geometry	area, rectangle, triangle	We find the area of a rectangle by multiplying length times width or ab. The area of a triangle is half that of a rectangle so the formula is ab ÷ 2.
Geometry	circle, circumference, diameter	The circumference is the length of the line that forms a circle. The diameter is a line that evenly divides a circle.

Figure 3.10

Measurement

KEYWORDS

Concept	Keywords	Word Problems or Statements
Measurement	inch, foot, yard	In the United States, we use the inch as a unit of measurement. Twelve inches equals one foot. When we put three feet together, we get a yard.
Measurement	centimeter, decameter, hectometer	In the metric system, a unit of measurement is the centimeter. Ten centimeters are a decameter and ten decameters are a hectometer. Every unit of metric measurement is based on a system of tens.

Figure 3.11

Composing With Keywords—Data Analysis and Probability

Choose three words related to data analysis and probability and compose statements using the words. You can change the forms of the words. For example, you can change *represent* to *representation.* The examples in Figure 3.12 are models of what to do.

Data Analysis and Probability

KEYWORDS

Concept	Keywords	Word Problems or Statements
Data Analysis and Probability	graph, represent, gather	After we gather data or information, we can show or represent that data on different kinds of graphs, such as bar graphs, line graphs, or circle graphs.
Data Analysis and Probability	pie graph, circle, sector	A pie graph is in the shape of a circle and is divided into sections called sectors. Each sector shows the percentage of the category that the graph is illustrating.

Figure 3.12

Composing With Keywords—Money

Choose three words related to money and compose statements using the words. You can change the forms of the words. For example, you can change the word *barter* to *bartering.* The examples in Figure 3.13 are models of what to do.

Money

KEYWORDS

Concept	Keywords	Word Problems or Statements
Money	currency, paper, coins	Most countries have two types of currency or money. They have coins or metal currency and paper money. Both coins and paper come in different amounts.
Money	money, barter, exchange	People are always exchanging goods for other goods or goods for services. A long time ago they did this in a system called bartering. Today most people use money as a medium of exchange.

Figure 3.13

Additional Models to Use or Adapt

Basic Examples

KEYWORDS		
Concept	Keywords	Word Problems or Statements
zero, backward, forward	If I count backward from ten I can get to zero, but when I count forward I can get to ten.	This is how it looks when I go backward: 10, 9, 8, 7, 6, 5, 4, 3, 2, 1, 0. This is how it looks when I go forward: 1, 2, 3, 4, 5, 6, 7, 8, 9, 10.
shape, triangle, circle	I made a shape called a triangle and then put a circle around it.	This is how what I wrote looks:
count, take away, less	I will count four pennies and take away two pennies so I will now have less pennies.	This is what my sentence shows: When I take away two pennies, I have just two pennies. That is less.

Figure 3.14

Advanced Examples

Concept	Words	Sentence	What My Sentence Shows or Illustrates
Number and Operations	number line, integer, difference	When I place integers on a number line, I can understand the difference between positive and negative numbers.	This is how my number line looks: —3 —2 —1 0 1 2 3 By placing integers on a number line, I can easily add and subtract positive and negative numbers.
Algebra	square, sequence, pattern	There is an interesting sequence of numbers when I set out perfect squares and look for the pattern.	This is how my sequence of perfect squares looks. Underneath I have written the pattern of numbers. 1 4 9 16 25 36 49 64 81 100 3 5 7 9 11 13 15 17 19
Geometry	quadrilateral, rectangle, sides	A rectangle has four sides and is only one type of quadrilateral.	This is how I have illustrated my sentence to show what I have said in words: Rectangle Quadrilateral
Measurement	tall, pound, weight	As I got taller, my weight went from 93 pounds to 115 pounds in one year.	This is how I looked before and after.
Data Analysis and Probability	graph, axis, gather	I gathered information about how much I grew in one year and then put this information on a graph that had a y-axis and an x-axis.	Here is my graph that shows my growth for one year. Some months I did not grow at all, but then from May to June I had a growth spurt. Sept. Oct. Nov. Dec. Jan. Feb. Mar. Apr. May Jun. Jul. Aug.

Figure 3.15

INTERNET LINKS

Mathematics for Parents Newsletter

http://www.wcer.wisc.edu/archive/mims/Parent_Newsletters/

The Math Forum @ Drexel

http://mathforum.org

Webmath

http://www.webmath.com/

4

Metacognition for Mathematical Thinking

"Can you do Addition?" the White Queen asked. "What's one and one and one and one and one and one?"

"I don't know," said Alice. "I lost count."

"She can't do Addition," the Red Queen interrupted.

—*Through the Looking Glass* (Carroll, 1965b, p. 142)

Learning mathematics requires that children create and re-create mathematical relationships in their own minds. (Burns, 1992, p. 24)

WHAT IS METACOGNITION?

The dialogue between Alice and the Red and White Queens is a humorous, yet insightful example of metacognition, which Costa and Kallick (2000) define as "thinking about thinking" or "know your knowing" (p. xvii). Notice the interesting play on words. The White Queen asks Alice whether she can do addition. Alice says, "I don't know." Then she gives her reason for not knowing: "I lost count." The Red Queen makes an immediate assessment based on Alice's response: "She can't do Addition."

Students who struggle with mathematics often feel like Alice. They might say, "I know how to add, but I can't do addition problems" or "I know the answer, but I don't know how I got it." Present-day assessments of mathematical achievement are likely to ask students how they arrived at the answer as well as what the answer is, giving students like Alice great difficulty. Ronis (1999) refers to the NCTM standards-based curriculum that "provides methods for getting at the reasons behind children's answers," further emphasizing the importance of having students learn how to be self-evaluative (p. 20).

To meet standards that expect students to provide reasons and do self-evaluation, students must question their responses, assess and reassess their understanding of mathematical concepts. The ability to assess and reassess one's knowledge is called metacognition, or knowing about knowing.

Ronis (1999) poses two questions that teachers must keep in mind: "What do we want students to understand?" and "What can they demonstrate . . . that they do understand?" (p. 26). Perkins (1992) elaborates on this concept of understanding and knowing. He uses the term metacurriculum, which refers to higher-order understanding "about how ordinary subject-area knowledge is organized," "about how we think and learn," and "about the way subject matter works" (p. 101).

The strategy Metacognition, which can be simply stated as "I know that I know," helps students develop their reasoning, thinking, and self-evaluation skills so that they gain higher-order knowledge. In the Metacognition strategy, students respond to a variety of metacognitive starters that are variations of "I know that I know" and are designed to bring about reflection and personal assessment.

One of the essential aspects stressed in the Everyday Mathematics program (Tangretti & Liptak, 1995, p. 4) is for students to focus on three (metacognitive) questions in solving mathematics problems: How did I get my answer? Is there another way to get the answer? Is there another right answer? We view these questions as metacognitive because they can be restated by the students: I know (or don't know) how I got my answer; I know (or don't know whether) there is another way to get the answer; and I know (or don't know whether) there is another right answer.

Paired with metacognition is "thinking flexibly," which gives students the opportunity to "look at a situation another way; find alternatives; find a way to change perspectives, generate alternatives, and consider options" (Costa & Kallick, 2000, p. xvii).

Figure 4.1 lists our recommended metacognitive starters, followed by suggestions for their use in the primary, intermediate, and middle grades. We suggest that students have visual access to these starters—that they appear on the classroom board or wall, and be copied into students' notebooks. Students can refer to the starters daily (or very frequently) and share the starters in collaborative groups. You may add to and adapt these starters according to your students' needs. At the end of this chapter is a sample lesson plan that includes Taxonomies, Composing With Keywords, and Metacognition and shows how these three strategies become linked.

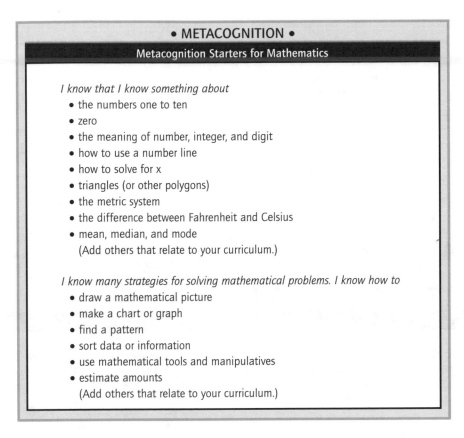

Figure 4.1

INTRODUCING METACOGNITION

Modern mathematics does not negate the importance of learning basic arithmetic facts. It specifically emphasizes that mathematics is a problem solving tool that stresses "the precise definition of terms, the making of only those assertions which specifically apply to the issues or objects under discussion, and the application of careful reasoning" (Vernooy, 1997, p. 5). By teaching students to explain or write about their answers, we move them from rote learning to the application of reasoning to form the basis of mathematical learning. This "becomes the key . . . to a student's ability to understand not only how the process works, but also why" (Tangretti & Liptak, 1995, p. 3).

Let's consider an example. You might find the following problem (or more accurately, algorithm) in a mathematics textbook or on a worksheet:

Solve these equations. Explain how you know what to do.

$$9 + 6 = ? \quad 27 + 13 = ? \quad 8 - 3 = ? \quad 25 - 16 = ?$$

We expect students to solve the algorithm if they have learned the rules of computation. What is difficult for students is to "explain how you know what to do." Most students respond automatically to single-digit algorithms and would answer by saying, "I just know." To a degree, they do "just know," just as they know how to read "sight" words such as *right* or *eight*. Therefore, students need direct instruction in how to write an explanation. They need to learn how to analyze (or break down) the steps their brains are using to solve the algorithm.

Begin to teach Metacognition by using Figure 4.2. Give students a copy of Figure 4.2 and walk them through the steps.

You can use a variety of Metacognition statements with your students. Figure 4.3 shows two examples of Metacognition statements using a different set of starter phrases. (Please note: We do not suggest that your students write explanations for every algorithm. Select one algorithm from a group that students are practicing and ask them to write a Metacognition statement using the template in Figure 4.3). We also recommend that teachers model the process several times before having students work independently.

Figure 4.4 gives students more valuable practice in Metacognition by asking them to complete statements that include the words "how" or "why." You can also improve their Metacognition by using open-ended statements with the underlying question, "Is there more than one answer?" See Figure 4.5 for examples of open-ended statements.

• METACOGNITION •
How to Write Metacognition Statements

Metacognition means (1) knowing what you know or (2) knowing what you don't know or (3) knowing what you need to know. One way to express Metacognition is by using a Frame that helps you organize your writing.

1. Select a term that you know something about from one of your mathematical Taxonomies.

2. Follow the outline of the Frame* to write what you know about that term. The Frame has starter phrases that you must complete. For example, the starter phrases might be:

   I know that I know . . .

   First I know . . .

   In addition, I know . . .

   Finally, I know . . .

   Now you know something that I know . . .

Suppose you chose the word *zero*. Your Metacognition statement might look something like this:

   I know that I know something about zero.

   First I know that zero can mean nothing or having no amount.

   In addition, I know that zero is used to show place value, as in the number 101, where zero means that there are no tens in that number.

   Finally, I know that the idea of zero came from India and the Arab traders who learned about it when they were trading in India a long time ago.

   Now you know something that I know about zero.

*For a complete discussion of Frames, see Chapter 7.

Figure 4.2

• METACOGNITION •

Sample Metacognition Statements

I know that I know how to add 9 + 6.

First, I think of 9 and how much more I have to go when I have 6 more.

Second, I count 10, 11, 12, 13, 14, 15. That is 6 more.

Then, I write 9 + 6 and put an equal sign to show my answer.

Finally, I put the answer, 15, after the equal sign.

Following is another response to the same problem that reveals a different path of thinking:

I know that I know how to add 9 + 6.

First, I know that 9 + 1 equals 10 and I have 5 more to go because I have to add 6.

Then, I add 10 and 5 so I get 15.

Finally, I have my answer, which is 9 + 6 = 15.

Figure 4.3

• METACOGNITION •

Metacognition Statements That Use How and Why

I know how to add . . .

I know how to take away . . .

I know how to estimate . . .

I know how to measure . . .

I know how to round off . . .

I know how to make a graph that shows . . .

I know why 1/2 is greater than (or more than) 1/3 . . .

I know why 1/4 of 8 is more than 1/5 of 8 . . .

I know why 12 inches is less than 3 feet . . .

I know why 2 dimes is more money than 3 nickels . . .

I know why I use 0 when I write the number 10 . . .

Figure 4.4

Introducing Metacognition in the Upper Grades

You may use the earlier models to introduce Metacognition in the upper grades or you may use Figure 4.6. Emphasize to upper-grade students that these problem-solving examples encourage them to ask themselves, "What do I already know?" and

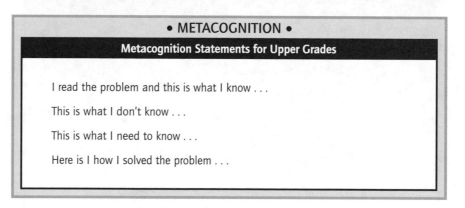

• METACOGNITION •

Open-Ended Metacognition Statements

The following Metacognition starters use three as a focal point. Students are asked to complete the starter, "I know three numbers that . . ."

I know three numbers that add up to 12.

I know three numbers that are odd and add up to 15.

I know three numbers that are less than 1.

Following are more open-ended starters that give students opportunities to create their own Metacognition statements and then think about how they can explain these statements.

I know three ways to subtract 8 from 21.

I know three shapes that have angles.

I know three coins that can make 20 cents.

I know three measuring tools that I use for cooking.

Figure 4.5

• METACOGNITION •

Metacognition Statements for Upper Grades

I read the problem and this is what I know . . .

This is what I don't know . . .

This is what I need to know . . .

Here is I how I solved the problem . . .

Figure 4.6

"What do I need to know?" Students often bypass these questions when they are learning rote responses. This happens not only in mathematics but in all subject areas.

Further Uses of Metacognition

Metacognition is the ability to conceptualize what you believe or understand that you know and then to prove that knowledge by "using it, representing it in multiple ways, or explaining it to others" (Rizzo et al., 1998). Because Metacognition statements are simple, students can practice writing them in every aspect of mathematics on a daily basis both in the classroom and as homework assignments. Figure 4.7 gives further examples of opening statements that involve use, representation, and explanation. When students become skilled at Metacognition, challenge them to create their own organizers and transitions.

• METACOGNITION •

Metacognition Statements for Use, Representation, and Explanation

Use
Begin with one of the following:
I know several ways to use a ruler . . .
I know several ways to use a calculator . . .
I know several ways to use a protractor . . .
I know several ways to use a compass . . .

Continue with these transitions:
If I need to, I . . .
I can also . . .
Furthermore, I . . .
By knowing how to use a _____ in these ways, I . . .

Representation
Begin with one of the following:
I know how to represent information on a bar (or other) graph . . .
I know how to represent fractions by drawing circles, rectangles, and other shapes . . .
I know how to represent the number __ in several ways . . .
I know how to represent miles or kilometers on a map . . .
I know how to represent letters, boxes, or other symbols to stand for a number or quantity.

Continue with these transitions:
I begin by . . .
After that . . .
Then . . .
Finally . . .

Explanation
Begin with one of the following:
I can explain how to add fractions with different denominators . . .
I can explain the difference between an analog clock and a digital clock . . .

I can explain the steps for solving a mathematical problem . . .
I can explain three ways to find the weight of a dog . . .
I can explain the meaning of this formula: area of a rectangle = length × width . . .

Figure 4.7

Responding to Students' Writing

Many teachers have expressed concerns about how to respond to student writing as it relates to the "grammar, organization, and conventions." They (rightfully) worry about the time it takes to respond to writing and how much they need to "correct," not just for the mathematics but for the "English."

You will find that one of the advantages of using the Metacognition templates in this chapter is the simplicity of their organization. Almost all students can follow the template layout that focuses on transitional statements in a logical or sequential order. By using these templates frequently, the students will internalize the organizational schema and you will find that you can focus on the substance (the mathematics) rather than the form. We have also included writing rubrics that can help you and your students produce clear mathematical writing (see Resource A).

Mathematics the Write Way

Writing Activities Related to Metacognition

(All Grades)

Following are examples of problems that can be explained or solved by using Metacognition. Examples are given concerning number and operations, algebra, geometry, measurement, and probability. Each example has a prompt and uses a Metacognition template to formulate a response. You may find similar problems in your mathematics curriculum, and we recommend that you adapt the Metacognition templates as necessary. You and your students may also create other problems and make appropriate changes to the templates.

Number and Operations

• METACOGNITION •

Prompt: Betty has quarters, dimes, and nickels to buy a notebook. If the notebook costs more than 50 cents and less than a dollar and she gave the storekeeper the exact change, what combinations of coins might she have used?

Sample Response Using Metacognition:

I read the problem and this is what I know:

I know that Betty has to have more than one quarter, dime, and nickel because the problem says quarters, dimes, and nickels. I also know that a quarter is 25 cents, a dime is 10 cents, and a nickel is 5 cents. And I know that the notebook is more than 50 cents but less than a dollar.

This is what I don't know:

I don't know how many of each coin she has.

This is what I need to know:

I need to know how many of each coin she has and how many of each coin she gave to the storekeeper.

I used a strategy of guess and check to solve the problem:

First I tried this combination:
2 quarters = 50 cents
2 dimes = 20 cents
2 nickels = 10 cents
This would mean that Betty paid 80 cents for the notebook.

Then I tried this combination:
2 quarters = 50 cents
3 dimes = 30 cents
2 nickels = 10 cents
So maybe the notebook cost 90 cents.

If she gave the storekeeper 3 nickels with 2 quarters and 3 dimes, the notebook would cost 95 cents. I don't think there are any other combinations.

Figure 4.8

Algebra

• METACOGNITION •

Prompt: Every day the farmer went to the chicken coop to count the new chicks. On Monday he found three chicks. On Tuesday he found five chicks. On Wednesday he found eight chicks. On Thursday he found twelve chicks. If this pattern continued for the rest of the week, how many chicks did the farmer have by Sunday?

Sample Response Using Metacognition:

I know how to find out how many chicks the farmer had on Sunday.

First, I know that the pattern is based on one week or seven days and that every day the farmer had more chicks.

Second, I made a table so I could see the pattern of how many more chicks the farmer had each day. The pattern looks like this:

Monday	3 chicks
Tuesday	3 chicks + 2 chicks = 5 chicks
Wednesday	5 chicks + 3 chicks = 8 chicks
Thursday	8 chicks + 4 chicks = 12 chicks
Friday	12 chicks + 5 chicks = 17 chicks
Saturday	17 chicks + 6 chicks = 23 chicks
Sunday	23 chicks + 7 chicks = 30 chicks

Finally, I figured out the pattern. Each day, the total number of chicks increased by one more than it increased the day before. I used my table to keep the pattern going until I reached Sunday. The farmer has 30 chicks because each day one more chick hatched compared to the day before and was then added on to the number of chicks that the farmer already had.

Figure 4.9

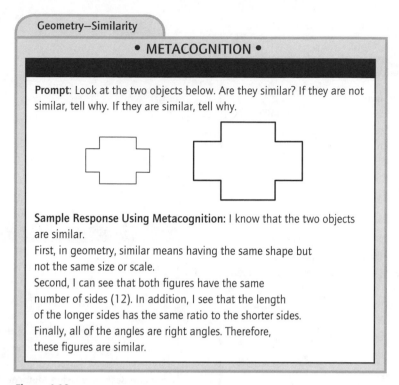

Geometry—Similarity

• METACOGNITION •

Prompt: Look at the two objects below. Are they similar? If they are not similar, tell why. If they are similar, tell why.

Sample Response Using Metacognition: I know that the two objects are similar.

First, in geometry, similar means having the same shape but not the same size or scale.

Second, I can see that both figures have the same number of sides (12). In addition, I see that the length of the longer sides has the same ratio to the shorter sides. Finally, all of the angles are right angles. Therefore, these figures are similar.

Figure 4.10

Measurement

• METACOGNITION •

Prompt: Mrs. Bennett is 65 inches tall. Mr. Bennett is 72 inches tall. Eight-year-old Sally Bennett is 48 inches tall and twelve-year-old Charles Bennett is 60 inches tall. Boys and girls grow about the same amount until age twelve—approximately 2 inches each year. If Sally grows two inches each year until she is fourteen, will she be as tall as her mother? How tall might she be if she grew two inches a year until she was sixteen? How many inches a year does Charles have to grow between twelve and sixteen to be as tall as his father? Write what you can predict from this information.

Sample Response Using Metacognition:

I know that I can predict several pieces of information about how tall Sally and Charles will be in a few years.

First, I know that if Sally grows 2 inches between the ages of eight and fourteen she will be 12 inches taller than she is now. I found this by creating an equation: $(2 \times 6) + 48 = 60$ inches ($60" - 48" = 12"$). I also know that if Sally is 60 inches when she is fourteen, she will be 5 inches shorter than her mother. I found this by subtracting Sally's height from her mother's ($65" - 60" = 5"$). She needs to grow 2 1/2 inches for two more years to be 65 inches tall or the same height as her mother.

Then I know that Charles is twelve years old and is 12 inches shorter than his father. I found this out by subtracting Charles's height from his father's ($72" - 60" = 12"$). If he grows 2 inches per year, he will have to grow until he is eighteen to be as tall as his father. I found this by creating a pattern of equations: $60 + 2 = 62$, $62 + 2 = 64$, $64 + 2 = 66$, and so on.

Finally, I know that this is the best I can predict since people's growth rates are only approximate and people stop growing at different ages when they are in their teens.

Figure 4.11

Additional Writing Activities Related to Metacognition

(All Grades)

Use the following activities, when appropriate, to further challenge your students. The examples cover number and operations, algebra, geometry, measurement, data analysis and probability, and money.

Metacognition for Number and Operations

• METACOGNITION •

Prompt: Select any number from three to nine. Write an opening statement: I know that I know several things (concepts) about the number (five). Write three statements using these transitions: first, second, last. Write a concluding statement, such as "Now you know . . ."

Sample Response Using Metacognition:

I know that I know several concepts about the number five.

First, five is an odd number between the even numbers four and six.

Example: 4, 5, 6

Second, five multiplied by an odd number results in a number that has five in the ones place.

Examples: $5 \times 3 = 15$, $5 \times 25 = 125$, $5 \times 45 = 225$

Last, five is a prime number, meaning it can only be divided by one or itself.

Now you know what I know about five.

Prompt: Write three statements telling what you know about the number 809.

Sample Response Using Metacognition:

I know that I can write three statements about the number 809.

First, 809 has three digits: 8, 0, 9.

Second, the number 809 has nine ones, no tens, and eight hundreds.

Last, it cannot be evenly divided into two whole numbers since it is an odd number.

These three statements tell something that I know about the number 809.

Figure 4.12

• METACOGNITION •

Prompt: Look carefully at the array of squares on the right. Write three sentences about this picture. Start your writing with a Metacognition statement.

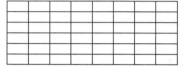

Sample Response Using Metacognition:
I know that I can write three statements about this array of squares. First, I know that this array forms a rectangle because all four sides are squares that have right angles.

Second, I know that there are twenty-four squares because $4 \times 6 = 24$.

Finally, since each square has four sides, I know that there are 96 edges or sides because $24 \times 4 = 96$.

These are three statements related to this array of squares that show what I know.

Prompt: Look at the grid on the right. Fill in the grid with 2 As, 4 Bs, 6 Cs, 8 Ds, 12 Es, 16 Fs. Write a Metacognition statement telling three pieces of information that you realized by filling in the grid.

Sample Response Using Metacognition:
As a result of filling in the rectangles with different amounts of letters, I know three facts or pieces of information.

First, each letter takes up a different fraction of the grid. For example, 1/24 of the grid are As; 1/12 are Bs; 1/8 are Cs; 1/6 are Ds; 1/4 are Es; 1/3 are Fs. I found this by creating fractions and reducing them. I used the number of squares for each letter as the numerator and the total number of squares as the denominator before I reduced the fractions.

Second, I notice that the larger the denominator is, the smaller is the fraction. For example, 1/24 of the grid is taken by 2 As, but 1/3 of the grid is taken by 12 Fs.

Last, I noticed that when the common denominator of all fractions was 48, the denominators were 24, 12, 8, 6, 4, and 3. These numbers are all factors of 48.

By filling the grid, I noticed many ideas that I had not thought of before.

Figure 4.13

Metacognition for Algebra

• METACOGNITION •

Prompt: Write a Metacognition statement for solving this algebraic equation: 66/x = 11. Begin your statement with "I know that I know how to solve 66/x = 11."

Sample Response Using Metacognition:

I know that I know how to solve 66/x = 11.

First, I know that the amounts on each side of the equal sign are the same. That means that any operation I do on one side of the equation must be done on the other side to keep them equal.

Therefore, if I multiply 66/x times x, I have to multiply 11 times x. I know that if I can get 66 to stand alone, I will be able to solve for x. So I multiplied both sides of the equation by x and got 66 = 11x.

Finally, I know that once the equation reads 66 = 11x, you can divide both sides by 11 to get x by itself. Then you can divide 66 by 11 to find the numerical value of x. In this equation, x = 6.

Figure 4.14

• METACOGNITION •

Prompt: There are several properties you have to know in algebra. Here are three of them:

1. One property is A = B. This is called the property of substitution.
2. Another property is A + B = B + A. This is called the commutative property.
3. A third property is A + (B + C) = (A + B) + C. This is called the associative property.

Write a Metacognition statement for each of these properties. Begin each statement with "I know that I understand the _____ property."

Sample Response Using Metacognition:

Property of Substitution

> I know that I understand the property of substitution.

> First, I know that if you are given that A = B, then anywhere you see A in an equation you can substitute B.

> Additionally, I know that if A = B, then B = A.

> Finally, I know that before you can solve the equation, you need to know which letters are equivalent or represent the same amount.

Commutative Property

> I know that I know about the commutative property.

> First, I know that the order of the terms in addition problems doesn't change the sum.

> Second, I also know that the order of factors in multiplication problems does not change the product.

> Finally, I know that I have to follow the order of operations when the equation includes more than one sign.

Associative Property

> I know that I know something about the associative property.

> First, I know that if all of the operations in an equation are addition, it does not matter which numbers you add first.

> Second, I also know that when there are parentheses in the equation, we have to do the operations in parentheses first, then do the rest of the problem.

> Finally, I know that there can be many operations in one problem.

Figure 4.15

Metacognition for Geometry

• METACOGNITION •

Prompt: The formula for the area of a rectangle is Area = Length × Height. The formula for the area of a right triangle is Area = ½(L × H). Write a Metacognition statement that tells why the formula for the right triangle is half the formula for a rectangle. Begin your statement with "I understand why . . ."

Sample Response Using Metacognition:

> I understand why a right triangle has half the area of a rectangle.

> I know that when you draw a diagonal line from corner to corner in a rectangle you will have two equal right triangles.

> I also know that if you draw a diagonal line from one corner of a rectangle to another, you divide the rectangle in half.

> Therefore, I understand that to compute the area of a right triangle, I must divide the area of the rectangle in half.

Figure 4.16

• METACOGNITION •

Prompt: A figure has a line of symmetry if it can be folded so that two parts are congruent (or meet at all points). Find figures from the group below that have symmetry. Write a Metacognition statement for each item, telling its points of congruence. Begin your statement with "I can explain why Figure _____ is congruent."

Figure A ◆   Figure B)(Figure C ☐

Sample Response Using Metacognition:
I can explain why Figure A has symmetry. When Figure A is folded in half, it changes its shape from a square to a triangle with all points meeting. I can also explain why Figure B has symmetry. When Figure B is folded along the horizontal line, the ends of the crescent lines meet on the other side. Finally, I know how to explain why Figure C is symmetrical. When you fold Figure C in half, the corners of the square meet.

Figure 4.17

Metacognition for Measurement

• METACOGNITION •

Prompt: Many times stores show the unit price for two different brands but in different units. For example, a box of corn flakes and a box of wheat flakes both cost $4.49. The box of corn flakes weighs 300 grams. The box of wheat flakes weighs 12 ounces. Both boxes appear to be the same size. How do you know which cereal is the better value? Write a Metacognition statement beginning with the sentence, "I know how to determine which cereal is the better value."

Sample Response Using Metacognition:

I know how to determine which cereal is the better value.

First, I know that an ounce equals 28.349 grams.

I also know that if I multiply 12 by 28.349, I will know how much a box of wheat flakes weighs in grams.

Therefore, I know that the box of wheat flakes weighs 340.188 grams and a box of corn flakes weights 300 grams. If I subtract 340.188 grams from 300 grams, I find out that I get 40.188 more grams of wheat flakes than corn flakes.

Finally, I know that you get more wheat flakes for $4.49 than you get corn flakes.

Figure 4.18

• METACOGNITION •

Prompt: When Maria was born she weighed 7 pounds. At one year of age she weighed 14 pounds. At age two she was 21 pounds. Her older brother Shawn weighed 8 pounds at birth, 16 pounds at one year, and 24 pounds at age two. Her younger sister Michele was 6 pounds at birth, 12 pounds at a year, and 18 pounds at age two. Write three Metacognition statements that show what you can infer from this story. Use these statements: "From this story, I first know that...," "I also know that...," "I can guess or estimate that..."

Sample Response Using Metacognition:

From this story, I first know that Shawn is the heaviest of the children and Michele is the lightest.

I also know that each of the three children gained as many pounds as they were born with for each year of their lives through age two.

Finally, I know that if this pattern continues until each child is nine years old, Maria will weigh 70 pounds, Shawn will weigh 80 pounds, and Michele will weigh 60 pounds. I can figure this out by making a table.

Age	Maria	Shawn	Michele
Birth	7 lbs.	8 lbs.	6 lbs.
1 year old	7 + 7 = 14 lbs.	8 + 8 = 16 lbs.	6 + 6 = 12 lbs.
2 years old	14 + 7 = 21 lbs.	16 + 8 = 24 lbs.	12 + 6 = 18 lbs.
3 years old	21 + 7 = 28 lbs.	24 + 8 = 32 lbs.	18 + 6 = 24 lbs.
4 years old	28 + 7 = 35 lbs.	32 + 8 = 40 lbs.	24 + 6 = 30 lbs.
5 years old	35 + 7 = 42 lbs.	40 + 8 = 48 lbs.	30 + 6 = 36 lbs.
6 years old	42 + 7 = 49 lbs.	48 + 8 = 56 lbs.	36 + 6 = 42 lbs.
7 years old	49 + 7 = 56 lbs.	56 + 8 = 64 lbs.	42 + 6 = 48 lbs.
8 years old	56 + 7 = 63 lbs.	64 + 8 = 72 lbs.	48 + 6 = 54 lbs.

Figure 4.19

Metacognition for Data Analysis and Probability

• METACOGNITION •

Prompt: Below is a grid showing Pat's piano practice schedule. Write three Metacognition statements that this graph could be about. Begin your statement with "I believe that I know the following information about Pat's piano practice schedule."

PIANO PRACTICE SCHEDULE							
	Sunday	Monday	Tuesday	Wednesday	Thursday	Friday	Saturday
10 am		x		x		x	
11 am		x		x	x	x	
12 pm	x	x	x	x	x		
1 pm	x		x		x		
2 pm			x		x		
3 pm							x

Sample Response Using Metacognition:

I believe that I know the following information about Pat's piano practice schedule.

First, I believe that Pat practices the most on Thursday.

Second, I believe (infer) that Pat is not going to school at this time because he is practicing during normal school hours.

Finally, I believe that Pat is a serious piano student because he is practicing 18 hours a week.

Figure 4.20

• METACOGNITION •

Prompt: Below is an alphabetical list of student names from a third-grade classroom. Write a Metacognition statement telling three things that you know from this list in addition to the number of students in the classroom.

• TAXONOMY •

A	Alison, Andy	
B	Ben	
C	Charlene, Cara, Chuck, Chris	
D	Donna	
E		
F	Francisco	
G	Gina, Geraldo, Giro	
H	Hanna	
I		
J	Jorge, Juan, Jaime, Jeanine	
K		
L		
M	Marta, Makira	
N		
O	Omar	
P	Penny, Penina, Philip	
Q		
R	Rudy, Rachel, Rachelle	
S	Sami, Sammi, Sam	
T	Thalia, Teneka, Terrance	
U		
V	Valeria, Victor	
W	Willy, William	
X	Xena	
Y		
Z	Zesta, Zena, Zacharia	

Sample Response Using Metacognition:

I believe that I know something about the names from these third-grade classes.

First, the names come from different languages or places.

I also think that the teachers will need a way to call on students whose names sound the same but are spelled differently.

Finally, I know that we can't tell how many boys or girls there are because names like Chris and Jaime and some others can be for either boys or girls.

Figure 4.21

Metacognition for Data Analysis and Probability—Baseball Statistics

• METACOGNITION •

Prompt: Tell what you know about baseball statistics from the data statement below.

Data Statement

PLAYER	AVG	G	AB	R	H	1B	2B	3B	HR	RBI	BB	SO
Wilson	.333	23	39	2	13	16	3	0	0	6	2	11
Reed	.294	105	262	35	77	117	22	0	6	25	25	58
Pinetta	.293	123	440	69	129	243	21	0	31	78	63	75
McWinn	.284	101	257	37	73	112	15	3	6	25	15	51
Allen	.277	91	296	28	82	118	14	2	6	27	36	73
Wang	.271	105	332	36	90	140	21	1	9	47	21	54
Zane	.266	133	467	55	124	169	22	1	7	54	64	87
Paul	.247	87	295	34	73	108	12	1	7	29	16	45
Perez	.246	70	203	22	50	69	8	1	3	20	12	22
Ramirez	.246	108	395	55	97	163	210	15	46	43	59	31
Martinez	.240	130	405	24	97	134	23	4	2	37	29	37
Johnson	.238	59	105	13	25	45	3	1	5	16	13	28
Valdez	.233	125	403	64	94	165	14	0	19	52	76	87
Lewis.	.231	32	117	16	27	39	6	0	2	7	16	23
Harris	.213	99	127	12	27	33	4	1	0	9	8	8

Legend:

Avg: Batting Average
G: Games Played
AB: Times at Bat
H: Hits
1B: Singles
2B: Doubles

3B: Triples
HR: Home Runs
RBI: Runs Batted In
BB: Bases on Balls (Walks)
SO: Strike Outs

Sample Response Using Metacognition:

I know that baseball uses a lot of statistics to figure out how well the players are doing. I understand how to read a data statement about baseball.

I also know that the top row uses abbreviations for each statistic. For example, "AVG" means batting average. I know that the batting average is an important baseball statistic because it is the ratio of hits to times at bat. Furthermore, I know that a higher batting average is better than a lower one. Finally, I know that it takes a lot of "at-bats" for an average to be helpful in predicting the chances of a player getting a hit in the future.

Finally, I can tell that Reed is the most likely player on the team to get a hit because he has a high batting average (.294) while playing in a lot of games (105). I also know that Pinetta is one of the better hitters because his average (.293) is almost as high as Reed's and he has played in more games (123). Pinetta's chances of getting a hit are about the same as Reed's.

This is just some of the information I can get from a baseball data statement.

Figure 4.22

Metacognition for Money

• METACOGNITION •

Prompt: Below is a monthly food budget for a family of two adults and two school-age children. The family decides that it wants to eat more healthful foods and also reduce how much money it spends each month. The family has come to you for advice on how to do this. Write a Metacognition statement that begins with "I know several ways that your family can eat better and spend less."

	Cost Per Month	Cost Percent
Food		
Meat (beef, chicken)	113.96	19.0%
Beverages (soda, coffee, juice)	86.40	14.4%
Fruits and vegetables	62.27	10.4%
Dairy (milk, butter, cheese, eggs)	53.31	8.9%
Desserts and snacks (ice cream, cookies, potato chips)	42.47	7.1%
Bread products	29.83	5.0%
Sauces and dressings (ketchup, syrup, salad dressing)	23.73	4.0%
Cereals, rice, pasta	17.53	2.9%
Miscellaneous items (oil, sugar, flour, salt)	10.67	1.8%
Other items		
Pet food	70.26	11.7%
Drugs and vitamins	40.07	6.7%
Soaps, shampoo, toothpaste	17.61	2.9%
Miscellaneous	31.89	5.3%
Total	$600.00	

Sample Response Using Metacognition:

I know several ways that your family can eat better and spend less.

First, I know that the family could save money by not drinking soda and coffee. They could cut their spending and save $86.40.

In addition, I know that the family could eat a healthier diet and save money by cutting back on the desserts. By eating less dessert, they would save about $22.00. So far, the family has saved over $108.40.

Finally, the family could shift some of the money it spends on meat and dairy products to fruits and vegetables. The family could spend $30.00 less on meat, spend $20.00 more on fruits and vegetables, and still save $10.00 a month and eat better.

Figure 4.23

• METACOGNITION •

Prompt: A person from a foreign country wants to know the values of U.S. coins: penny, nickel, dime, quarter, and half-dollar. Write a Metacognition statement that begins, "I understand you want to know about U.S. coins."

Sample Response Using Metacognition:

I understand you want to know about U.S. coins.

First, you need to know that the words *penny, nickel,* and *dime* will not help you remember what the coins are worth because the words do not tell you what portion of a dollar they represent.

Therefore, you have to remember that a penny is 1/100 of a dollar (one cent), a nickel is 1/20 of a dollar (five cents), and a dime is 1/10 of a dollar (ten cents).

Finally, it is easier to remember the value of a quarter because the quarter is 25% of a dollar (25 cents).

Figure 4.24

Sample Lesson Plan Using Taxonomies, Composing With Keywords, and Metacognition

With these three writing strategies, you can plan numerous lessons from simple to complex and for students with a wide range of abilities. Before we introduce the rest of the writing strategies in Chapters 5 through 11, we have included a sample lesson plan that illustrates how the first three writing strategies—Taxonomies, Composing With Keywords, and Metacognition—can be incorporated into a mathematics activity. The boldfaced words are terms that are discussed in detail throughout this book and demonstrate how writing and mathematics are fully integrated. (Note: This lesson was adapted from *About Teaching Mathematics* [Burns, 1992, pp. 215–217]. The original lesson did not include writing activities.)

Lesson Plan

Instructional Objective: Students will demonstrate that they understand the concept of equivalent fractions.

Prerequisite Knowledge: Students know that a fraction has a numerator and a denominator and that fractions represent parts of a whole.

Method: Three writing strategies will be incorporated into the instructional objective for expanding knowledge about fractions. Each strategy relates to the other strategies and helps build a developmental system for writing and learning. By following the plan in order, students will be able to combine the strategies in their writing. In this lesson students will create a **Taxonomy**, move to **Composing With Keywords**, and complete their writing using a **Metacognition statement.**

Materials:

>   Composition books, writing paper, and utensils
>   4" × 12" construction paper strips in at least five colors
>   Scissors, rulers

Step 1: Pre-Assessment Using a Taxonomy (approximately 10 minutes)

Tell the class that they are going to be working with fractions. Ask students to create a blank **Taxonomy** page for the topic of fractions. Ask the students to work **solo** and write as many words as they can think of that they associate with the topic of fractions (3 minutes). Walk around the classroom while students write the words. Get a sense of how many words individual students know. Confirm that all students have written the words *numerator* and *denominator* on their Taxonomies. Have students form groups of four or five to **collaborate**. Ask them to share their Taxonomies and add other words that come to mind as they share. Introduce the slogan **"Words are free!"** so that the students will readily exchange words.

Step 2: Composing With Keywords (about 10–15 minutes)

Ask students to select three words from their Taxonomies that they can use to write a sentence about fractions. Have them put a check mark next to each selected word and then write those words on a separate piece of paper. Tell them that they will use a second strategy (after Taxonomies) called **Composing With Keywords.** The task is to write one sentence about fractions that uses all the three words. For example, if the student selects the words *line, numerator,* and *number,* his or her sentence might read, "The *numerator* is a *number* that is placed above the *line* that is over the denominator.

Step 3: Sharing Sentences (15–20 minutes)

After the students have written their sentences, tell them to read their sentences aloud to their collaborative groups. They should begin sharing by saying, "These are my words. This is my sentence."

After all students have shared in their groups, ask students in each group to nominate a member of their group to share their sentence with the entire class. Write the sentence on the board. Be sure to make positive comments about the sentence. Use the sentence to promote a discussion of both fractions and sentence writing. Be sure to solicit one sentence from each group. Post the sentences on the walls in the classroom and possibly in the hallways.

Step 4: Present New Information

Explain and demonstrate how equivalent fractions have numerators and denominators that are the same. Ask students to create equivalent fractions using paper strips or manipulatives.

For example, you might ask students to use strips of colored construction paper that are of equal size. First, one strip should be labeled **one whole.** Next to the words, students should write the number in fractional form (1/1). Second, the strip should be folded in half. Each side of this strip should be labeled **one half.** Next to the words, the students should write the number in fractional form (1/2). Third, they should make a 1/4 strip. Each strip can be a different color. Finally, when students have made all of the strips, they should staple the strips together into a pack.

Step 5: Write Metacognition Statements (15–20 minutes)

Tell the students that they are now going to write three sentences about what they know about fractions and equivalence of fractions. Advise them to use the words from their **Taxonomies.** Suggest that each sentence contain more than one word from the **Taxonomy.** Tell students to be sure to skip lines so that they may go back and **revise** and **edit** their writing.

Give students this format for their **Metacognition statements:**

I know that I know something about equivalent fractions.

First . . .

In addition . . .

Finally . . .

Now you know what I know about equivalent fractions.

Students may wish to illustrate their work.

Step 6: Post-Assessment Closure (approximately 15 minutes)

Ask students to share their **Metacognition statements** in their groups. After all students have shared in their groups, ask them to nominate one person in the group to share her or his writing with the class.

INTERNET LINKS

How Do You Write a Good Math Solution?

http://mathforum.org/elempow/writing.html

Using Writing in Mathematics

http://www2.ups.edu/community/tofu/lev2/journaling/writemath.htm

5

Defining Format for Mathematical Clarity

"Can you show me the biggest number there is?" asked Milo.

"I'd be delighted," replied the Mathemagician.

Inside was the biggest 3 Milo had ever seen.

"No, that's not what I mean," objected Milo.

—*The Phantom Tollbooth* (Juster, 1964, p. 189)

Real world competencies depend on communication learning abilities, which in turn depend upon a broad vocabulary. The linguistic prerequisite is a foundation for a whole range of competencies in domains such as mathematics, art, history, ethics, politics, and science. (Hirsch, 1996, p. 146)

WHAT IS DEFINING FORMAT?

The Defining Format strategy shows students how to explain the detailed and precise meanings of the major terms they use to communicate their understanding of mathematics. We have chosen the chapter slogan "Write to a Martian!" as a metaphor for trying to explain a vocabulary term to an audience that is supposedly totally unfamiliar with that term. Often mathematical words can be one of the most confusing aspects of mathematics. One reason for this confusion is that while we use numerous mathematical words in everyday speech, these same words can take on very specialized and often complex meanings when used in mathematics. The following paragraph demonstrates how mathematical words that are used in everyday speech require much more precise use in mathematics.

> For a *number* of days, I was only able to eat a *fraction* of what I usually ate. I *estimated* that my *weight* was dropping by a *couple* of *pounds* each day and that my strength was only *half* of what it had been before. If this *problem* kept up for *more than a week*, I would *weigh less* than what I had weighed when I was in my *teens*.

While this statement makes sense figuratively, it is mathematically general, and to understand mathematics the learner must use mathematical words with accuracy and precision. Even the word *number*—a word we often assume students know—can be difficult to define accurately. For example, some students may define number by giving examples: 1, 2, 3, 4, and so on. Other students might say, "A number tells you how much." While both are true, there is much more to know about a number, especially if we have to explain what it is to a "visiting Martian."

The Defining Format strategy and template show students how to accurately define specific mathematical terms. Defining Format challenges students to ask a question about a word, find a category for the word, and list characteristics that describe the word and the category (see Figure 5.1). Note that defining the term begins by asking a question (e.g., "What is a number?") and writing the first part of the response directly below it (e.g., "A number is a"). Next, the student moves to the second column and writes the name of the category (e.g., symbol), followed by the word *that* in order to complete the sentence by writing the characteristics (of a number) in the third column (e.g., "can be written as 0, 1, 2, etc."). By answering the question in this format, the student avoids colloquial responses such as "a number is something" or "a number is like when."

> The . . . argument for more student writing is the improvement of academic performance in every . . . academic area. . . . Students who write more frequently perform better not only on essay exams . . . but also on multiple-choice tests across a range of subjects. . . . In order to write well, students must think in a logical manner, proceeding from beginning to middle to end. They must think in an analytical manner. . . . when they write well, they think well. And when students think well, they perform better in any context. (Reeves, 2002, p. 5)

INTRODUCING DEFINING FORMAT IN MATHEMATICS

Defining Format is the link between vocabulary (Taxonomies) and fluency (the ability to "speak or write fluently" [Random House, 2001, p. 739]).

The various Taxonomies that the students have created to serve as "holders" of words often need to be defined. Defining Format teaches students the process of defining in clear, unambiguous ways, focusing on the *distant or unknowing audience,* metaphorically called "The Martian."

Defining Format can be introduced by the middle of first grade, and certainly early in second grade, and should be an integral part of the third-grade mathematical repertoire. Students can set up the Defining Format template in their mathematics journals by following these directions:

• DEFINING FORMAT •		
Question	**Category**	**Characteristics**
What is a number?		
A number is a	symbol that	1. can be written as 0, 1, 2, 3, 4, 5, 6, 7, 8, 9. 2. can be used for counting, putting items in order, and identifying places or people. 3. may be cardinal or ordinal, positive or negative, whole or a fraction, odd or even, prime or non-prime, rational or irrational, among other qualities. 4. may be written in different bases such as base 10, base 5, or others.

Figure 5.1

1. Turn to the Table of Contents in your mathematics journal. Write the date in the first column; write "Defining Format" in the second column; write the page number in the third column (see Figure 5.2).

2. Open to the blank pages where you will start your Defining Format chart. Be sure that you have two blank pages facing each other.

3. Divide the left-hand page in half. Keep the right-hand page as it is.

4. At the top of the first column on the left-hand page, write "Question." At the top of the second column, write "Category." At the top of the right-hand page, write "Characteristics." (See example in Figure 5.3.)

		Table of Contents	
	Date	Mathematics Topic and Strategy	Page
	Dec. 12	What is a square? Defining Format	6

Figure 5.2

• DEFINING FORMAT •		
Question	Category	Characteristics
What is a triangle?		
A triangle is a	polygon that	1. has three angles and three sides. 2. is a closed plane. 3. can be isosceles, equilateral, or right. 4. can have angles that are acute, scalene, or right, depending on the number of degrees.

Figure 5.3

Use this template every time you are asked to use Defining Format:

a. Start in the first column. Write a question about your word, skip a line, and then write the beginning of the answer to the question. For example, if your word is a number, go to the first column, write "What is a number?" and then skip a line and write "A number is a."

b. Move to the second column. Choose a category for the word. Write the category name, followed by the word "that." For example, if your category is "symbol," go to the second column and write "symbol that."

c. Move to the last column. Think of some characteristics of the word. Write these characteristics in the third column. Number each characteristic separately. Be sure that your responses complete the sentence you began in columns 1 and 2. For example, you might say that a number is a symbol that "can be written as 0, 1, 2, 3, etc."

5. Notice that when you have completed the chart, you have a set of sentences (a paragraph) that completely answers the question and defines the word.

When you first introduce Defining Format, guide the students through each of the steps. After three or four examples, most students will be able to independently set up their template and enter (at least) the question. In Resource B you will find a template that you can share with your students to illustrate the format.

One difficulty students may have is in choosing a category. For example, if the question is "What is addition?" young, or even older, students are likely to say, "Addition is when you put numbers together." Or if students are asked, "What is a fraction?" they may say, "It's something that has a numerator and denominator." Therefore, it is important to take the time to guide students in their thinking about categories. For example, help students realize that addition can be categorized as a *mathematical operation* and fraction as a *type of number*. Students will become aware of categories through their Taxonomies, since each Taxonomy is usually labeled by category (e.g., types of numbers, measurement tools, polygons). You may also help students recognize categories by helping them create a list of terms and their category, as illustrated in Figure 5.4. If possible, keep this chart posted so that students can easily refer to it when defining terms, and add to it as you introduce new terms.

Examples of Defining Format in the Primary Grades

One of the ways to introduce students to Defining Format is to have them define a familiar term that uses numbers or mathematical concepts (the category is shown in parentheses):

- clock (timepiece),
- calendar (time organizer),
- penny (coin), or
- plus sign (symbol).

You will find that while students know and can identify these items, they will initially have difficulty defining them mathematically. However, if you guide students through the Defining Format process, they will learn the vocabulary of defining and will understand that mathematics requires precise terminology. Figures 5.5 through 5.8 give examples of Defining Formats for the words suggested above. Use these examples to guide your instruction, but do not copy them. Allow students to contribute their own definitions. Defining Format requires students to construct meaning and works best when the class works cooperatively to contribute to the definitions and clarify their meanings. (Note: Figures 5.5 to 5.8 were created through group discussion by students in Grades 2, 3, and 4.)

Mathematical Terms and Categories	
Terms (other terms may apply)	Category
addition, subtraction, multiplication, division	mathematical operations
triangle, square, rectangle, parallelogram, quadrangle	polygons
circle, pyramid, prism, cone, cylinder	geometric shapes
ruler, tape measure, protractor, thermometer, odometer	measuring tools
inch, foot, yard, mile, ounce, pound, ton, pint, quart, gallon, millimeter, centimeter, decimeter, dekameter, meter, kilometer, liter, gram, kilogram, degree, acre	(types of) weights or measurements
area, plane	surfaces
sum, difference, product, quotient	arithmetic results
zero, numeral, plus sign, minus sign, times sign, division sign	symbols
algebra, geometry, trigonometry, calculus, statistics	branches of mathematics

Figure 5.4

What Is a Clock?

• DEFINING FORMAT •

Question	Category	Characteristics
What is a clock?		
A clock is a	type of timepiece that	1. uses numbers to tell time. 2. may have two hands, a minute hand and an hour hand. 3. may have a hand to tell seconds. 4. has twelve numbers. 5. has a face. 6. can be round or square or other shape. 7. is analog or digital.

The teacher pointed out that this is true for the analog clock or the clock in the classroom.

Added by the teacher.

Figure 5.5

What Is a Calendar?

• DEFINING FORMAT •

Question	Category	Characteristics
What is a calendar?		
A calendar is a	time organizer that	1. shows days, weeks, months, and years. 2. can be made into a book. 3. helps people keep track of what they have to do. 4. has numbers and words. 5. tells holidays and other events.

> This is the category one of the teachers selected.

Figure 5.6

What Is a Penny?

• DEFINING FORMAT •

Question	Category	Characteristics
What is a penny?		
A penny is a	type of coin that	1. is one cent. 2. is less than a nickel, dime, or quarter. 3. is made of copper. 4. has a picture of Abraham Lincoln. 5. has words such as "e pluribus unum."

> These are examples of the teacher guiding the students to focus on value first, rather than appearance, which is often more difficult for young students.

Figure 5.7

What Is a Plus Sign?

• DEFINING FORMAT •

Question	Category	Characteristics
What is a plus sign?		
A plus sign is a	symbol that	1. is used in addition. 2. shows that there is more than there was before. 3. is the opposite of a minus sign. 4. is one of many signs used in mathematics, such as equal (=), greater than (>), and less than (<).

> The teacher may provide this term, but after this example, students will begin to use the word *symbol* for all the operational and other mathematical signs.

Figure 5.8

Examples of Defining Format in the Intermediate and Middle Grades

Every area of mathematics has its specialized terms that overlap with the other areas. It is important, therefore, that students define terms regularly and apply their meanings when doing mathematical tasks. Figures 5.9 through 5.13 give examples of Defining Formats for the five content areas outlined by NCTM (2000). You (and your students) may find that there are additional (or different) characteristics for each area. Constructing definitions is often a lively class activity and leads to forming habits of striving for accuracy, persisting, and thinking interdependently—habits of the mind that define intelligent behavior (Costa & Kallick, 2000).

What Is an Integer?

• DEFINING FORMAT •

Question	Category	Characteristics
What is an integer?		
An integer is a	type of number that	1. can be plus or minus, also called positive or negative (e.g., +9, −9). 2. can be zero. 3. uses the basic symbols: 0, 1, 2, 3, 4, 5, 6, 7, 8, 9. 4. can go to infinity. 5. identifies spaced points on a line.

Figure 5.9

What Is Algebra?

• DEFINING FORMAT •

Question	Category	Characteristics
What is algebra?		
Algebra is a	branch of mathematics that	1. uses alphabetic symbols to represent numbers that are real, imaginary, or complex. 2. gives symbols precise meanings. 3. uses equations (expressions) as a short cut to lengthy verbal statements. 4. is based on the same laws or rules of arithmetic with letters replacing numbers and no restrictions on the numbers the letters represent.

Figure 5.10

What Is a Quadrilateral?

• DEFINING FORMAT •

Question	Category	Characteristics
What is a quadrilateral?		
A quadrilateral is a	polygon that	1. has four sides closed and four angles. 2. may be a rectangle, square, parallelogram, or trapezoid. 3. has angles equaling 360 degrees.

Figure 5.11

What Is a Meter?

• DEFINING FORMAT •

Question	Category	Characteristics
What is a meter?		
A meter is a	type of measurement that	1. is 100 centimeters. 2. is one-tenth of a kilometer. 3. is equal to 39.38 United States inches. 4. has been defined as equal to one ten-millionth of the distance from the equator to the pole measured on a meridian.

Figure 5.12

What Is a Median?

• DEFINING FORMAT •

Question	Category	Characteristics
What is a median?		
A median is a	(type of) measure that	1. represents the middle number in a sequence of numbers. 2. can be considered a halfway mark between numbers that are smaller and numbers that are larger. 3. shows the central tendency of a sequence of numbers.

Figure 5.13

To ensure accuracy of definitions, we recommend that students check the glossaries of their textbooks, dictionaries, and Internet sources. We realize that "all this checking" requires lots of extra time, so we suggest that you set up rotating "research committees"—small groups of students who undertake the task of "accuracy and clarity." Rewards of extra credit and recognition often go a long way to motivate the important habit of accuracy.

Mathematics the Write Way

Writing Activities Related to Defining Formats

(All Grades)

Standards throughout the United States require that students understand mathematical vocabulary and terminology, as implied in the NCTM learning principle that "students must learn mathematics with understanding, actively building new knowledge from experience and prior knowledge" (NCTM, 2000, p. 28ff). For example, one curriculum guide specifies that a third-grade student might be asked to "identify alternative forms of expanding whole numbers less than 1000 using expanded notation" (West Hartford Public Schools, 2000). According to this curriculum guide, the student must know the terms *expanded notation, means the same as,* and *value.* So while the mathematical task may seem easy, the mathematical terms or words are certainly not.

The following activities help students define mathematical terms and meet mathematical standards for each of the content areas—number and operations, algebra, geometry, measurement, data analysis and probability—and money. In these activities, students imagine that they are writing to a Martian, the intrepid visitor to Earth who is puzzled by the mathematics of Earthlings and who keeps asking questions. Each model dialogue is followed by suggestions to students for creating their own dialogue, and embedded in these dialogues are opportunities for using Defining Format. Use these activities as models or adapt them to meet your grade-level curriculum and students' needs. We have given examples that students can complete in a relatively short time and others that can serve as models for lengthier mathematical projects. Pick, choose, or modify as suits your students' needs and interests.

> A suggestion: You might want to read one of these dialogues aloud to your students as an example of writing to a Martian and then have your students create a Taxonomy of terms that they would want to explain to this visitor.

Dialogues Related to Defining Formats for Number and Operations

Number and Operations

• DIALOGUE: EXPANDED NOTATION •

The Martian wants the Earthling to answer this question: "What is expanded notation?" Following is a possible response focusing on the term **expanded notation.**

Martian: I have looked at a lot of mathematics books in your schools and see the term **expanded notation.** What does that mean?

Earthling: First, I will give you an example of a whole number: 345. This is a number that appears to be merely three digits—3, 4, and 5. However, on Earth mathematicians figured out that the words we use to express that number—three hundred, forty, five—means that there are 3 hundreds, which we write as 300; there are 4 tens or 4 times 10, which we write as 40; and there are 5 ones.

Martian: That seems complicated to me.

Earthling: I'll show it to you in a simple way. Think of the words we say for 345: three hundred, forty, five. In expanded notation (or the long way), we write those words in numbers, using a plus sign: $300 + 40 + 5$.

Martian: I get it. It's like adding

$$
\begin{array}{r}
300 \\
+ 40 \\
+ 5 \\
\hline
345
\end{array}
$$

Earthling: Show me how you would write the following numbers in expanded notation:

633
4204
30,602
450,641
8,392,901

Martian: That's easy now. Here they are:

$600 + 30 + 3$
$4000 + 200 + 4$
$30,000 + 600 + 2$
$400,000 + 50,000 + 600 + 40 + 1$
$8,000,000 + 300,000 + 90,000 + 2,000 + 900 + 1$

Earthling: You're a fast learner.

Martian: Thanks. But I sure am glad that there is a short cut to expanded notation because it's too tiring to write out all these numbers.

Figure 5.14

Number and Operations

• SUGGESTED DIALOGUE: FRACTIONS (NUMBERS) •

The Martian wants the Earthling to answer this question: Why are the fractions 2/4, 4/8, 5/10 called "the same" or, as you say, "equivalent"? And by the way, what is a fraction?

Figure 5.15

Number and Operations

• DIALOGUE: ARRAY, EQUATION, NUMBER SENTENCE •

The Martian has heard the words **array, equation,** and **number sentence.**
The Martian asks the Earthling, "What do you mean by the words array, equation, and number sentence on Earth?" Following is a possible dialogue on these terms:

Martian: What do you mean by the words array, equation, and number sentence?

Earthling: An array is a type of arrangement that shows items (objects) or numbers, as in this array of telephones:

If we divide the number of telephones by two we get two equal arrays. There are twelve telephones in the total array. By dividing the total array into two arrays, we have six telephones in each array. We can now write an equation to express the division of the array:

12 (telephones) ÷ 2 (arrays) = 6 (telephones in each array). This equation can be simplified as a number sentence to look this way: 12 ÷ 2 = 6.

Martian: I think I now understand. But could you give me a definition of *equation*?

Earthling: Of course. An equation is a set of numbers or value on the left side of an equal sign that equals the same number or set of numbers or value that are on the right side.

Figure 5.16

Number and Operations

• SUGGESTED DIALOGUE: ARRAYS •

The Martian has posed this problem to the Earthling: "When I get back to Mars, I would like to have a tile floor like I have seen in some Earthlings' kitchens. Could you draw a tile pattern array for me and explain what I need to do to put that pattern in my own kitchen? And by the way, what is a good measuring tool to measure my floor?" Write a dialogue between you and the Martian answering this problem.

Figure 5.17

Dialogues Related to Defining Formats for Algebra

Algebra

• DIALOGUE: WHAT IS ALGEBRA? •

The Martian is visiting the algebra class and asks, "What is algebra?" A friendly Earthling gives the Martian this explanation:

Earthling: First, you have to think of algebra as a branch or form of mathematics. Algebra explains the relationships among different values.

Martian: Please give me an example of what you mean.

Earthling: Well, let's talk about what *equals* means. The = sign is important to understanding arithmetic. It means that what is on one side of the = sign has the same value as what is on the other side. For example, if I say 1 + 5 = 2 + __, you would have to find what goes in the blank that makes the value of the left side the same as the value on the right side.

Martian: What makes algebra different from arithmetic?

Earthling: In algebra, we can substitute a letter for a number, but we still have to know that = still means that the values on both sides are the same. For example, in algebra, we can say that 8 + 1 = 3x (when a letter is placed next to a number, it means we multiply them together). Whatever we say "x" is worth has to make both sides of the = sign the same value.

Martian: So this is like saying 3 times "what" equals 9.

Earthling: Great.

Martian: But how do I get the answer?

Earthling: Well, there are a couple of ways to go about it, but in algebra, we try to get the letter to stand by itself on one side of the = sign. We call that isolating the letter, in this case, x.

Martian: Show me what you mean.

Earthling: OK. When we do this, don't forget what the = sign means. We start with 8 + 1 = 3x. What do you think we mean when we say we want to isolate the x?

Martian: To get the x by itself.

Earthling: Good. If we are going to keep both sides of the = sign the same value, we have to treat both sides of the = sign the same way. Otherwise, the two sides won't have the same value. If I want 3x to become just x, I have to divide it by 3. Since I am dividing one side of the = sign by 3, I have to divide the other side by 3, too. It looks like this:

$$8 + 1 = 3x$$
$$9 = 3x$$
$$\frac{9}{3} = \frac{3x}{3}$$
$$3 = x$$

What has happened?

Martian: If we divide both sides by 3 as shown in the equation, the 9 changes to a 3 and the x is isolated. Yea! So now does x = 3?

Earthling: That's it. Both sides of the = sign still have the same value. Come back soon. You're ready for your next algebra lesson.

Figure 5.18

Algebra

• DIALOGUE: SIMPLIFYING EQUATIONS IN ALGEBRA •

The Martian wants the Earthling to answer this question: "What do Earthlings mean when they say there are rules for simplifying equations?" Following is a possible response of the Earthling to the Martian.

Martian: Before I arrived on Earth, a fellow Martian told me that Earthlings have six rules for simplifying equations. Are they hard to learn?

Earthling: Well, you learn them by practicing one at a time. For example, we use the usual order of operations when we see parentheses and exponents. We also use the associative and distributive properties.

> **Note to Teacher:** In learning algebra, the student learns that the rules of arithmetic are transformed into the rules of algebra. When students understand these rules (or laws), they can solve increasingly complex equations.

Martian: Of course, that makes sense. What's next?

Earthling: Something else that you have to do is combine like terms. For example, if you have $5x + 6x$, you can combine the 5 and 6 and keep the x. So it simplifies to $11x$.

Martian: Seems easy. Well, I know that $11 = 5 + 6$. So I can do that type of simplifying. Tell me more.

Earthling: Well, you can add the same value to either side of an equation.

Martian: Very easy. When does algebra become harder?

Earthling: How about allowing you to subtract the same value from both sides of an equation?

Martian: Just as easy as addition.

Earthling: Multiplying both sides by any number except 0?

Martian: A little harder.

Earthling: Dividing both sides by the same number except 0?

Martian: A bit more of a challenge.

Earthling: Good. I'm glad you are finding your start in algebra easy. Later on, we will try some things that are more difficult.

Martian: Thanks.

Figure 5.19

Algebra

• DIALOGUE: LAWS OF ALGEBRA •

The Martian wants the Earthling to answer this question: "What do Earthlings mean when they say there are laws for writing equations?" Following is a possible response of the Earthling to the Martian.

Martian: Before I arrived on Earth, a fellow Martian told me that Earthlings have seven laws for writing equations. Are they hard to learn?

Earthling: Well, you learn them by practicing one at a time. For example, the reflexive law is the easiest. It says that $A = A$ or, in numbers, $4 = 4$.

Martian: Of course, what else could it be? What's next?

Earthling: Then there is the substitution law. It says if $A = B$, then B can be used in place of A. See if you can do this with numbers.

Martian: Seems easy. Well, I know that $5 = 3 + 2$. So I can always use $3 + 2$ to mean 5. Tell me more.

Earthling: This is a law you always learn in arithmetic. It's called the commutative law. It says that $A + B = B + A$. In multiplication it's the same: $A \times B = B \times A$.

Martian: Very easy. That means $3 + 2 = 2 + 3$ or $2 \times 3 = 3 \times 2$. When does algebra get harder?

Earthling: Let's try this one, called the associative law. In addition we can write, for example, $A + (B + C)$. The parentheses only group items together. So $(A + B) + C$ is the same as $A + (B + C)$. Try this with numbers.

Martian: $6 + (4 + 3) = (6 + 4) + 3$. I see now. Both arrangements equal 13. I wonder if the associative law works with multiplication. $(6 \times 2) \times 3 = 6 \times (2 \times 3)$. Yes, they both equal 36. How interesting. Tell me more.

Earthling: The next one is the distributive law, which means you can distribute the symbols in different arrangements but get the same answer. Watch. $A \times (B + C) = (A \times B) + (A \times C)$. How does this equation look with numbers?

Martian: Hmm. I just learned my times tables, so let's see if this works. $4 (3 + 2) = (4 \times 3) + (4 \times 2)$. So $3 + 2$ is 5 and $4 \times 5 = 20$. Then $4 \times 3 = 12$ and $4 \times 2 = 8$ and $12 + 8 = 20$. Just two more to go.

Earthling: The sixth law is the law of equal addition and subtraction. First, we must remember the substitution law.

Martian: That says that $A = B$.

Earthling: Good. So if $A = B$, then $A + C = B + C$.

Martian: Got it. $A = 6$, $B = (2 + 4)$. So $6 + 3 = (2 + 4) + 3 = 9$. I see this works for addition.

Earthling: Now do this law of equal addition and subtraction for subtraction.

Martian: OK. $A = 8$. $B = (5 + 3)$. So $8 - 4 = (5 + 3) - 4$. That means in algebra $A - C = B - C$. I'm ready for the last law.

Earthling: This is the law of equal multiplication and division. Since $A = B$, then $A \times C = B \times C$.

Martian: Yes, because what happens in addition, happens in multiplication. So that means that since $7 = (3 + 4)$, then $7 \times 3 = (3 + 4) \times 3 = 21$. So will this work for division?

Earthling: Let's try it. First, we remember that $A = B$. So $A \div C = B \div C$.

Martian: Division is hard for me. But let's see. $10 \div 2 = (5 + 5) \div 2 = 5$.

Earthling: Well done. You are now ready to learn more algebra.

Martian: Thanks.

Figure 5.20

Algebra

• SUGGESTED DIALOGUE: ALGEBRAIC REPRESENTATIONS •

The Martian is puzzled and poses this question: "I was visiting an Earthling classroom when the teacher asked me to write six different representations of 36. How do I do that?" Write a dialogue between you and the Martian answering this problem.

Figure 5.21

Dialogues Related to Defining Formats for Geometry

Geometry

• DIALOGUE: POLYGONS •

The Martian asked the Earthling to describe and compare polygons in an organized way, so the Earthling made a grid of the polygons. When the Earthling finished the grid and showed it to the Martian, the Earthling asked the Martian to tell a story about polygons from the information in the grid.

Earthling: Look at the grid. It has a lot of words on it. I want to be sure you know what they mean.

Martian: I see that each polygon has its own name. It looks like the names change whenever the number of angles and sides change.

Earthling: That's right. Do you see any patterns in the names?

Martian: Yes. This is interesting. I see that the word for a three-sided polygon has the form -**angle** and the word for a four-sided polygon has the form -**lateral.**

Earthling: Nice observation.

Martian: Then it looks like the rest of them end in -**agon.** Is that right?

Earthling: Excellent. Notice anything about the parts of the words that come before -**agon?**

Martian: I think the first part of the word tells us how many sides there are. For example, **pent-** must mean five, **hex-** means six, and so on. Is that it?

Earthling: I couldn't have said it better myself. What do you notice about the number of degrees?

Martian: It seems that the more sides and angles there are in a polygon, the more degrees there are. In fact, I see a **progression.**

Earthling: Good word, but could you explain what you mean by a **progression?**

Martian: Well, each successive polygon has 180 degrees more than the previous polygon.

Earthling: I couldn't have said it better myself. You are a mighty sharp Martian.

> **Note to Teacher:** Among all the aspects of mathematics, geometry has the most natural affinity with writing. Geometry was one of the earliest forms of mathematics. The ancient Babylonians, Egyptians, and Greeks applied geometry to measure land (hence the word), but gradually they became interested in the subject beyond its applications. They began studying it for its abstraction and beauty of form and symmetry, subsequently writing detailed descriptions of this special aspect of mathematics.

POLYGONS

Picture of Polygon	Name of Polygon	Number of Angles	Number of Sides	Degrees of Each Angle	Number of Degrees
	triangle	three	three	can be less than 90°, just 90°, or more than 90°, but all three angles must equal 180°	180°
	quadrangle	four	four	can be less than 90°, just 90°, or more than 90°, but all four angles must equal 360°	360°
	pentagon	five	five	in a regular pentagon each angle is 108°, adding up to 540°	540°
	hexagon	six	six	in a regular hexagon each angle is 120° adding up to 720°	720°
	heptagon	seven	seven	in a regular heptagon each angle is 128 7/8° totaling 902 1/8°	902 1/8°
	octagon	eight	eight	in a regular octagon each angle is 135° adding up to 1080°	1080°
	nonagon	nine	nine	in a regular nonagon each angle is 140° totaling 1260°	1260°
	decagon	ten	ten	in a regular decagon each angle is 144° totaling 1440°	1440°

Figure 5.22

Geometry

• SUGGESTED DIALOGUE: POLYGONS AND PAPER •

The Martian is curious about paper used in the classroom and questions the Earthling: "I noticed that the paper you write on in the classroom is almost always the shape of a rectangle. Why don't you use paper that has the other shapes, such as a triangle or a hexagon or octagon?

Note to Teacher: The open-ended question on paper requires the students to think of both use of space and efficiency of handling.

Figure 5.23

Geometry

• DIALOGUE: CONGRUENT AND SIMILAR •

The Martian has heard the terms **congruent** and **similar** in relation to geometry and spatial sense.
The Martian is confused and has asked the Earthling to define these terms as clearly as possible. Following is a model of the dialogue between the Earthling and the Martian.

Earthling: Here are two sets of figures. What do you notice about them?

Martian: Let's see. In each set the figures seem to be the same.

Earthling: What do you mean by the **same**?

Martian: I mean that one is just like the other. The first arrow looks like the second arrow. They are also facing in the same direction and look to be the same size. The next two arrows are also the same size and are facing in the same direction.

Earthling: I'll try to make it easy by asking you a question. If both sets of figures face the "same way," could you place one figure in a set over the other figure so that they fit exactly over each other?

Martian: Yes, but only if they were also the same size.

Earthling. You got it. Two or more figures have to be the same shape and the same size and all their points have to fit over each other.

Martian: So that's what you mean by **same.**

Earthling: Yes, but we have a more accurate word called **congruent.** Now look at these figures. Do you think they are congruent?

Martian: Mmm. This is tricky. The triangles look to be the same size, but they are not pointing in the same direction, and the arrows are facing opposite directions. So I'm not sure.

Earthling: But what is the rule to be congruent?

Martian: Oh yes, the points of both figures have to fit over each other. If I turned one of the triangles upside down it would exactly fit over the other triangle. And if I had both arrows go in the same direction, they would be congruent because all of their points would fit.

Earthling: Well, to be congruent, the figures don't have to "go the same way," but sometimes it's easier to see the congruence if they are pointing the same direction. Just to be sure you understand, here's another set of figures. Tell me whether or not these are congruent.

Martian: These are sort of the same.

Earthling: Can you explain exactly what you mean?

Martian: Well, in each set one figure is smaller than the other, but they have the same shape, if they all faced the same way.

Earthling: Good. So while they are the same shape, they are not the same size. That means they are **not congruent** because their vpoints will not match. But they are similar.

Martian: Thanks, Earthling. Now I get the difference between **congruent** and **similar.**

Figure 5.24

Geometry

• SUGGESTED DIALOGUE: CONGRUENCE, SIMILARITY, AND GEOBOARDS •

The Martian wants to better understand congruence and similarity. The Martian asks the Earthling, "Could you show me how to use the geoboards so that I could know more about what is congruent and what is similar? And by the way, what exactly is a geoboard?"

Note to Teacher: The response to the first question in Figure 5.25 requires the Earthling to have a geoboard and write a dialogue between the Martian and himself or herself that includes illustrations of congruence and similarities on the geoboard. It's a challenging task, but the task is valuable because it requires students to both explain and illustrate.

Figure 5.25

Dialogues Related to Defining Formats for Measurement

Measurement

• DIALOGUE: WEIGHTS AND MEASUREMENT •

(This model is recommended for a long-range student project or a joint effort of two or more students.)

Martian: When I visited a classroom, I noticed that students were measuring everything—the size of the room, themselves, water, sand, time. How can I show my fellow Martians all these measuring systems?

Earthling: To help you get started, I will set up a grid with some measuring information that we use on Earth. If you want all of the information, you can check the Internet or look in the back of any unabridged dictionary.

Note to Teacher: Many composition books include types of measurements on their inside covers. Some will be familiar to the students, but others will not because they are rarely used today. If you have time, have your students look over these measurements and discuss the different ways they have been used. Suggest to your students that they do some research about their history and present their findings to the class. Acknowledgment of effort is always an incentive.

Martian: I think I will like this.

Earthling: I have created two grids of measurements. The first grid shows commonly used measurements in the metric system. The other grid shows commonly used measurements in the United States system. Each grid is divided into linear measures (used for surfaces and distance), liquid measures, and weights. After you have studied these grids, write an explanation of the differences you notice between these systems.

WEIGHTS AND MEASURES IN THE METRIC SYSTEM		
Linear Measures	**Liquid Measures**	**Weight Measures**
10 millimeters = 1 centimeter	10 milliliters = 1 centiliter	10 milligrams = 1 centigram
10 centimeters = 1 decimeter	10 centiliters = 1 deciliter	10 centigrams = 1 decigram
10 decimeters = 1 meter	10 deciliters = 1 liter	10 decigrams = 1 gram
10 meters = 1 decameter	10 liters = 1 decaliter	10 grams = 1 decagram
10 decameters = 1 hectometer	10 decaliters = 1 hectoliter	10 decagrams = 1 hectogram
10 hectometers = 1 kilometer	10 hectoliters = 1 kiloliter	10 hectograms = 1 kilogram

Figure 5.26

(Continued on page 92)

Measurement

• DIALOGUE: WEIGHTS AND MEASUREMENT •

WEIGHTS AND MEASURES IN THE UNITED STATES SYSTEM		
Linear Measures	**Liquid Measures**	**Weight Measures**
12 inches = 1 foot	2 pints = 1 quart	16 ounces = 1 pound
3 feet = 1 yard	4 quarts = 1 gallon	2000 pounds = 1 ton
5,280 feet = 1 mile	31 gallons = 1 barrel	
	2 barrels = 1 hogshead	

Martian: Very interesting. This is what I notice. First, am I right when I say that some Earthlings measure weights and measures with the metric system and others use the United States system?

Earthling: True, although some people use both systems.

Martian: Why don't all Earthlings use the same system?

Earthling: It would take a very long time for me to explain that, but right now study the different tables, and see what sense you can make of them.

Martian: Hmm. The words and patterns in the metric system are easier to understand. For example, all the linear measures end with **-meter**. Then it looks like there is another word in front to tell what part of a meter or how many meters we have. Is that right?

Earthling: Good observation. What else do you notice?

Martian: All the metric liquid measures end with **-liter** and all the weight measures end with **-gram**.

Earthling: Another good observation. Anything else?

Martian: The number 10 looks important in the metric system. Ten is all over the table and my guess is that multiples of 10 are the key to knowing what the weights and measures mean.

Earthling: Well done. Let's go on.

Martian: I don't see any patterns in the United States system.

Earthling: What do you see?

Martian: It appears that each measure in the United States system has a unique name that does not sound like any other measure in the system. Right?

Earthling: Yes. Anything else?

Martian: And the number 10 won't help much in understanding the values. It appears that each measure uses a different number.

Earthling: Think of it as a challenge. You won't believe this at first, but it actually works.

Martian: I think that it is probably best to pick one or the other when doing a problem.

Earthling: That works for me and most of the Earthlings. Now that you understand the most important part, we can learn how to use both systems.

Figure 5.26 (*Continued from page 91*)

Measurement

• DIALOGUE: METRIC MEASUREMENT •

The Martian has been shopping in the supermarket and is really confused about weights. The Martian says to the Earthling, "I bought three items. The first was a small box of baking soda that weighed 544 grams. Then I bought a big box of corn flakes that weighted 340 grams. I also bought a box of spaghetti that was much smaller than the box of corn flakes, but it weighed 454 grams and the corn flakes weighed only 340 grams. I drew the picture below for you to help me with this problem. How could a very small box have so much more weight than a bigger box?"

Note to Teacher: While the problem in Figure 5.27 has more to do with the concept of volume than weight or size, it makes students think about the connection between mathematics and physical objects and how weight, density, and volume are related.

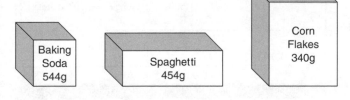

Suggested Dialogue: Have students work in pairs examining a food package. Ask them to write a dialogue between an Earthling and a Martian in which the Martian asks questions about the mathematical aspects of the package and the Earthling responds to those questions.

Figure 5.27

• COMPARING A RULER TO A PROTRACTOR •

In this writing activity, the Martian wants to know the uses of the ruler and the protractor. The Martian and the Earthling have their usual dialogue.

Martian: I have tried using the ruler and the protractor, but I still need help to understand what they measure and how to use them.

Earthling: First, let's look at each one.

Now, let's set up a Defining Format template with the question and category. Write all the characteristics you notice about a ruler. Put a number next to each characteristic.

Martian: This seems easy. Here are the characteristics of the ruler that I think I already know:

- has a straight edge; can be marked with the metric or United States system or both
- is used for linear measurement; has numbers to allow you to measure distances
- is a foot long in the United States system

Earthling: Write these in the column on characteristics.

Martian: OK. Here goes.

Earthling: Can you tell me the category and characteristics of a protractor?

Martian: That's easy. I'll do the whole thing in the Defining Format template.

Earthling: Tell how the ruler and the protractor are similar. Tell me how they are different. Here is how to get started: A ruler and a protractor are both measuring devices with similar and different characteristics.

Martian: I can do the rest myself. I'll just compare and contrast the characteristics.

• DEFINING FORMAT •

Question	Category	Characteristics
What is a ruler?		
A ruler is a	type of measuring device that	1. has a straight edge. 2. can be marked with either the metric or United States system, or both. 3. is used for linear measurement. 4. has numbers to allow you to measure distances. 5. is a foot long in the United States system

• DEFINING FORMAT •

Question	Category	Characteristics
What is a protractor?		
A protractor is a	type of measuring device that	1. is shaped like a semicircle. 2. is used for measuring degrees and distances. 3. can be used like a ruler by using the straight part. 4. can measure degrees in angles by using the curved part. 5. is divided into different linear measures. 6. can be used in both the United States and metric systems.

Figure 5.28

• SUGGESTED DIALOGUE: HEIGHT AND WEIGHT •

Note to Teacher: The answers to the questions in Figure 5.29 will require student research and make an excellent project for two students (a Martian and an Earthling, of course).

The Martian has seen a height and weight chart in the nurse's office. The Martian has asked the Earthling many questions: Could you explain the difference between height and weight? Why do you measure weight in pounds and height in feet and inches? Could you use the metric system to get your height and weight?

Figure 5.29

Dialogues Related to Defining Formats for Data Analysis and Probability

Data Analysis and Probability

• DIALOGUE: PREDICTION ABOUT THE WORLD SERIES •

The Earthling and the Martian have been working very hard on learning to write about mathematics. They agree that they need some recreation. The Earthling invites the Martian to watch a World Series game with him. The Martian accepts the invitation but does not know much about baseball and the World Series. The Earthling tells the Martian not to worry because the Earthling is an expert on the topic.

Just before the game begins, the Earthling and the Martian get ready with some popcorn and soft drinks. As they settle in, the Earthling makes a prediction about which team will win the series. The Martian is curious about how the Earthling made the prediction.

Martian: What makes you think the team you picked will win the World Series?

Earthling: The baseball season always ends with a World Series. It is a best-of-seven series, meaning that the first team to win four games is the champion. When teams of equal strength meet, there is a probability that the home team will win. In the history of the World Series, 60% of the winners have been the teams with an extra game at home. My team happens to have the home field advantage this year.

Martian: You said that the home team wins 60% of the time. That means that there must be other factors that affect who wins. If I wanted to make a prediction, what else could I look at?

Earthling: Of all the factors that help us predict which team will win baseball games, pitching is the most important. We have a statistic that measures the quality of

> **Note to Teacher:** Of all the popular sports played in the world, baseball has the greatest amount of counting (or statistics). A commonly stated axiom is that "baseball is a game of statistics."

pitching. It is called the earned run average. Teams with the lowest earned run averages win the World Series 65% of the time. As it turns out, my favorite team and the opponent have approximately the same earned run averages.

Martian: Fascinating. Is there anything else I would consider in making a prediction on the World Series?

Earthling: There are a lot of statistics about baseball that might help. My third choice would be looking at which team had the best winning percentage during the regular season. The team with the best winning percentage wins the World Series about 55% of the time.

Martian: I think I get it, but I am not sure I know what some of the words mean. For example, what are statistics, percentages, and averages?

Earthling: When you see how much fun we are going to have tonight second guessing the manager, you will see why I love writing and learning about mathematics. Now just for practice, define these terms using the Defining Format template by answering these questions: What is a statistic? What is a percentage? What is an average?

Martian: Well, I'll begin by saying that each one is a type of number. Then I'll come back to you so you can help me with the characteristics.

Earthling: Great. Come back after the game.

Figure 5.30

Data Analysis and Probability

• SUGGESTED DIALOGUE: MATHEMATICS TERMS IN BASEBALL •

Martian: Would you please help me create Defining Format templates for the terms statistic, percentage, and average? I want to take them back to Mars.

Earthling: Of course.

Figure 5.31

Dialogues Related to Defining Formats for Money

Money

• DIALOGUE: CHECKS AND SAVING MONEY •

Note to Teacher: Understanding the more abstract or hidden information about money (e.g., checks, credit cards, interest, mortgages) requires a combination of instruction (from school and family) and extensive experience. Because knowledge of money (and having money) is inequitable, students, regardless of age, vary greatly in their knowledge of this subject. For her book *Money Talks,* Fairley (1998) interviewed African Americans who have had successful careers in money industries such as accounting, banking, and investments. She asked each interviewee what advice he or she would give to young people regarding money. Each mentioned saving money and learning how to make money grow.

I.M. Earthling
3 Solar System Way
Milky Way Galaxy, Universe 123456789

Date _____

Pay to the Order of _____ $ _____

_____ Dollars

Universal Bank
Milky Way Galaxy

For _____
000666 0444444812 4321001345

Martian: Why must you sign the check?

Earthling: I sign the check with my name so the bank knows it's me. The bank has a copy of my signature on file so no one else can give away my money.

Martian: But isn't the bank giving me their money?

Earthling: No, it's my money. I put money in a particular bank and the bank holds the money for me. So if I write a check to you for $100, the bank has to be holding at least $100 of my money.

Martian: It's getting clearer. But why would a bank hold your money and let someone else have it just because you ask the bank?

Earthling: You have asked an intelligent question. While the bank is holding my money and I am not using it, the bank gets interest.

Martian: Interest?

Earthling: Yes. The bank invests my $100 and the money of thousands of other people—hundreds of thousands of dollars—and makes money on that money.

Martian: How much does the bank make?

Earthling: I can just give you an example. Suppose my bank has $100 from 1,000 customers. It now has $100,000.

Martian: Sounds like a lot to me.

Earthling: Then it invests (puts) this $100,000 into a new building that is being built.

Martian: Why would the bank do that?

Earthling: Because the builders need to borrow the $100,000 for their building. The bank lends the builders the money but charges the builders 6% interest. Can you do the mathematics?

Martian: Yes, I just learned how to do percents. So 6% of $100,000 is $100,000 × .06 = $6,000.00. That's not bad. Maybe I should go into the banking business.

Earthling: Well, this is just the beginning of the story about checks and banks and interest and money. We'll continue later.

Martian: I like this story. Thanks.

This dialogue is built on the concept of saving money and making it grow, a topic that is of great interest to the Martian. The Martian, like many young Earthlings, has heard the word *check* but can't grasp how a check works. The Martian expresses this confusion.

Martian: I've been on Earth for many months now and have seen people write checks. How can a check be like money? Can an Earthling just write a check for any amount? Why does a bank give a person money in exchange for a check? Can I pay for my food and rent by just writing a check?

Earthling: Whoa! You have too many questions at once. Let's start with defining what a check is.

Martian: Well, it looks like paper with lines and a place to sign.

Earthling: That's what it looks like, but that doesn't say what it is. First we'll set up a Defining Format template. Then you can ask me questions.

• DEFINING FORMAT •

Question	Category	Characteristics
What is a check?		
A check is a	written order that	1. gives a bank instructions about money. 2. gives the name of the person who is to get the money. 3. has to be signed by the person making the request. 4. must be "backed up" by at least the amount of money written on the check.

Earthling: Any questions?

Martian: What do you mean by instructions?

Earthling: Let's look at one of my checks. Notice it says, "Pay to the order of." Now suppose I put in your name: U. R. Martian. That tells the bank to pay you and no one else.

Figure 5.32

Money

• SUGGESTED DIALOGUE: INTEREST ON MONEY •

Martian: I need help to save money so that I can go back to Mars and then come back to Earth again. I already have $5,000, but each trip costs me $10,000. You said that I can earn interest on my money. Could you show me how I can get my $5,000 to become $10,000 and how long that would take?

Earthling: We can do it. All we need is a calculator and some time together.

Figure 5.33

INTERNET LINKS

Adventures in Statistics

http://mathforum.org/trscavo/statistics.html

Cybersleuth Kids

http://cybersleuth-kids.com/sleuth/Math/

The Prime Glossary

http://www.utm.edu/research/primes/glossary/index.html

Thirteen Ed Online

http://www.thirteen.org/edonline/lessons/index_math.html

6

Morphology and Etymology for Expanding Mathematical Vocabulary

"Everyone understands numbers. No matter what language you speak, they always mean the same thing. A seven is seven anywhere in the world."

—*The Phantom Tollbooth* (Juster, 1964, p. 199)

Use the language of mathematics to express mathematical ideas precisely. (NCTM, 2000, p. 159)

WHAT IS MORPHOLOGY?
WHAT IS ETYMOLOGY?

Morphology is the study of word patterns and formations in a particular language. For example, the English noun *number* can be formed into numeral, numeracy, numeration, enumeration, numerous, numerously, numerator; and the verb *number* has the forms numbers, numbered, numbering. English is a predominantly morphological language. Therefore, many mathematical words in English can take many forms or "morphs." To "know" English means to know its morphological construction and apply that knowledge in every subject or content area.

Etymology, often a handmaiden of morphology, is the study of the derivations of words and the history of the changes of words. Wells (1997) points out that only a handful of centuries ago, numbers were smaller, fewer, and simpler. People had little need or reason to count beyond a few thousand. For example, the Greek word *myriad*, which now means a great amount, once referred to the number 10,000. It has also become a synonym for *countless, numerous, infinite,* and *a vast horde*.

WHY STUDY MORPHOLOGY
AND ETYMOLOGY IN MATHEMATICS?

A study in the 1980s, referring to the "math crisis" in American education, stated that "students learn mathematics well only when they *construct* their own mathematical understanding. To understand what they learn, they must enact for themselves verbs that permeate the mathematics curriculum: 'examine,' 'represent,' 'transform,' 'solve,' 'apply,' 'prove,' 'communicate'" (Mathematical Sciences Education Board, 1989, pp. 58–59).

In a chapter titled "Assessing Thought and Curriculum in Student Work," Strong et al. (2001) present a "rubric for thought" in which they name the levels of achievement as "novice, apprentice, practitioner, and expert." In this rubric, the expert "effectively balances clarity, interest, and insight . . . and refines communication to meet the audience's needs" (p. 58). This is a process that can only occur when the student has the "words" and can use those words and understand syntax (structure) and semantics (meaning) (Pinker, 1994).

Numerous educators and researchers have addressed the importance of learning through patterns. Jensen (1998) states that "patterns give context to information that otherwise would be meaningless" and further points out that the "desire [of humans] to form some kind of meaningful pattern . . . seems innate" (p. 95). Caine and Caine (1991), in their discussion of brain-based learning, explain that one of the exceptional features of the brain is its capacity to "detect patterns and to make approximations" (p. 3). Therefore, these authors are critical of teaching that ignores the capacity of the brain to search for common patterns and relationships.

According to Skuy and Mentis (1999), categorization is another important "instrument" of learning. (Their work is based on Feuerstein's Instrumental Enrichment (IE) program and categorization is one of Feuerstein's instruments.) Categorization is the "grouping of elements according to relevant principles" that builds on previous learning and establishes new learning (p. 34).

Merging Morphology and mathematics enhances learning because mathematics requires students to recognize and understand patterns and Morphology is the study of word patterns. Blending Morphology and mathematics particularly helps students who have difficulty making connections.

Etymology exposes students to the history of mathematical words. While knowing the history of a word may not directly enhance a student's ability to do specific mathematical procedures, it often leads the student to a deeper understanding of the word's meaning. Countryman (1992), in her practical book *Writing to Learn Mathematics*, says that mathematics is "all words. . . . Words are tools with which we think, and thinking is the central concern of mathematics teaching" (p. 54). Morphology and Etymology are ways for the teacher to provide direct instruction in mathematical (and other) vocabulary. Substantial research has indicated that "direct instruction on words that are critical to new content produces the most powerful learning" (Marzano et al., 2001, p. 127). A further study by Stahl and Fairbanks (1986) showed that student achievement can increase by 33 percentile points when students are given vocabulary instruction on the specific words of the content. The above citations make the case for studying Morphology and Etymology in the mathematics curriculum.

INTRODUCING MORPHOLOGY IN MATHEMATICS

A good way to begin using Morphology is to have the students create or update a Taxonomy (see Chapter 13 in Rothstein & Lauber, 2000). The sample Taxonomy in Figure 6.1 includes many terms with interesting Morphologies, which we have italicized.

Choose words from the Taxonomy that have large Morphologies. You can determine which words have large Morphologies by using a CD-ROM version of an unabridged dictionary. CD-ROM dictionaries allow the user to type in a word and obtain a complete listing of related words. For example, if you typed in the word *add* on the Random House *Webster's Unabridged Dictionary* CD-ROM, you would find the following forms of the word.

> add, adds, adding, added, addition, additional, additionally, addend, additive, addendum

Begin by having the students set up for Morphology by opening to a double-page spread in their notebook (two blank pages facing each other). Have them fold each sheet of the notebook in half so that there are now four columns. Ask students to label each column with a part of

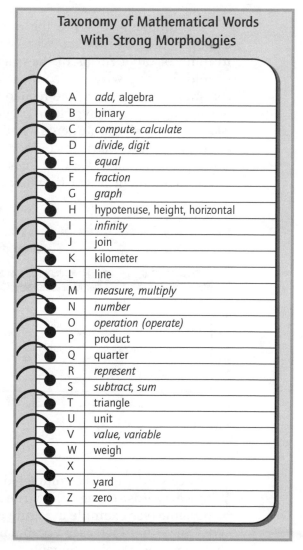

	Taxonomy of Mathematical Words With Strong Morphologies
A	*add*, algebra
B	binary
C	*compute, calculate*
D	*divide, digit*
E	*equal*
F	*fraction*
G	*graph*
H	hypotenuse, height, horizontal
I	*infinity*
J	join
K	kilometer
L	line
M	*measure, multiply*
N	*number*
O	*operation (operate)*
P	product
Q	quarter
R	*represent*
S	*subtract, sum*
T	triangle
U	unit
V	*value, variable*
W	weigh
X	
Y	yard
Z	zero

Figure 6.1

speech, as shown in Figure 6.2. (Remember to make an entry of "Morphology" in the Table of Contents.)

• MORPHOLOGY •			
Noun	Verb	Adjective	Adverb

Figure 6.2

Tell students to write the original word in the appropriate column. In this example, the students should write the word *add* in the verb column. Ask students to think of other forms of the original word. For example, for the word *add*, they should come up with the words *addition, additional, added*, and possibly others. Guide the students in placing the related words in the appropriate columns. Explain that verbs such as *add* have three other forms or "morphs," such as *adds, adding*, and *added*. Then, ask the students whether they can think of other "morphs" that should be added to the chart. Encourage students to also include the plural forms of any nouns, such as *addend* and *addends*. All the forms for *add* are illustrated in Figure 6.3. Other mathematical words will have more forms, as illustrated below.

• MORPHOLOGY FOR *ADD* •			
Noun	Verb	Adjective	Adverb
addition, additions	add	additionally	additional
addend, addends	adds		
additive, additives	adding		
addendum, addenda	added		

Figure 6.3

After students have completed the Morphology, have them use the Composing With Keywords strategy and write sentences that include as many of the word forms as possible (see example in Figure 6.4). Composing With Keywords can be a form of word play that increases vocabulary and expands the student's syntactic ability to make mathematical statements.

• MORPHOLOGY FOR *ADD* •

Composing With Keywords for the Morphology of *Add*

Addition, from the verb **add**, is a mathematical operation that requires us to **add** at least two **addends** to get a sum. The word **addition** can also become plural, such as when we think of **adding additions** to a house. The same word, **add,** can be found at the end of certain books that have **added** information, which is called an **addendum**. But if there is more than one **addendum**, we say there are **addenda**. Sometimes an **additive** is added to food, but if there are too many **additives**, the food can become unhealthy.

Figure 6.4

Figure 6.5 shows an example Morphology for the mathematical word *multiply*. A Composing With Keywords statement is shown in Figure 6.6. When using Morphology, choose words that are appropriate for your students, although you may want to reach for the stars.

• MORPHOLOGY FOR *MULTIPLY* •

Noun	Verb	Adjective	Adverb
multiplication	multiply	multiplicative	
multiplier,	multiplies	multiplicational	
multipliers	multiplying		
multiplicand	multiplied		
multiple, multiples			
multiplicity			

Figure 6.5

• MORPHOLOGY FOR *MULTIPLY* •

Composing With Keywords Using the Morphology of *Multiply*

The process of **multiplying** is called **multiplication**. To **multiply**, we need a number called a **multiplier**. For example, in the problem 6 × 5, 6 is the **multiplier** of 5 (or vice versa). For example, a **multiple** of 12 is 2. 12 can be **multiplied** by 2 to get 24.

Figure 6.6

Figures 6.7 to 6.9 give some more examples of Morphologies for mathematical words. *Multiply, equal,* and *divide* are verbs with extended Morphologies; *infinity* is a noun with adjectives and adverbs.

• MORPHOLOGY FOR *EQUAL* •

Noun	Verb	Adjective	Adverb
equation, equations	equal	equal	equally
equality, equalities	equals	equitable	equitably
equalization,	equaling	inequitable	
equalizations	equaled		
	equalize		
	equalizes		
	equalizing		
	equalized		

Figure 6.7

• MORPHOLOGY FOR *DIVIDE* •

Noun	Verb	Adjective	Adverb
division, divisions	divide	divisive	divisively
divider, dividers	divides	divisible	
dividend, dividends	dividing	indivisible	
divisiveness	divided		
divisibility			
indivisibility			

Figure 6.8

• MORPHOLOGY FOR *INFINITY* •

Noun	Verb	Adjective	Adverb
infinity		infinite	infinitely
infiniteness		infinitesimal	infinitesimally
finiteness*		finite	finitely

*Finiteness is opposite in meaning to the main word but is part of the Morphology.

Figure 6.9

INTRODUCING ETYMOLOGY IN MATHEMATICS

Students are generally fascinated by word meanings, and the Etymology of mathematical words is particularly interesting. Some of you may feel that learning the Etymology of mathematical words takes time away from the actual teaching of mathematics. However, knowing the "stories" behind the words adds interest and excitement and, of course, increases knowledge of vocabulary and history. Figure 6.10

includes the stories of 10 mathematical words. Figure 6.11 lists suggested books for researching mathematical Etymologies, and there is a wonderful Etymology resource on the Internet (see Internet Links).

• ETYMOLOGY •

The Etymological Story of Ten Important Mathematical Words

Mathematics comes from the Greek word *mathanein*, which means "learn." The word is also related to an older form, *mem*, from which we get the word *memory*. The English word *mathematics* comes from the French form *mathematiques*, which, in turn, is from the Latin plural *mathematica*.

Algebra comes from the Arabic term *ilm aljebra*, which originally meant the setting of broken bones or fractures. When large numbers of Arabs lived in Spain in the late Middle Ages, the word became *algebra*, which then was used to refer to the science of reunion and equation, gradually becoming a mathematical term.

Algorithm is another word from Arabic that took a long route of change. It began with an Arab mathematician named Abu Ja'far Mohammed ibn Musa al-Khwarizmi. He lived in Baghdad (Iraq) and wrote many works on numbers. Eventually his works were translated into Latin, which was the language used by many mathematicians in the Western world. As users of Latin, these mathematicians pronounced the name al-Khwarizmi as *alkhwaris-mus*, which then became pronounced *algorismus*. The word then became associated with the Greek word *drithmos*, meaning "number," so that *algorism(us)* again changed, this time to *algorithm*. Today this word means a set of rules for solving a finite problem.

Digit is from the Latin word *digitus*, which means "finger" (or toe) and also means "pointer." It began to be used as a measure of length equaling the size of a finger. Mathematicians then began to use the word to designate numbers from 0 to 9, which (except for 0) can be counted on the fingers.

Equal is from the Latin *aequus*, which means "level" or "even." This word has had a traveling history—it became *egal* in French, *uguale* in Italian, and *igual* in Spanish. In English, there are many words related to *equal* such as *equation, equator, equate, equilibrium,* and *adequate*. The word also has taken on many opposite meanings such as unequal, disequilibrium, and inadequate.

Fraction is from the Latin *fractus* meaning "to break." Today it has come to mean "parts of a whole" in mathematics. It still carries its original meaning in words such as *fracture, fragile,* and *frail*. And when one has a fraction of understanding, it means a small part that has broken off from the whole.

Hypotenuse is originally from the Greek word *hypoteinousa*, a compound word that means "to stretch." The Greeks used this word to mean a line that is "stretched under" the right angle of a triangle. In Latin the word became *hypotenusa*, and the English words *tend* and *tense* are from the second half of the compound form—*teinusa*.

Line is from the original Latin form *linea* meaning "string." It came to English through the French word *ligne* in the fourteenth century. Several English words relate to this word. Among them are *lineage, align, linen* (a thread of flax), and ocean *liner*, from the custom of a line of ships going into a port.

Measure is an old word from the original Indo-European basis of the English language. The early base of the word was *mat-* or *met-* and became the Latin word *metiri*, which had *mens* as one of its morphological forms. This form became *mensura*, changed to *mesure* in Old French, and passed into English as *measure*. This history of this important mathematical word eventually gave us a huge vocabulary including *commensurate, dimension, immense, month,* and even *moon*. Of course, all the words that carry the form *meter* have evolved from this ancient word.

Ratio is another Latin word that began with the meaning of "think" or "calculate." This Latin form comes from the verb *reri*. We also have the word *rational* related to *reason*, another word that is related to thinking. The words *rate* and *ratify* are from *ratio*, as is *rations*, meaning an amount given to a soldier. Word detectives (called etymologists) have also traced the form *–red* in the word *hundred* as coming from a very old German word meaning "number," which came originally from the Latin *ratio*.

Figure 6.10

• ETYMOLOGY •

Suggested Books
Suggested Books for Researching Etymologies of Mathematical Words
Ayto, J. (1990). *Dictionary of word origins.* New York: Arcade.
Berlitz, C. (1982). *Native tongues.* New York: Grosset & Dunlap.
Funk, W. (1989). *Word origins and their romantic meanings.* New York: Grosset & Dunlap.
McArthur, T. (Ed.). (1992). *The Oxford companion to the English language.* New York: Oxford University Press.

Figure 6.11

Your students might enjoy researching the etymology of the following mathematical words and showing how they are used in both mathematics and general speech: *height, horizontal, join, kilometer, multiply, number, operation* (or *operate*), *products, quarter, subtract, sum, temperature, unit, vertical, weight, yard, zero.*

When students begin studying algebra, they encounter numerous words that have a "number" suffix, such as binomial. These algebra words have complex meanings that are specifically related to formulas and equations and must, of course, be taught within the context of this subject. However, knowing the literal meanings of algebraic words can help students learn and remember algebraic tasks. Following is a sample of these terms and their definitions:

Polynomial is formed from the Greek form *poly,* which means "much" or "many." In algebra, the word refers to an expression consisting of the sum of two or more terms. For example, in the equation $ax + bx + c$ where a, b, and c are constants, x is the variable.

Binomial is from the Greek *bi* meaning "two." In an algebraic equation, binomial refers to the sum or difference of two terms, as $3x + 2y$ or $3x - 2x$.

Monomial is from the Greek *mono* meaning "one" and refers to one term only, as in $3x$.

Adding Morphology and Etymology to your mathematics program will clearly show students the relationship between words and mathematics and will open up areas of research, study, word play, humor, and the integration of subjects. Following are activities for Morphology and Etymology that you can use with your students.

Mathematics the Write Way

Morphology

Our numeric symbols are the basis for hundreds of words in the English language. For example, the symbol 3 is not only the base for the words *three* and *third* but is also the base for the words *triangle, tricycle, triplets, tricorn, trio,* and *triplicate.* Each of the digits from 1 to 10, in fact, forms the basis for an array of words.

The Numerology Chart (Figure 6.12) includes each digit and its derivative words. Students can do creative and lively writing by using the number words from the Numerology Chart. You can use the suggested activity or create an activity to suit your students' needs. A sample response to the activity is included.

Writing Number Stories

Study the charts below. Then write a "One Story"—a story about the numeral 1 using words related to the numeral. Use as many words related to 1 as you can (see Figure 6.13).

Etymology

According to Menninger (1969), the basis of English can be traced to India's early language, Sanskrit. The speakers of this language, known as Aryans, migrated across the Indian subcontinent into Persia, Greece, Rome, and north across the steppes into what are now Slavic lands. They also migrated northeasterly into lands known as Germanic areas, reaching what we now call England, Norway, Denmark, and Sweden. These people brought with them their numbers, and since "number words are among the words of a language that most strongly resist change" (Menninger, 1969, p. 100), we can still recognize relationships among number words in Indo-European languages.

> Menninger (1969) was a great mathematician and linguist. In his writing he includes detailed descriptions of the origins of number words. These descriptions make interesting lessons for combining mathematics with language.

• ETYMOLOGY •

Writing Number Stories

Numerology Chart

Symbol	Cardinal	Ordinal	Shapes	Cycles	People	Song Groups	Animals	Ages
1	one	first		unicycle	singleton	soloist	unicorn	
2	two	second		bicycle	twins	duet, duo	bicorn, biped	
3	three	third	triangle	tricycle	triplets	trio	tricorn	
4	four	fourth	quadrangle	quadricycle	quadruplets	quartet	quadruped	quadrigenarian
5	five	fifth	pentagon		quintuplets	quintet		quinquagenarian
6	six	sixth	hexagon		sextuplets	sextet		sexagenarian
7	seven	seventh	heptagon or septagon		septuplets	septet		septuagenarian
8	eight	eighth	octagon		octuplets	octet	octopus, octopod	octogenarian
9	nine	ninth	nonagon					nonagenarian
10	ten	tenth	decagon					centenarian

Additional Words Related to Numerical Symbols*

Symbol	Number Words
1	once, only, unique, unit, united, solo, solitude, solitary, solely, soliloquy, monologue, monogram, monocle, monarchy, monolingual, university
2	twice, duplicate, duplex, double, bifocal, bilingual, bimonthly, binary, bilateral, couple, dialogue, diameter, diarchy
3	thrice, triplicate, triple, trimester, triumvirate, triarchy, trilingual, trinity
4	quadruple, quadrant, quadratic, quadrille
5	quintuple, quintessential, quintessence, pentagonal, pentagram, pentahedron, pentaprism
6	sextant, sextile, sextillion, sexagesimal
7	September,** Septuagent, septennial, septenary, septimal
8	October,** octave, octennial, octillion
9	November,** novena, nonary
10	December,** decade, decimal, decametric

*Check out an unabridged dictionary for other words.

**Students are likely to be interested in why these months are the ninth, tenth, eleventh, and twelfth. Suggest that your students research the reason by checking the word *calendar* in the library or on the Internet.

Figure 6.12

• ETYMOLOGY •

Writing Number Stories: Sample Response

Once a day a **unique unicorn** rode his **unicycle** to the **university**. On his shirt he had his **monogram** UU (for **unique unicorn**), and on his left eye he wore a **monocle**. He had been born a **singleton** and remained a **solitary** type who preferred at least **one** hour of **solitude** once a day. He was a **soloist** in the school chorus and was also famous for his **monologues** and **soliloquies**. Unfortunately, he was only **monolingual**, limited **solely** to speaking English. Yet in spite of his **solitary** ways, his **monolingualism**, and his **unique** style of wearing a **monogram** and **monocle**, this **unicorn** was beloved by the whole **university**, not only in the **United** States but across the entire world where there was a **united** belief in the ways of **unicorns**.

Note to Teacher: If students enjoy writing a "One Story," they can continue by writing stories about other numbers. This activity works well when students work in *dyads* or even *triads*.

Figure 6.13

Two activities in Etymology follow. The first activity asks students to compare the English names for numbers with the German, Spanish, French, and Italian names for numbers. Students who speak or know a language other than English can teach fellow students numbers in their native language and do a similar comparison or contrast to English numbers. You can adapt this activity to your students' needs (Figure 6.14).

The second activity focuses on geometric words with the suffix *-hedron* (Figure 6.15). This is a Greek form that means "face," and when it is combined with different prefixes, it refers to certain types of figures. Students can learn about these *-hedron* words by doing the activity. (For an example of a polyhedron "character," see *The Phantom Tollbooth* [Juster, 1964]. In this book, the Dodecahedron is a delightful twelve-faced humorous character who lives in the city of Digitopolis.)

Learning Numbers in Another Language and Using Them in a Story

Study the chart of Numbers in Different Languages (Figure 6.14). Find the similarities and differences among the names for the numbers. What connection can you make between number words in different languages and mathematics?

• ETYMOLOGY •

Using Numbers in a Different Language

Numbers in Different Languages

English	German	Spanish	French	Italian
one	eins	uno, una	un, une	uno, una
two	zwei	dos	deux	due
three	drei	tres	trois	tre
four	vier	cuatro	quatre	quattro
five	fünf	cinco	cinq	cinque
six	sechs	seis	six	sei
seven	sieben	siete	sept	sette
eight	acht	ocho	huit	otto
nine	neun	nueve	neuf	nove
ten	zehn	diez	dix	dieci

Now, learn the numbers in one of the languages you don't know. Complete the following framed story to help you learn the numbers. Fill in the spaces with numbers from the language you have chosen. Use as many different numbers as you can. You will also have to do some mathematics to complete the story. See if you can find someone to help you pronounce the numbers. Then, if you can, read your story aloud to a friend.

FRAMED STORY:

Once there were _____ children who lived in a house with _____ dogs and _____ cats. Another family came to visit. They had _____ children, _____ parakeets, and _____ gerbils. The children divided themselves into _____ groups, with _____ children in each group. Each group picked _____ animals. They all played together for _____ hours. They started playing at _____ o'clock and finished playing at _____ o'clock. The children had so much fun that they decided to meet every _____ weeks for a whole year. They would now see each other approximately _____ times in the same year.

You may need a number that is greater than 10 for the last sentence. How do you think you can find out that number?

Figure 6.14

• LEARNING ABOUT POLYHEDRONS •

A polyhedron is a solid geometric figure with many faces. The suffix - *hedron* is from the Greek and means "*face.*" The prefix before - *hedron* tells you how many faces the figure has. For example, *tetra*- means "four," so a tetrahedron has four faces. Here are some common polyhedrons (*poly*- means "many").

Tetrahedron – four faces

Pentahedron – five faces

Octahedron – eight faces

Dodecahedron – twelve faces

Icosahedron – twenty faces

Imagine that you are one of the polyhedrons shown above. Write a letter to another polyhedron.
*In this letter include

- your address,
- the address of the polyhedron you are writing to,
- a description of your faces,
- the advantages of having so many faces,
- one or two questions you have for the polyhedron you are writing to,
- an illustration of yourself.

*See Chapter 11 on Personifications and Interactions for this type of writing.

Figure 6.15

INTERNET LINKS

Etymology

http://www.etymonline.com

Information About Zero

http://mathforum.org/library/drmath/sets/select/dm_about_zero.html

Mathematics in Specific Cultures, Periods, or Places

http://www.maths.tcd.ie/pub/HistMath/Links/Cultures.html

Origin of Zero

http://www.sciam.com/askexpert_topic.cfm?topicID=11

7

Profiles and Frames for Organizing Mathematical Information

"One of the nicest things about mathematics . . . is that many of the things which can never be, often are. . . . It's very much like trying to reach Infinity. You know that it's there, but you just don't know where."

—*The Phantom Tollbooth* (Juster, 1964, p. 175)

Organize instruction around a few core ideas. (Strong et al., 2001, p. 69)

WHAT ARE PROFILES AND FRAMES?

Zinsser (1990), in his chapter "Science Writing and Technical Writing" (which includes mathematics), points out that the writer's job is to lead "a reader who knows nothing, step by step, to a grasp of the subject" (p. 116). We have combined two formats—Profiles and Frames—to help students do this job. Profiles and Frames serve as text organizers and outlines that help students keep to the topic and follow a plan, so that they, in turn, can guide the reader. Profiles are templates into which students plug appropriate information to solve a problem or explain a mathematical concept. A Profile allows the student to either organize or reorganize information based on both prior knowledge and research. For example, when a student reads a text and has to summarize or retell the information, the Profile guides the student in selecting key ideas and essential information. After students have gathered the essential information and entered it on the Profile, they can now "tell it" or write it "in their own words." Frames are also a form of outline. In Frames, however, the students are given the syntactic structure, which includes stem or partial sentences. Completing these partial sentences helps students focus on the content of their writing without concern for grammatical or structural aspects of the text.

THE PURPOSE OF PROFILES AND FRAMES

The rationale for using Profiles and Frames is found in *Teaching With the Brain in Mind* (Jensen, 1998): "The brain's susceptibility to paying attention is very much influenced by patterning. We are more likely to see something if we are told to look for it or prompted to its location" (p. 43). Jensen also discusses the importance of context and patterns, emphasizing that "patterns give context to information that otherwise would be dismissed as meaningless" (p. 95). He believes that the human desire to create patterns is innate, pointing out that even very young children arrange items in groups rather than leaving them random.

Bomer (1995) points out that students who are learning to write (and read) must discover and then follow the patterns of organization that give text meaning, either within their own or someone else's text. Young writers, or those writing about newly learned concepts, often need organizers to help them get started, to help them follow a sequence or arrangement, and to stay focused on the topic. When students use Profiles and Frames as text organizers, they can concentrate on the mathematical information they need to impart with minimum concern about the beginning, middle, and end of their writing. Furthermore, when students learn to write text that is consistently organized, they learn to internalize the "sound" of good writing, so that eventually they can organize their writing independently and in their own voice.

There is another critical application of Frames. Most state tests and curricula expect students to respond to open-ended and multistep problems. Of particular importance is the students' ability to fully explain how they arrived at their results. The end of this chapter has a Frame (Figure 7.26) that is specifically designed to support students in addressing this requirement.

INTRODUCING PROFILES AND FRAMES

In this chapter, we begin with Mathematics the Write Way, which provides a variety of Profiles and Frames. As in the previous chapters, we present the models for students in six content areas—number and operations, algebra, geometry, measurement, data analysis and probability, and money—followed by examples of completed writings. There are also blank templates of Profiles and Frames for your use in Resource B. Most of the models in this chapter cover a range of grade levels and can serve as ways to provide differentiated instruction. For example, Profile of a Number (Figure 7.1) represents information on numbers that students learn from Grade 2 through Grade 7 or higher. So we suggest that you can use these Profiles as they are or modify them to meet your students' needs. They can be adapted for various grade levels by deleting or adding information, and you can also use the examples in this chapter to create your own Profiles.

Frames serve as text outlines that provide the writer with a pre-established sequence for writing. Similar to Profiles, Frames allow the writer to concentrate on the content with minimum concern about organization. Two ideas stated by Saltzman (1993) apply to Frames. One is that writers need to "warm up" (p. 134) and the other is that "imitation is a smart idea" (p. 137). By giving Frames to the student writer, we provide stepping stones to focused writing and remove the worry about format. In addition, when students use Frames frequently with a variety of topics or concepts, they begin to internalize sequential formats, a necessary requisite for good writing (Zinsser, 1990). As suggested for Profiles, modify them as appropriate to your students' needs, but allow for a wide range of abilities.

Mathematics the Write Way

Writing Activities Related to Profiles

Students who understand the structure of numbers and relationships among numbers can work with them flexibly. (NCTM, 2000, p. 149)

Each Profile below is followed by one or two examples of how to use it. There is an example of a completed Profile and, in some cases, an example or model of a story written from the completed Profile. The models given in this section are fuller length forms of writing than in the previous chapters and represent the developing ability of students to write more on mathematical topics. We suggest that, if possible, you duplicate or make a transparency of an appropriate Profile and show your students the sequence of its use.

Number and Operations

• PROFILE •

Profile of a Number (Blank Template)

Complete the information in this Profile. Then write a story or an article about the number you have selected. Be sure to follow the organization of the Profile. You can also use this Profile to write about other numbers.

Select any number from 1 to 9: _____

Is the number odd or even? _____

Write the ordinal name. _____

Write the Roman numeral. _____

Affix a zero to the number. _____ Write this number in words. _____

Affix two zeros. _____ Write this number in words. _____

Write the number with six zeros affixed. _____ Write this number in words. _____

Write the factors of this number. _____

Use this number in a fraction. _____ Show the fraction as a decimal. _____

Does this number have a square root that is a whole number? _____ If yes, what is the number? _____

Does this number have a square root that is not a whole number? _____ What is this number? _____

Write the negative of this number. _____ Add a positive number to it. _____
What is the answer? _____

Write the negative of your number again. _____ Add a negative number to this number. _____
What is the answer? _____

Is there any geometric figure associated with your number? _____ What is the geometric figure (or figures)? _____

Is there any other information you can add to this Profile?

Figure 7.1

Number and Operations

• PROFILE •

Profile of a Number (Sample Response)

Complete the information in this Profile. Then write a story or an article about the number you have selected. Be sure to follow the organization of the Profile. You can also use this Profile to write about other numbers.

Select any number from 1 to 9: _____7_____

Is the number odd or even? _____odd_____

Write the ordinal name. _____seventh_____

Write the Roman numeral. _____VII_____

Affix a zero to the number. _____70_____ Write this number in words. _____seventy_____

Affix two zeros. _____700_____ Write this number in words. _____seven hundred_____

Write the number with six zeros affixed. _____7,000,000_____

Write this number in words. _____seven million_____

Write the factors of this number. _____1 and 7_____

Use this number in a fraction. _____1/7_____ Show the fraction as a decimal. _____.1429_____

Does this number have a square root that is a whole number? _____no_____ If yes, what is the number? _____N/A_____

Does this number have a square root that is not a whole number? _____yes_____ What is this number? _____2.6458...____

Write the negative of this number. _____−7_____ Add a positive number to it. _____−7+ (+8)_____ What is the answer? _____1_____

Write the negative of your number again. _____−7_____ Add a negative number to this number. _____−7 +−3_____ What is the answer? _____−10_____

Is there any geometric figure associated with your number? _____yes_____ What is the geometric figure (or figures)? _____heptagon_____

Is there any other information you can add to this Profile? *There are seven days in the week, seven wonders of the world, and the seventh-inning stretch in a baseball game.*

Figure 7.2

Number and Operations

• PROFILE •

Profile of a Number (Sample Story)

Every number in our numbering system has a story. Here is part of the story related to the number seven:

Seven is an odd number, which means it cannot be divided in half to make two whole numbers. In addition to its cardinal name, seven, it has the ordinal name seventh, as in the seventh day. Like all our numbers, we can write 7 as a Roman numeral using letters—VII—but when we use Roman numerals we lose the system of place value, making it very hard to add and subtract, except in our heads. That's because we need zero for place value.

Speaking of place value, we can place zero (0) to the right of the seven (7) and get seventy (70) or two zeros (00) and get seven hundred (700) or six zeros (000000) and get seven million (7,000,000). We can keep placing zeros to infinity.

Seven is a number that has only two factors, 1 and 7. This means that 7 can be divided only by 1 where the answer is 7. Or it can be divided by itself (7 divided by 7) and the answer is 1. This type of number that only has two factors is called a prime number and is similar to the numbers 1, 3, and 5. When seven is a fraction, as in 1/7, we can convert that fraction to a decimal, and if we take it to four places we get .1429. Of course, we can go beyond four places and in the case of 1/7 we would go on forever.

The square root of 7 is not a whole number. By using a calculator to get the square root of 7, the answer is 2.6458, and can be continued.

All numbers can be positive and negative so that negative seven is written as −7. When we add a positive number such as +8, the answer is +1. The idea of positive and negative numbers is easier to understand when we look at a number line, as illustrated below.

Negative Numbers   Positive Numbers

−10 −9 −8 −7 −6 −5 −4 −3 −2 −1 0 1 2 3 4 5 6 7 8 9 10

Now we can see that −7 + −3 = −10.

The geometric figure that represents seven is called a heptagon, from the Greek word *hept,* meaning seven. The number seven is used in many ways, such as seven days in the week. In ancient times, there were the seven wonders of the world. Today, when we go to a baseball game, we have the seventh-inning stretch—after six-and-a-half innings everyone stands up and stretches to relax their legs and arms.

As we can see, a number is more than just a number. It is symbol of mathematical, historical, and geographic information.

Figure 7.3

Algebra

• PROFILE •

Profile of Pascal's Triangle

A pattern is an arrangement of items or numbers that has a sequence or organization. Some patterns are easy to figure out, such as $1 + 2 + 3 + 4 + 5 + \ldots$ You can easily follow this pattern to infinity. Other patterns, especially in mathematics, can get very complicated.

Below is a pattern discovered by Blaise Pascal. Pascal was a brilliant French mathematician who lived during the 1600s. One of his mathematical discoveries was the symmetrical arrangement of numbers (or binomial coefficients) that raised each number to a higher power. This arrangement formed a triangle that could continue to infinity. Study the illustration of Pascal's Triangle and complete the information on the Profile.

Pascal's Triangle

```
                            1
                        1       1
                    1       2       1
                1       3       3       1
            1       4       6       4       1
        1       5      10      10       5       1
    1       6      15      20      15       6       1
1       7      21      35      35      21       7       1
1   8      28      56      70      56      28       8       1
1   9   36      84     126     126      84      36       9       1
```

Profile

Location of the number that appears the most frequently:

Location of numbers that are in consecutive order:

Progression of the third row of numbers diagonally (Write the progression vertically):

Patterns of addition in the triangle:

Patterns of multiplication:

Other patterns or information:

Figure 7.4

Algebra

• PROFILE •

Profile of Pascal's Triangle (Sample Response)

Location of the number that appears the most frequently: *On the left and right outer sides of the triangle.*

Location of numbers that are in consecutive order: *Second interior rows running diagonally.*

Progression of the third row of numbers diagonally (Write the progression vertically):

1 + 2

3 + 3

6 + 4

10 + 5

15 + 6

21 + 7

28 + 8

36 + 9

Patterns of addition in the triangle: *The sum of any two consecutive numbers in any row can be found between these numbers in the row below (e.g., 15 + 20 = 35)*

Patterns of multiplication: *Begin in the third row from the pinnacle. Multiply 2 × 3 to get 6; multiply 2 × 10 to get 20; multiply 2 × 35 to get 70; multiply 2 × 126 to get 252 and so forth*

Other patterns or information: *Each diagonal has its own pattern. It has a symmetry. There are an infinite number of triangles. The interior numbers get progressively larger as the triangle grows.*

Figure 7.5

Geometry

• PROFILE •

Profile of a Rectangle

An excellent way to understand more about polygons is to observe and write about their characteristics in a Profile. Then, if you use the Profile to write a description of a polygon, you will deepen your understanding even more and you will also improve your writing skills.

Complete the following Profile of a rectangle. When you have completed the Profile, write several paragraphs telling someone what a rectangle is. To make the writing interesting, you might want to imagine that you are a rectangle describing yourself to either humans or other geometric shapes. This type of writing is called Personification.*

Type of polygon:

Number of sides: Number of angles:

Total number of degrees: Number of degrees in each angle:

Types of rectangles:

Formula for finding the perimeter:

Formula for finding the area:

Rectangular objects or items in our environment:

Write instructions on how to use a rectangle to create other polygons.

*Personification writing is discussed in detail in Chapter 11.

Figure 7.6

Geometry

• PROFILE •

Profile of a Rectangle (Sample Response)

An excellent way to understand more about polygons is to observe and write about their characteristics in a Profile. Then, if you use the Profile to write a description of a polygon, you will deepen your understanding even more and you will also improve your writing skills.

Complete the following Profile of a rectangle. When you have completed the Profile, write several paragraphs telling someone what a rectangle is. To make the writing interesting, imagine that you are a rectangle describing yourself to either humans or other geometric shapes. This type of writing is called Personification.

Type of polygon: *rectangle*

Number of sides: *four*   Number of angles: *four*

Total number of degrees: *360°*   Number of degrees in each angle: *90°*

Types of rectangles: *squares, quadrangles, parallelograms, rectangular prisms*

Formula for finding the perimeter: *Add the lengths and widths of all four sides or P = W + W + H + H*

Formula for finding the area: *Multiply the length times the width or L × W*

Rectangular objects or items in our environment: *windows, picture frames*

Write instructions on how to use a rectangle to create other polygons.

1. *Draw a diagonal line from one angle to its opposite angle. This will form two triangles.*
2. *Divide a rectangle into as many triangles as you can.*
3. *Divide a rectangle into as many smaller rectangles as you can.*
4. *Rotate a square to form a rhombus.*

Figure 7.7

• PROFILE •

Profile of a Rectangle (Sample Story)

Following is an example of a description of a rectangle written from the point of view of a rectangle. The rectangle has taken the information from the Profile and is telling about itself to a triangle.

Meet a Rectangle

My name is B. A. Rectangle and I am seen everywhere from windows to picture frames. First you should know that I have four sides and four angles. My sides may be equal in length and height or my height may be greater than my width or vice versa. In any case, I always have four right angles, with each angle measuring 90 degrees. If you add up my angles, they equal 360 degrees.

When all my four sides are equal, I am called a square even though I am still a rectangle. Some mathematicians like to call me a quadrangle, which simply means I have four (quad) angles, or a quadrilateral, which means I have four sides. I can also be referred to as a parallelogram, which means that the length sides and the width sides are parallel.

It is very easy to find my perimeter, a word that means to "measure around." All you have to do is add the length of both sides to the width of both sides and you will have the perimeter. If you want to find my area—that is, the space I take up—you will have to multiply my length times my width.

What I find very interesting about myself is that I can form triangles. Just draw a diagonal line from one angle to the opposite angle and you will get two triangles. Even more curious is that you can divide me up into many triangles. If you do not want triangles, you can divide me into more rectangles or into the rectangles that are called squares. I can also be rotated so that I take on a new name called a rhombus.

Even though I already know that you can be formed within me, I would like some details about your life as a triangle. For example, how many degrees do you have and what kind of angles can you form? I would love to know exactly what you are since we are close in so many ways.

Figure 7.8

Measurement

• PROFILE •

Profile of an Analog Clock

Today we are likely to use two types of clocks to keep track of time. One is called an analog clock, which has hands and twelve numbers or indicators. The other is called a digital clock, which is computerized. Complete the Profile of an analog clock. Then write a description of this clock imagining that you are creating a brochure on clocks. You can also write a Profile of a digital clock and compare both analog and digital clocks in your brochure.

Numbers shown on the clock:

Reason for the numbers:

Time markers other than numbers:

Reason for markers other than numbers:

Name of small hand:

Name of large hand:

Name of third hand:

Number of hours represented:

Number of seconds represented:

Power sources for an analog clock:

Other possible features on an analog clock:

Reasons for a clock:

Other information about an analog clock:

Figure 7.9

Measurement

• PROFILE •
Profile of an Analog Clock (Sample Response)

Today we are likely to use two types of clocks to keep track of time. One is called an analog clock, which has hands and twelve numbers or indicators. The other is called a digital clock, which is computerized. Complete the Profile of an analog clock. Then write a description of this clock imagining that you are creating a brochure on clocks. You can also write a Profile of a digital clock and compare both analog and digital clocks in your brochure.

Numbers shown on the clock: *1, 2, 3, 4, 5, 6, 7, 8, 9, 10, 11, 12*

Reason for the numbers: *Each number represents five minutes of an hour.*

Time markers other than numbers: *tally marks or dots*

Reason for markers other than numbers: *to show minutes*

Name of small hand: *hour hand*

Name of large hand: *minute hand*

Name of third hand: *second hand*

Number of hours represented: *12*

Number of seconds represented: *60*

Power sources for an analog clock: *internal spring, electricity—either plug or a battery*

Other possible features on an analog clock: *date, alarm, light, must be set, needs dials to change the time*

Reasons for a clock: *wake up on time, time a race or a test, time cooking*

Other information about an analog clock: *May use Roman numerals instead of Arabic numerals; may use dots instead of numbers; can also be watches; shows the manufacturer's name; may sit on a table or stand like a grandfather clock.*

Figure 7.10

Measurement

• PROFILE •

Profile of an Analog Clock (Sample Story)

How do you know an analog clock when you see one? There are many things to look for. Most clocks have numbers on them that tell what hour of the day it is. Usually, clocks break the 24 hours of the day into two groups of 12. So the numbers run from 1 to 12. These same numbers help us figure out how many minutes of each hour have gone by. The distance between each number represents five minutes. In between the numbers are tally marks or dots for each minute.

Analog clocks come with three hands (but no fingers). The short or little hand on a clock marks the hours of the day. The longer or big hand marks the minutes in each hour. Some clocks have a third hand to mark the seconds in each minute. There are 60 minutes in each hour and 60 seconds in each minute.

Good clocks run at the same speed as time. If clocks run too slowly, then people will be late. If they run too fast, people will be early. All machines need power, and clocks are time measuring machines. The power for clocks can come from two sources. Some analog clocks get their power from wound-up springs. As the springs slowly unwind, they provide power to make the hands go around. Other clocks use electricity to make a motor turn their hands. The electricity can come from either a plug or a battery. Almost all analog clocks have dials to set the time and alarms.

Some people like their clocks simple and others like them fancy. The simple clocks just tell you the time and call it a day (so to speak). Others have a lot of features that make them more useful. Some will tell you the day and the date. Some will wake you up with an alarm. Some will light up at night so you can see how much past your bedtime it is.

A few other pieces of information might help you recognize a clock. Some clocks use Roman numerals instead of Arabic numerals. The Roman numerals are the ones that look like letters (I, II, III, IV). Just in case you were wondering, the Romans who invented these letter-numbers lived a long time ago when their clocks had no hands, and they used light from the sun to tell time. Some clocks don't use numbers of any kind. They think telling time should be a little like a game of charades. Just look at the pose and guess the time without numbers.

Most clocks have the manufacturer's name on them. They can sit on a table or on the floor. Tall clocks on the floor are sometimes called grandfather (or grandmother) clocks. Some clocks are in big towers of large buildings. Maybe you could invent the mother or father or sister or brother clock and become famous. After all, it isn't just grandfathers and grandmothers who need to tell time.

Figure 7.11

Data Analysis and Probability

• PROFILE •
Profile of Dice

Dice are small cubes that are often used in games. One of these cubes is called a die; two are called dice. Mathematicians often use dice to study probability. For example, a mathematician might want to know the probability (chances) of getting a double when throwing the dice (e.g., two threes). One way to do this is to record how many times you have to throw the dice to get a double. The more trials you do, the closer you get to an accurate probability. Knowing the probability of dice is also helpful in playing games. If possible, use actual dice to get your answers. Complete the Profile to learn more about dice, outcomes, and probability.

Number of faces on a die:

Range of dots on a die:

Odd numbers on a die: Even numbers:

Odd number combinations, using two dice (for example, 1 + 2 = 3):

Even number combinations, using two dice (for example, 1 + 1 = 2):

Total number of possible combinations (even and odd):

Combinations of doubles, using two dice (for example, 6 + 6 = 12):

Games that use dice:

Reason(s) for using dice in games:

Figure 7.12

Data Analysis and Probability

• PROFILE •

Profile of Dice (Sample Response)

Dice are small cubes that are often used in games. One of these cubes is called a die; two are called dice. Mathematicians often use dice to study probability. For example, a mathematician might want to know the probability (chances) of getting a double when throwing the dice (e.g., two threes). One way to do this is to record how many times you have to throw the dice to get a double. The more trials you to do, the closer you get to an accurate probability. Knowing the probability of dice is also helpful in playing games. If possible, use actual dice to get your answers. Complete the Profile to learn more about dice, outcomes, and probability.

Number of faces on a die: *6*

Range of dots on a die: *1 to 6*

Odd numbers on a die: *1, 3, 5*   Even numbers: *2, 4, 6*

Odd number combinations, using two dice (for example, 1 + 2 = 3): *1 + 2 = 3; 1 + 4 = 5; 1 + 6 = 7; 2 + 3 = 5; 2 + 5 = 7; 3 + 4 = 7; 3 + 6 = 9; 4 + 5 = 9; 5 + 6 = 11*

Even number combinations, using two dice (for example, 1 + 1 = 2): *1 + 1 = 2; 1 + 3 = 4; 1 + 5 = 6; 2 + 2 = 4; 2 + 4 = 6; 2 + 6 = 8; 3 + 3 = 6; 3 + 5 = 8; 4 + 4 = 8; 4 + 6 = 10; 5 + 5 = 10; 6 + 6 = 12*

Total number of possible combinations (even and odd): *21*

Combinations of doubles, using two dice (for example, 6 + 6 = 12): *1 + 1 = 2; 2 + 2 = 4; 3 + 3 = 6; 4 + 4 = 8; 5 + 5 = 10; 6 + 6 = 12*

Games that use dice: *Monopoly, Yahtzee, Clue, Trivial Pursuit*

Reason(s) for using dice in games: *The results are random so they are fair to all the players.*

Figure 7.13

Data Analysis and Probability

• PROFILE •

Profile of Dice (Sample Story)

Dice are really fun to play with. We use them in all kinds of games, such as Monopoly, Yahtzee, Clue, and Trivial Pursuit. One of the reasons they are fun is that they cannot be controlled by the thrower. This makes them fair for all players. But it also means that we have to know something about probability when we play with them.

Dice were invented a long time ago and are still used today. Each die is a cube with six sides. Each side is called a face. The faces of the die do not have noses, eyes, or mouths, just dots. The range of the number of dots is from 1 to 6 and no two faces have the same number of dots. Therefore, there are three sides with even numbers and three sides with odd numbers.

When you throw the dice (two die), you get a combination of two numbers. When added together, the sums can be odd or even. There are 21 combinations; 9 different combinations make odd sums and 12 different combinations make even sums. Six of the combinations are doubles, meaning that the same number of dots appear on each of the dice.

Next time you play a game using dice, take some extra time to keep track of the numbers you and your partners get and see if you discover any patterns.

Figure 7.14

Money

• PROFILE •

Profile of a United States Coin

There are six types of United States coins: penny, nickel, dime, quarter, half dollar, dollar. Each coin is worth a different amount, is made of metal, and has a variety of information on it. Choose a coin and complete the Profile of a United States Coin. (You may need a magnifying glass to clearly see the items on the coin.) After you finish the Profile, write a description of that coin to someone from another country.

Name of coin:

Value of coin in cents:

Metal used for coin:

Number of coins needed to equal one dollar:

Number of coins needed to equal ten dollars:

Number of coins needed to equal one hundred dollars:

Year this coin was minted:

Person represented on the coin:

Words or phrases written on the face and reverse side of the coin and their meanings:

Illustrations or symbols on the reverse side of the coin:

Other information:

Figure 7.15

Money

• PROFILE •

Profile of a United States Coin (Sample Response)

There are six types of United States coins: penny, nickel, dime, quarter, half dollar, dollar. Each coin is worth a different amount, is made of metal, and has a variety of information on it. Choose a coin and complete the Profile of a United States Coin. (You may need a magnifying glass to clearly see the items on the coin.) After you finish the Profile, write a description of that coin to someone from another country.

Name of coin: *quarter*

Value of coin in cents: *25 cents*

Metal used for coin: *cupro-nickel*

Number of coins needed to equal one dollar: *4*

Number of coins needed to equal ten dollars: *40*

Number of coins needed to equal one hundred dollars: *400*

Year this coin was minted: *1997*

Person represented on the coin: *George Washington*

Words or phrases written on the face and reverse side of the coin and their meanings:

> *"Liberty" means that there is freedom for Americans.*
>
> *"In God We Trust" means that we have confidence in God.*
>
> *"E pluribus unum" means that out of many people we are one nation.*
>
> *"United States of America" is the country in which the coin was minted and is used.*

Illustrations or symbols on the reverse side of the coin: *Eagle—the eagle is the bird that symbolizes the United States, also called its emblem.*

Other information: *Two quarters equal one half dollar. The word quarter means a quarter or one-fourth of a dollar.*

Figure 7.16

Money

• PROFILE •

Profile of a United States Coin (Sample Story)

Dear Francisco:

I recently read that many of the countries in Europe are going to use the same money, called Euros. That should be handy.

You have asked me to describe one of the coins I use in the United States and to explain the reasons for the illustrations and the words on that coin. I am enclosing a coin that we call a quarter and would like to tell you as much as I can about it.

I think the most useful coin in the United States is the quarter. I say this because you can use it in all the coin-operated machines here. That means that you can buy drinks and candy, make phone calls, park the car, and do a lot of other things with a quarter.

The quarter is worth 25 cents, which is why the coin has the words "quarter of a dollar" on it. Some quick calculating tells you that four quarters equal a dollar. Therefore, 40 quarters equal 10 dollars and 400 quarters equal 100 dollars.

Quarters are made of several metals, such as nickel and copper, that give the appearance of being silver. The English word we use for making coins is minting. Each quarter has the year it was minted under the picture of George Washington. President Washington was our first president and you see his face and name all the time, even on the dollar bill.

We put a lot of words on our coins. The words remind us of ideas we believe in. For example, "liberty" is on the quarter to show we believe in freedom. "In God we trust" is there because during the Civil War a number of Americans asked the government to place these religious words on the coin.
All our coins use the Latin words "e pluribus unum" (out of many, one) to remind us that out of many people we are one nation. These words became the motto of our country in 1776 when the American colonies united against Great Britain. And, of course, we put "United States of America" on our coins to identify our country.

There are also pictures on the quarter. I already mentioned George Washington's. On the other side is a picture of the American bald eagle, our national bird. This bird was selected early in American history because it is a bird that is unique to North America and now is a symbol for freedom and a strong spirit.

Tell me about the Euro when you get a chance. Hope we see each other soon.

Sincerely,

Jaime

Figure 7.17

Writing Activities Related to Frames

Teacher Notes

Following are Frames for each of the content areas—number and operations, geometry, measurement, data analysis and probability—and money. Adapt these Frames to your students' needs. You will find that by using Frames, your students will write with greater ease and organization and will be able to better focus on mathematical explanation. Frames will also allow you to more easily assess your students' writing because there is an existing grammatical framework. Each Frame is followed by a sample of a completed Frame.

Number and Operations

• FRAME •

Frame

Many times you will need to solve mathematical problems, either in school or outside of school. One way to solve a number problem is to use a Frame. A Frame is similar to an outline but is written in sentence form and can often be used to solve similar problems. Below is a number problem. Solve it by using the Frame that follows the problem.

Problem:

Beth had to read a book for her class report. The book was 80 pages long. She had to finish it in five days. She read eight pages the first day. The next day she read two pages more than the first day. On the third day she read the same number of pages as she read on the first day. On the fourth day she read two more pages than she read on the second day. On the fifth day she read the same number of pages she read on the fourth day. How many pages had she read by the fifth day? How many more pages did she have to read?

Frame:

Beth had to read a book that was _____ pages in _____ days.

On the first day she read _____ pages.

     She now had _____ more pages to read.

On the second day she read _____ plus two more pages, making _____ pages.

     She now had read a total of _____ pages.

     She now had _____ more pages to read.

On the third day she read _____ pages.

     She now had read a total of _____ pages.

     She now had _____ more pages to read.

On the fourth day she read _____ pages plus two pages, making _____ pages.

     She now had read a total of _____ pages.

     She now had _____ more pages to read.

On the fifth day she read the same number of pages as on the fourth day. That was _____ pages.

     She now had read a total of _____ pages.

     She now had _____ more pages to read.

The teacher gave Beth two more days to finish her book.

     She read _____ pages on the next day and _____ pages on the day after to finish the book.

Figure 7.18

Number and Operations

• FRAME •

Frame (Sample Response)

Many times you will need to solve mathematical problems, either in school or outside of school. One way to solve a number problem is to use a Frame. A Frame is similar to an outline, but is written in sentence form and can often be used to solve similar problems. Below is a number problem. Solve it by using the Frame that follows the problem.

Problem:

Beth had to read a book for her class report. The book was 80 pages long. She had to finish it in five days. She read eight pages the first day. The next day she read two pages more than the first day. On the third day she read the same number of pages as she read on the first day. On the fourth day she read two more pages than she read on the second day. On the fifth day she read the same number of pages she read on the fourth day. How many pages had she read by the fifth day? How many more pages did she have to read?

Frame:

Beth had to read a book that was __80__ pages in __7__ days.

On the first day she read __8__ pages.

      She now had __72__ more pages to read.

On the second day she read __8__ plus two more pages, making __10__ pages.

      She now had read a total of __18__ pages.

      She now had __62__ more pages to read.

On the third day she read __8__ pages.

      She now had read a total of __26__ pages.

      She now had __54__ more pages to read.

On the fourth day she read __10__ pages plus two pages, making __12__ pages.

      She now had read a total of __38__ pages.

      She now had __42__ more pages to read.

On the fifth day she read the same number of pages as on the fourth day. That was __12__ pages.

      She now had read a total of __50__ pages.

      She now had __30__ more pages to read.

The teacher gave Beth two more days to finish her book.

      She read __15__ pages on the next day and __15__ pages on the day after to finish the book.

Figure 7.19

Geometry

• ΓΓΔΜΕ •

Frame for a Rectangular Prism

Problem: Most boxes are in the shape of rectangular prisms. One of the most commonly used rectangular prisms is the cereal box, which contains a great deal of mathematical and other information. Look at a cereal box and complete the Frame.

Frame:
Most cereal boxes are in the shape of rectangular prisms for the following reasons:

Cereal boxes also contain a great deal of information, such as:

A person's major reasons for buying a particular cereal, besides its taste, might be:

To understand some of the information on a cereal box, you would have to know the following mathematics:

Figure 7.20

• FRAME •

Frame for a Rectangular Prism (Completed Story)

Problem: Most boxes are in the shape of rectangular prisms. One of the most commonly used rectangular prisms is the cereal box, which contains a great deal of mathematical and other information. Look at a cereal box and complete the Frame.

Frame:

Most cereal boxes are in the shape of rectangular prisms for the following reasons:

Rectangular prisms have space, known as volume, so the cereal can fill the whole volume.

Rectangular boxes of different heights and widths can fit into one cabinet because their edges can touch each other without leaving space.

Rectangular prisms have a great deal of space on the exterior for writing information about the cereal.

Cereal boxes also contain a great deal of information, such as:

Listing the ingredients so you know whether the ingredients are healthy for you.

Giving you the name and address of the company in case you want to contact the company because you are satisfied, dissatisfied, or have questions.

Coupons available with discounts, bar codes, contests, and prizes or premiums

A person's major reasons for buying a particular cereal, besides its taste, might be:

Get the vitamins and nutrients to build a strong body.

Pay less for it than for similar cereals.

Take advantage of the coupons and premiums.

To understand some of the information on a cereal box, you would have to know the following mathematics:

The percentage daily value for vitamins that children of different ages or adults of different ages need.

The amount of grams of fat the cereal has and if that amount is too much, too little, or just right for most children or adults.

How many grams in a pound or the ratio of grams to ounces.

Figure 7.21

Measurement

• FRAME •

Frame for Measurement

Problem: You have three empty containers. One container holds 3 liters, a second holds 5 liters, and a third holds 9 liters. How can you use these containers to measure exactly 7 liters of water? The steps in the problem have been "framed out." Follow the steps and write what you did to get 7 liters.

Step	3-Liter Container	5-Liter Container	9-Liter Container	Total Number of Liters
Step 1				
Step 2				
Step 3				
Step 4				
Step 5				

To get exactly 7 liters from three containers each holding 3 liters, 5 liters, and 7 liters, I did these steps:

First,

Second,

Third,

Fourth,

Finally,

By following these steps, I . . .

Figure 7.22

• FRAME •

Frame for Measurement (Sample Response)

Problem: You have three empty containers. One container holds 3 liters, a second holds 5 liters, and a third holds 9 liters. How can you use these containers to measure exactly 7 liters of water? The steps in the problem have been "framed out." Follow the steps and write what you did to get 7 liters.

Step	3-Liter Container	5-Liter Container	9-Liter Container	Total Number of Liters
Step 1	0	0	Fill container with 9 liters	9 liters
Step 2	Fill container with 3 liters	0	Still has 9 liters	12 liters
Step 3	Pour 3 liters into 5-liter container; now has 0 liters	Now contains 3 liters	Still has 9 liters	12 liters
Step 4	0	Fill container to the top using water from 9-liter container; now has 5 liters	Pour water from this container to fill 5-liter container; now has 7 liters	12 liters
Step 5	0	Empty container; now has 0 liters	7 liters	7 liters

To get exactly 7 liters from three containers each holding 3 liters, 5 liters, and 9 liters, I did these steps:

First, I filled the 9-liter container, giving me 9 liters of water.

Second, I filled the 3-liter container, giving me 12 liters of water total.

Third, I emptied the contents of the 3-liter container into the 5-liter container. I still have 12 liters of water total and room for 2 more liters in the 5-liter container.

Fourth, I emptied 2 liters of water from the 9-liter container into the 5-liter container. I still have 12 liters of water in total, but only 7 in the 9-liter container.

Finally, I emptied the 5-liter container and have exactly 7 liters of water left.

By following these steps, I used 3-liter, 5-liter, and 9-liter containers to measure exactly 7 liters of water.

Figure 7.23

Money

• FRAME •

Frame for Making Money From the Tooth Fairy

Complete this Frame using whatever amount of money you want, but it must be under $10.00 per tooth. When you have finished the Frame, compare your results with one of your classmates.

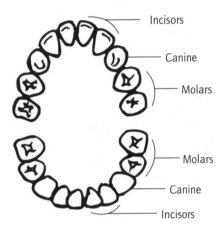

When I was about two years old, I had a full set of twenty baby teeth, which began to come loose when I was _____ years old. When I began to lose these baby teeth, I was told that the Tooth Fairy would give me a different amount of money for different types of teeth that came out and that I should save that money for my future education.

For each of my central incisors, the tooth fairy gave me $_____.

For my lateral incisors, she doubled the amount. She gave me $_____ for each lateral incisor.

For my canines, she doubled the amount of my lateral incisors. She gave me $_____ for each canine.

When I lost my first molars, she doubled the amount of my canines. She gave me $_____ for each first molar.

For losing my second molars, I received the same amount of money that I had received for my lateral incisors and first molars combined. She gave me $_____ for each second molar.

The Tooth Fairy had made _____visits. On her last visit she gave me a list of my baby teeth and how much money she had left me. It looked like this (set up a list showing all of the teeth and the total amount of money you received):

Figure 7.24

Money

• FRAME •

Frame for Making Money From the Tooth Fairy (Sample Response)

Complete this Frame using whatever amount of money you want, but it must be under $10.00 per tooth. When you have finished the Frame, compare your results with one of your classmates.

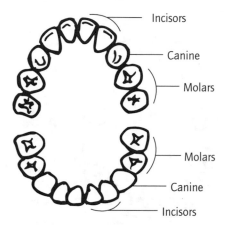

When I was about two years old, I had a full set of twenty baby teeth, which began to come loose when I was _5_ years old. Soon I began to lose these baby teeth. I was told that the Tooth Fairy would give me a different amount of money for different types of teeth that came out and that I should save that money for my future education.

For each of my central incisors, the tooth fairy gave me _$.50_.

For my lateral incisors, she doubled the amount. She gave me _$1.00_ for each lateral incisor.

For my canines, she doubled the amount of my lateral incisors. She gave me _$2.00_ for each canine.

When I lost my first molars, she doubled the amount of my canines. She gave me _$4.00_ for each first molar.

For losing my second molars, I received the same amount of money that I had received for my lateral incisors and first molars combined. She gave me _$5.00_ for each second molar.

The Tooth Fairy had made _10_ visits. On her last visit she gave me a list of my baby teeth and how much money she had left me. It looked like this (set up a list showing all of the teeth and the total amount of money you received):

Tooth Name	Number of Teeth	Price per Tooth	Total
Central Incisors	4	$.50	$2.00
Lateral Incisors	4	$1.00	$4.00
Canines	4	$2.00	$8.00
First Molars	4	$4.00	$16.00
Second Molars	4	$5.00	$20.00
Total	4		$50.00

Figure 7.25

Responding to Open-Ended and Multistep Problems

As indicated at the beginning of this chapter, it has become essential for students to demonstrate their ability to respond to open-ended and multistep problems. This expectation is also consistent with NCTM standards.

Students are expected to write out the steps they have taken to arrive at a solution. Most states have developed rubrics for assessing student responses to such questions that generally focus on elements such as accuracy, completeness, and organization. Most states give more credit for demonstrating complete mathematical thinking than getting the right answer. However, getting the answer correct should continue to be the goal.

A common feature of open-ended questions is that there may be various ways to solve the problem. Therefore, students need a repertoire of problem-solving strategies as well as an organized approach to explaining their results.

The Problem-Solving Frame (Figure 7.26) was specifically developed to help students meet this demand. The Frame guides students through each of the steps in solving an open-ended or multistep problem. Teachers are advised to model the application of the Problem-Solving Frame prior to having students use it independently. With practice, students will internalize the steps and be able to follow them without the Frame when they encounter problems on state tests. The strategies contained in the Frame are common to most mathematical problems, but teachers should feel free to add or change the strategies included.

Note that the Problem-Solving Frame specifically asks students to consider that some of the information presented in the problem may be extraneous to finding the solution and that there is an emphasis on labeling the answer (which our experience indicates is a common lapse).

Measurement

• FRAME •

The Problem-Solving Frame

Restate the problem _____

_____

_____

_____

Understanding the problem

Complete the Understanding table below

What We Already Know	What Is Not Important	What We Need to Find Out

How will the solution be labeled? _____

Do you think there could be more than one correct answer? _____

Choose a strategy. If you use more than one strategy, put them in the order you used them.

Look for a pattern	Use objects
Construct a table	Guess and check
Make an organized list	Work backwards
Act it out	Solve a simpler (or similar) problem
Draw a picture	Make a model
Write an equation	

Solve the problem here:

Now use the frame below to explain the results:

There were three (or other number) of strategies I used to solve this problem.

The first was _____

_____

_____

Then I _____

Finally I _____

By following these steps, I found that _____

Figure 7.26

INTERNET LINKS

Facts About United States Currency

http://www.treas.gov/education/fact-sheets/currency/in-god-we-trust.shtml
http:www.usmint.gov/about_the_mint/mint_history

Math Problem Solving

http://www.rhlschool.com/math.htm

8

Reasons, Procedures, and Results to Explain Mathematical Ideas and Concepts

Ginger and Pickles retired into the back parlour. They did accounts. They added up sums, and sums, and sums.

"What is seven pounds of butter at 1/3, and a stick of sealing wax, and four matches?"

—*The Complete Tales* (Potter, 1997, p. 216)

Mathematical reasoning develops in classrooms where students are encouraged to put forth their own ideas for examination. (NCTM, 2000, p. 189)

WHAT ARE REASONS, PROCEDURES, AND RESULTS?

While most students have come to believe that mathematics deals mainly with computation, mathematicians are almost always involved in stating the reasons, procedures, and results related to mathematical problems and ideas. Strong et al. (2001) distinguish "novices from experts" in how these problems and ideas are communicated, commenting that "novices view communication as a simple telling, experts view communication as a complex process of examining what they know" (p. 37). In the strategy we call Reasons, Procedures, Results we combine the basic format of the *essay* (usually taught in language arts and English classes) with writing in mathematics. Many students may have not had explicit instruction in essay writing (and may not even know what an essay is). It is important, therefore, that we take instructional time to teach a major form of writing within the content area of mathematics. In the Washington State Essential Academic Learning Requirements for Mathematics (Office of Superintendent of Public Instruction, 2004), three expectations are cited that relate to communication and are specific to the essay:

- using mathematical reasoning and justifying thinking;
- communicating knowledge and understanding in both everyday and mathematical language;
- connecting mathematical ideas within mathematics, or other subject areas, to real-life situations. (p. 3)

THE ESSAY IN MATHEMATICS

The *Random House Webster's Unabridged Dictionary* defines an essay as "a short literary composition on a particular theme or subject, usually in prose and generally analytic, speculative, or interpretive."

The basic essay has three features: an opening statement, three (or more) supporting statements, and a concluding statement.

- The opening statement clearly explains the problem, concept, or issue.
- The three or more supporting statements (or arguments) are used to describe, explain, or enlarge upon the opening statement. These statements give reasons, procedures, results, or purposes to support the opening statement.
- The concluding statement recapitulates the problem, procedure, concept, or issue described in the opening statement.

By using the strategy Reasons, Procedures, Results, students can become proficient in consolidating their mathematical thinking, communicating coherently and clearly, and expressing mathematical ideas precisely, three of the standards emphasized throughout *Principles and Standards* (NCTM, 2000) and recapitulated in *Standards and Curriculum. A View From the Nation* (NCTM, 2004).

To guide students in becoming "experts" in mathematics and communication, this chapter provides essay formats for

- giving reasons for mathematical ideas and procedures,
- showing the steps to solve mathematical problems,
- explaining mathematical ideas, and
- persuading others about mathematical concepts or beliefs.

Essay Formats—Personal, Persuasive, Explanatory

An essay can be written in a personal, persuasive, or explanatory format or can be a combination of any two or three (Rothstein & Lauber, 2000). All three formats are used in mathematics and are an essential part of NCTM and state-mandated standards. Students, therefore, *need* to be taught how to write essays in all subject areas.

Personal Essays

In the personal essay, the writer writes from a personal perspective, using his or her own voice. Unfortunately, many students have been told to be objective, to reserve their opinion or judgment, and to avoid using the word "I" in an essay. Yet nothing in the definition of an essay indicates that it is to be without opinion or judgment. In fact, professional essayists often write from a personal perspective (Strunk & White, 2000).

Writing personal essays helps students formulate their own ideas or find their own solutions to problems. In essence, this type of essay allows students to personalize mathematics (or any subject) by connecting them with the topic and helping them to discover personally relevant connections to the topic (Tangretti & Liptak, 1995). If your students have been using the strategies of Metacognition and Profiles and Frames, they will easily move into writing the personal essay (and the other essay formats).

These are some basic starters for students writing personal essays:

- There are three reasons why I . . .
- I believe that there could be three ways . . .
- I was able to obtain the following results . . .
- I have used estimation (or multiplication, etc.) in three different ways (or situations).
- I want to understand geometry (or other mathematics) for the following three reasons.
- I solved this problem by following these steps or procedures.

Persuasive Essays

In the persuasive essay, the writer seeks to sway the reader's opinion. The writer hopes to change the reader's mind so that the reader comes to believe what the writer believes. However, the writer does not use the word "I." Instead, he or she uses the editorial "we" in order to include everyone and to convince the reader of a premise or idea. Students who have had opportunities to create and solve problems in groups will often come up with naturally occurring persuasive ideas that they can share with their classmates in "mathematical forums" or "mathematical conferences."

Students can use these starters when writing persuasive essays:

- There are three reasons why we should (or have to) . . .
- We need to consider these three ways . . .
- In order to solve _____, we must do the following . . .
- We must understand three concepts . . .
- To achieve the correct results, we should . . .

By using these and similar starters, students are able to write expanded statements and they do not get "stuck" in one idea or solution (Marzano et al., 2001) and can begin to think interdependently (Costa & Kallick, 2000).

Explanatory Essays

In the explanatory essay, the writer takes an impersonal, "textbook" approach to the subject. The writer usually takes a neutral stance and offers few, or no, opinions on the topic, striving for accuracy and clarity in the explanation. The explanatory essay in mathematics often has a "how to" voice and, like the strategy Defining Format, requires the writer to think of the audience (a Martian).

Students can use these starters when writing explanatory essays:

- There are three reasons why . . . (e.g., There are three reasons why Roman numerals are mathematically limited.)
- Here are three ways to . . .
- We can solve for x using the following steps . . .
- To understand decimals (rectangles, etc.), you need to know (1) _____, (2) _____, and (3) _____.
- A _____ and a _____ are similar (or different) in these ways . . . (e.g., A rectangle and a polygon are similar in these ways . . .)
- To convert _____ to _____, first . . . , then . . . , after that . . . (e.g., To convert Fahrenheit to Celsius, first . . . , then . . . , after that . . .)

If students learn these basic formats, they will be able to write mathematical explanations with clarity and precision, thereby uniting good writing with good mathematics. Essays can be friendly and personalized, even in mathematics. The next section, Mathematics the Write Way, provides models of personal, persuasive, and explanatory essays for each of the mathematics content areas (NCTM, 2000) plus money. Modify or adapt the examples for your students' needs.

If your students haven't as yet created a Taxonomy of Verbs for Mathematicians (Figure 2.13), be sure to have them set one up. Below is a Mathematical Verb Taxonomy (Figure 8.1) listing the verbs from Washington State's Essential Academic Learning Requirements (2004) and which also are in state standards across the country. You can now combine the words from both Taxonomies (Figures 2.13 and 8.1).

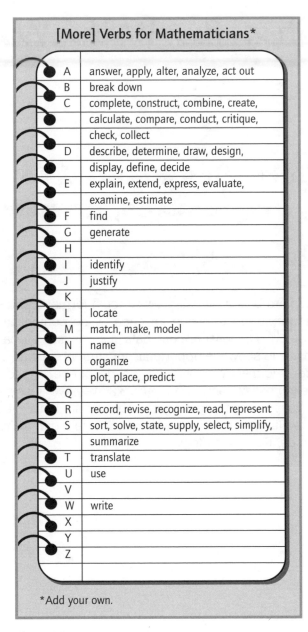

[More] Verbs for Mathematicians*

A	answer, apply, alter, analyze, act out
B	break down
C	complete, construct, combine, create, calculate, compare, conduct, critique, check, collect
D	describe, determine, draw, design, display, define, decide
E	explain, extend, express, evaluate, examine, estimate
F	find
G	generate
H	
I	identify
J	justify
K	
L	locate
M	match, make, model
N	name
O	organize
P	plot, place, predict
Q	
R	record, revise, recognize, read, represent
S	sort, solve, state, supply, select, simplify, summarize
T	translate
U	use
V	
W	write
X	
Y	
Z	

*Add your own.

Figure 8.1

Mathematics the Write Way

Writing Activities Related to Reasons, Procedures, Results

(All Grades)

The following activities are based on using a prompt, a format found on many state and local assessments. Prompts are provided for each of the content areas—number and operations, algebra, geometry, measurement, data analysis and probability—and money. The essays are extensive to show the opportunity for student growth. You may modify the prompts or requirements to meet your students' needs, but be sure to use the framework that is illustrated for each essay genre. (In Figure 8.2, we have italicized the framework.) You can also create your own prompts related to your students' needs and levels. In Figures 8.2 to 8.10, we illustrate problems and prompts that can be responded to using the Reasons, Procedures, Results strategy.

Number and Operations

• PERSONAL ESSAY •

Reasons, Procedures, Results for Fractions

Prompt: Write three reasons why you need to understand fractions.

Personal Essay Model

I need to understand fractions for several important reasons. [Opening sentence]

First, [transition] I must be able to use money, and money uses fractions. For example, four quarters equal a dollar. Therefore, a quarter is $\frac{1}{4}$ of a dollar. When I have two quarters, I have $\frac{2}{4}$ of a dollar. Now $\frac{2}{4}$ can be reduced to $\frac{1}{2}$, so two quarters are half a dollar or fifty cents. When I have three quarters, I have $\frac{3}{4}$ of a dollar or seventy-five cents. *This is just one example of using fractions with money.* [Summary or concluding sentence for first reason]

Second, [transition] recipes use fractions all the time, and since I love to bake I must know my fractions. Last week my mom and I were making chocolate chip cookies. The recipe we had was for 72 cookies. We wanted to make 36 cookies or $\frac{1}{2}$ the amount of the recipe. We had to do a lot of fractions. For example, the recipe called for $\frac{3}{4}$ of a cup of sugar. So we needed $\frac{1}{2}$ of $\frac{3}{4}$ or $\frac{3}{8}$ of a cup. That was less than a cup of sugar, so I had to measure very carefully. Then the recipe said to use $2\frac{1}{4}$ sixteen-ounce packages of chocolate chips. That came to 40 ounces of chocolate chips. I needed two sixteen-ounce packages and four ounces of a third package. *I was so glad that I had learned about fractions in school so that I could use this recipe.* [Second summary or conclusion]

Finally, [transition] I use fractions to measure. We are going to finish a large basement in my house. Because I have a sister and a brother, my mother said that we should divide the basement into three areas so that we can each have our own space for our computers and books. We measured the area of the basement and found that it was 4 meters long by 3 meters wide. That meant we had a room that was 400 centimeters long that we had to divide by 3. Each of us would get a space that was a little more than 133 centimeters long. But since 133×3 equals 399, we agreed that my brother would get a space that was 1 centimeter more than mine or my sister's. That was easier than trying to measure $\frac{1}{3}$ of a centimeter to get the space even. Because the width of the room was 300 centimeters, two of us had a room that was 133 centimeters by 300 centimeters, and one of us had a room that was 134 centimeters by 300 centimeters. *We were all happy with having $\frac{1}{3}$ or slightly more than $\frac{1}{3}$ of the basement.* [Summary or conclusion]

In order to use money, bake cookies, and measure a room, I need to have a lot of information about fractions. [Concluding sentence]

Figure 8.2

• EXPLANATORY ESSAY •

Reasons, Procedures, Results for Division

Prompt: You have invited six friends to your birthday party. Your mother has baked 32 cookies. Explain three ways that you and your six friends can solve the problem of sharing the cookies.

Explanatory Essay Model (From a Personal Perspective)

Six friends and I make seven people who have to share 32 cookies. Here is an explanation of how I can do this task as fairly as possible.

First, I can find the nearest number to 32 that can be divided evenly by 7. The number is 28, so by dividing 28 by 7, each person will get four cookies. But now 4 cookies remain. If I break the four cookies in half, each person gets a half of a cookie and one half a cookie remains. Since a half of a cookie divided into seven pieces would end up in crumbs, we can draw lots. I would give out seven pieces of paper, one of which would have the number 7 on it. The person who gets the paper with the 7 gets the remaining half of the cookie.

Another way is to let everyone besides me have cookies, because my mother can always bake some more cookies for me on another day. This leaves 6 people to share 32 cookies. Again, I need the number nearest to 32 that can be divided by 6, and that number is 30. So 30 divided by 6 will give each person 5 cookies with 2 cookies left. If I split each cookie into three equal pieces or thirds, I can give each person $\frac{1}{3}$ of a cookie. Now everyone but me has received $5\frac{1}{3}$ cookies.

Finally, I can use 21 cookies and put aside 11 cookies. By dividing 21 by 7, I give each person, including myself, 3 cookies. Now 11 cookies are left. I give each person and myself 1 cookie and 4 cookies are left. Since I know that dividing 4 cookies by 7 people won't be even, I call my dog. I then can divide the four cookies in half and share the eight pieces with 7 people and one dog.

This is how I would solve the problem if my mother did not make an amount of cookies that could be evenly divided by the number of people who were at my birthday party.

Figure 8.3

Algebra

• PERSUASIVE ESSAY •

Reasons, Procedures, Results for Algebra

Prompt: Write a persuasive essay to a group of students convincing them to use three shortcut rules in algebra.

Persuasive Essay Model

Here are three shortcut rules that you should know in order to do well in algebra. By knowing these rules you will save time when doing the problems and you are more likely to be accurate in your answers.

One rule states that if a term stands alone on one side of an equation, it can be moved to the other side by changing its operational sign. By knowing this shortcut rule, you will not have to add the number to both sides of the equation. Nor will you have to regroup and then add. Here is an example of what you should do.

$$x - 55 = 370$$

Move − 55 to the right side of the equation and add it to 370. It now looks like this:

$$x = 370 + 55$$
$$x = 425$$

A second rule states that the positive or negative signs can be switched on both sides of an equation. Here is an example:

$$(-x) = 62 \text{ is the same as } (x = -62)$$

The advantage of this rule is that finding positive x is easier than finding negative x. Therefore, you should always switch the negative sign to the number rather than keeping it with the variable.

Another rule states that both sides of an equation can be inverted (turned upside down). By knowing this rule you will easily find the value of x, as in this example

$$\frac{2}{x} = 2$$

Now you have to invert both sides of the equation.

$$\frac{x}{2} = \frac{1}{2}$$

Then you must multiply both sides of the equation by 2, which is really $\frac{1}{2}$.

$$2\left(\frac{x}{2}\right) = 2\left(\frac{1}{2}\right)$$

Now 2 times $\frac{x}{2}$ gets reduced to x. So x = $\frac{1}{2}$ times 2, which equals 1. Therefore, x = 1.

By learning these shortcut rules for solving equations, you will work faster and be more accurate in getting the answers.

Figure 8.4

Geometry

• EXPLANATORY ESSAY •
Reasons, Procedures, Results for Geometry

Prompt: You have learned that the formula for finding the area of a right triangle is $A = (1/2) \times L \times H$ You now have to find the area of an oblique triangle. How do you use your knowledge about finding the area of a right triangle to find the area of an oblique triangle?

Explanatory Essay Model

To find the area of an oblique triangle, there are several steps you have to take based on your knowledge about a right triangle.

First, review your understanding of a right triangle. A right triangle is formed from a rectangle that has been divided into two right triangles. Since the area of a rectangle is $A = L \times H$, the area of a right triangle is $(1/2) \times L \times H$. This is an easy formula to remember.

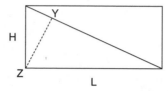

Second, you must remember that you can divide an oblique triangle into two right triangles. If you can figure out the area of two right triangles, you can add these areas together to get the area of the oblique triangle. Therefore, you now do the second step—divide the oblique triangle into two right angles.

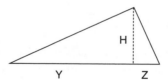

Write your formula. Keep in mind that you have two right triangles.

$$A = \left(\tfrac{1}{2}\right) \times H \times Y + \left(\tfrac{1}{2}\right) \times H \times Z$$

Third, rewrite your equation using the distributive law.

$$A = \left(\tfrac{1}{2}\right) \times H \times (Y + Z)$$

Now use the law of substitution. Because the base is the sum of y and z, you can substitute B for Y + Z. Your equation looks like this.

$$A = \left(\tfrac{1}{2}\right) \times H \times B. \text{ In other words, } \tfrac{1}{2} \text{ height times base.}$$

You now have used your knowledge about the area of a right triangle to find the area of an oblique triangle.

Figure 8.5

Measurement

• PERSUASIVE ESSAY •

Reasons, Procedures, Results for Measurement

Prompt: Your mathematics class is having a debate about whether to use liquid measures in the metric system or in the United States system. Half the class votes for the metric system and the other half votes for the United States system. You have been elected to write a persuasive essay arguing for the metric system. Present your case.

Persuasive Essay Model (With a Personal Perspective)

Although almost every country in the world today uses the metric system, the United States has stayed with its own system that is based upon English measurements. For example, we are likely to buy a quart of milk, but people in France and other countries buy a liter. When we buy two gallons of juice in America, people in Spain buy a decaliter. The Spaniards will have more than two gallons of juice in a decaliter. So which is a better system? Liters or quarts? Gallons or decaliters?

I have given great thought to this question, and I believe that we should switch to the metric system for several important reasons.

First, the metric system is simple to understand. Every measurement is based on the tens system. For example, if we line up ten liters of milk, we know we have a decaliter of milk, since *dec-* means ten. If we have ten decaliters, we have one hundred liters or one hectoliter. The term *hecto-* means one hundred in Greek. Fifty decaliters, therefore, equals half a hectoliter. Since the system we use in the United States only has pints, quarts, and gallons, we have no easy way to figure out large amounts of liquids. For example, 31 gallons equals one barrel, but not every barrel is the same size.

Second, the metric system allows us to measure very small amounts of liquid. A thousandth of a liter is a milliliter and a hundredth of a liter is a centiliter. Since the smallest United States liquid measure is a pint, or about two cups (which are not always the same size), we have to use the metric system to measure liquid accurately if it amounts to less than a pint.

Finally, the majority of countries in the world already use the metric system as a standard. Therefore, wherever you travel outside of the United States, you will use the same measurement system. Bottles and containers will always be in liters and units of liters, but in the United States you may find that liquids are sometimes in ounces (a measurement of weight) because they are not exactly a quart or a gallon. When measurements are not exact, you can't easily figure out how much you are paying for different measures of liquids or other products.

I hope my arguments for using the metric system will convince you about the usefulness of the metric system. All we need to do is to start learning and using them at an early age. Then we will know them as well as people everywhere.

Figure 8.6

Data Analysis and Probability

• PERSUASIVE ESSAY •

Reasons, Procedures, Results (Part I)

First, read the prompt. Second, answer the questions. Third, write your persuasive essay.

Prompt: Read the following advertisement carefully, including the small print.

Stuff's House of Goodies
THIS FRIDAY AND SATURDAY ONLY
$20 Days

Video Games	**Sports Watches**
Space Ninjas	TXX Multi-Function
Reg.: $40	Reg.: $25
Sale: $20	Sale: $20

Music Videos	**Toys**
All Titles	Electro-Friends
Reg.: $16	Reg.: $30 each
Sale: 20% off	Sale: $20

The More You Buy, The More You Save!!

Sales tax not included. May not be available in all stores. May not be purchased for resale.
Retailer reserves the right to limit purchase quantities.

The ad says you can save a lot of money. Decide whether you agree after you have answered these questions:

1. If you bought two of every item in the ad, what would be the total difference between the regular prices and the sale prices?
2. If the sales tax is 8%, what would the Electro-Friends actually cost you?
3. What are the percentage savings for each item?
4. What does the ad mean when it says you can "save money"?
5. What do the ad writers mean when they say, "The more you buy, the more you save"?
6. Read the small print at the bottom of the ad. Why do you think the store put these statements in the ad?

After you answer the questions, write a letter to the store. Tell them the reasons you like their offer or the reasons you think that this is not a good offer. To write a convincing essay, include your answers to the questions above.

Figure 8.7

Data Analysis and Probability

• PERSUASIVE ESSAY •

Reasons, Procedures, Results (Data for Response) (Part II)

1. If you bought two of every item in the ad, what would be the total difference between the regular price and the sale price?

Item	Regular Price	Sale Price
Space Ninjas	$40.00 ($80.00 for 2)	$20.00 ($40.00 for 2)
TXX	$25.00 ($50.00 for 2)	$20.00 ($40.00 for 2)
Music Videos	$16.00 ($32.00 for 2)	$12.80 ($25.60 for 2)
Electro-Friends	$30.00 ($60.00 for 2)	$20.00 ($40.00 for 2)
Total	$222.00	$145.60

The difference between the regular price and the sale price is $76.40.

2. If the sales tax is 8%, what would the Electro-Friends actually cost you?

    $21.60

3. What are the percentage savings for each item?

    Space Ninjas: 50%
    TXX: 20%
    Music videos: 20%
    Electro-Friends: 33%

4. What does the ad mean when it says you can "save" money?
    Answers will vary.

5. What do the ad writers mean when they say, "The more you buy, the more you save"?
    Answers will vary.

6. Read the small print at the bottom of the ad. Why do you think the store put these statements in the ad?
    Answers will vary.

Figure 8.8

Data Analysis and Probability

• PERSUASIVE ESSAY •

Reasons, Procedures, Results (Part II continued)

I saw your ad in the paper and there are some things I would like to buy. But I believe you should be clearer in what you are offering.

First, the ad says that there are a lot of sales on these things, and in some ways I think you are right. I could get Space Ninjas that are now $20.00 apiece or only $40.00 for two of them. That would save me 50% of the original price. And if I bought one TXX watch that would be $20, but if I bought two of them I could save $10.00.

But I'm still puzzled over how we can save money by buying. I think we can only save money by not buying. Maybe the ad means that we would spend more money if there wasn't a sale. So maybe the ad should say, "Our sale prices help you spend less money when you buy on sale."

There is also an 8% sales tax so that we have to add that amount to every purchase we make. For example, we have to add $6.40 to a purchase of $80.00. Now I know why the print for the sales tax is small. You should print this information in the same size as the other information.

I hope I have convinced you to change your ad so that you make it clear that "The More You Buy, The More You Save."

Figure 8.9

Money

• EXPLANATORY ESSAY •

Reasons, Procedures, Results for Money

Prompt: Bert Mitchell is a Certified Public Accountant. He is also the Chief Executive Officer of the largest minority-owned accounting firm in the United States. Here is a statement of advice that he gives to parents:

> "If kids start putting money into an IRA (Individual Retirement Fund) when they are 10 years old, 12 years old, or 15 years old, the dollars that they put in are worth tens of thousands of dollars when they are seventy years old" (Fairley, 1998, p. 8).

Write an Explanatory Essay giving three reasons why Mr. Mitchell's idea is good advice.

Note to Teacher: You can use this money activity with students in third or fourth grade who may not understand the mathematical principles of saving, interest, and compounding but can respond to the idea of saving money. Older students can incorporate whatever mathematical principles they have learned related to savings and investing.

Explanatory Essay Model

Mr. Mitchell gives very good advice to parents about saving money for their children. There are at least three good reasons why Mr. Mitchell is right about this idea.

First, parents who save money for their children's future are teaching their children good habits. When children see their parents save, they learn the same good habits and will pass them on to their own children. Every generation in the family will have learned an important lesson about money.

Second, Mr. Mitchell advises parents to save the money for their children in an IRA (Individual Retirement Account). In an IRA account, the child cannot take out the money until he or she is 59 years old. That means that if the parents open an account when their child is 10 years old, the money will not be touched for 49 years. Money in this account will earn interest for every year during 49 years. If the parents put in $1000 every year, when the child reaches 49 years old, he or she will have $49,000, plus all of the interest that would have been added on. This leads to the third reason.

Third, interest is earned on the principal. The principal is the original amount of money deposited into the account. Then that interest is added to the principal. Now the principal + interest earns more interest. The money begins to grow like a pyramid—interest is earned on principal + interest + interest, then interest is earned on principal + interest + interest + interest, then more interest is earned on principal + interest + interest + interest + interest, and so forth. We call this system compound interest. If parents start this system for their children, their children will be very rich senior citizens. Here is how much money a child would have if her parents made an initial deposit of $1000 and the account earned 5% interest each year:

Year 1	$1000.00 \times .05 = $50.00	$50.00 + $1000.00 = $1050.00
Year 2	$1050.00 \times .05 = $52.50	$52.50 + $1050.00 = $1102.50
Year 3	$1102.50 \times .05 = $55.12	$52.12 + $1102.50 = $1157.62

If we kept going for another 46 years, that child would have a LOT of money!

These are just three of the reasons why Mr. Mitchell's advice to a parent about saving money in an IRA is so important to a child's future.

Figure 8.10

Mathematical Topics for Personal, Persuasive, and Explanatory Essays

Here are prompts that your students can effectively respond to by using the essay formats illustrated in this chapter. The essay prompts in Figures 8.11 to 8.13 all relate to the topic of using a calculator. However, the opening sentence for each prompt determines whether the essay will be personal, persuasive, or explanatory.

• PERSONAL ESSAY •

Personal Essay Prompt

You have been asked to show students in a different classroom how you use your calculator for doing mathematics. Imagine that the students have not had as much experience as you have had. Write a personal essay in which you tell three ways that you use your calculator to help you do algorithms or assist you in solving mathematical problems. Remember to THINK IN THREES!

Figure 8.11

• PERSUASIVE ESSAY •

Persuasive Essay Prompt

A classroom of 20 students needs a set of calculators for each student. Each calculator costs $36.00. A generous member of your community has offered to pay for some mathematics equipment for the class, but the person is not sure about using the money for buying calculators. Write a persuasive letter to this person stating the reasons for buying a calculator for every student. Be sure to show how calculators can benefit mathematical learning and how the money will be wisely spent. Remember to THINK IN THREES!

Figure 8.12

• EXPLANATORY ESSAY •

Explanatory Essay Prompt

Your class is planning a Mathematical Conference in which groups of students will present different topics to students in other classes. You and several other classmates will give a presentation on "The Many Uses of the Calculator." Working with your group, prepare an explanatory essay outlining and detailing the different uses of a calculator and how this tool can be useful in becoming a better mathematician. Keep your audience in mind and remember to THINK IN THREES.

Figure 8.13

INTERNET LINKS

Discovery School

http://school.discovery.com

Funbrain

http://funbrain.com

MathsNet: Net Solutions Interactive

http://mathsnet.net/

9

Who's Who in Mathematics for Biographies and Careers Related to Mathematics

Professional mathematicians spend most of their time writing.

—*A Guide to Writing in Mathematics Classes* (Crannell, 1994)

One reason why mathematics enjoys special esteem . . . is that its propositions are absolutely certain and indisputable. (Albert Einstein in a lecture to the Prussian Academy of Sciences in 1921, cited in Wells, 1995, p. 85)

WHAT IS WHO'S WHO?

The National Council of Teachers of Mathematics standard on communication states that one of the purposes of mathematics is to "extend students' knowledge by considering the thinking and strategies of others" (NCTM, 2000). Yet often "others" are limited to other teachers or other students. Students often miss out on learning from mathematicians, men and women from different time periods, cultures, and locations who have contributed to mathematics and other fields dependent upon mathematics. NCTM (2000) also reminds us that mathematics is used in many workplaces and by many other people besides mathematicians—scientists, engineers, computer developers, navigators, and so on all use mathematics.

When students get to know who's who in mathematics, they can appreciate how much the field has evolved. They can begin to appreciate the magnificent history of discovery, proof, refutation, and further proof. Real-life mathematics differs greatly from textbook mathematics. Real-life mathematics is not a study in which answers are absolutely right or wrong. Rather, real-life mathematics evolves over time through countless discussions among mathematicians. Consider this example from Wells (1995): "Early Greek mathematicians thought they knew very well what a number was. Numbers were either integers, formed in a sequence starting from 1, or they were ratios of integers—what we call fractions" (p. 71). Yet, Pythagoras moved beyond this understanding when he made the amazing discovery of irrational numbers.

In this chapter we focus on the NCTM communication standard and suggest strategies that guide students in

- relating mathematics to their own lives and personal development,
- learning and writing about careers related to mathematics, and
- researching and writing about mathematicians who have developed advanced mathematical ideas.

Relating Mathematics to the Students' Personal Lives

In almost every mathematics classroom, there are students who find the subject matter to be easy and students who find the subject matter to be painfully difficult. The chasm between these learners frustrates both the fast learner—who is held back by the slower learner—and the slower learner, who sees himself or herself as a "math dummy." Strong et al. (2001) cite four principles for addressing this diversity in the classroom, principles that particularly affect learning mathematics:

- Build in quality instruction by setting "high content and skill standards."
- Use rotation; that is, "demand [that] instruction and assessment include a variety of teaching strategies and activities."
- Allow focused and supported choice that "sensibly limits the range of student choice."
- Provide validation and compensation to students. Validate the strengths and compensate for the weaknesses of students who are having difficulty. (p. 70)

The above principles play an important role in the concepts of differentiation and multiple intelligences because while not everyone can be good at everything, everyone can be good at something. So while your mission may be to teach the *same* mathematics to all your students, some of the students will do well in the subject, while others can do well in learning *about* the subject. Learning about mathematicians may be one of those topics that will engage students in the subject of mathematics. Students of varying abilities and diverse multiple intelligences can use their talents to learn about mathematicians as well as about careers and opportunities related to mathematics. Through focused writing, students can use their interpersonal intelligence ("connecting with people") and intrapersonal intelligence ("invention and creativity") while learning about mathematics (Strong et al., 2001, p. 71).

Learning and Writing About Careers Related to Mathematics

As students learn mathematics, they often want to know why they are studying this subject. Aside from basic, practical uses (counting, budgeting, checking), mathematics is used in numerous careers. Many young students are unaware of these careers and their connections to mathematics. Therefore, integrating the study of careers with the study of mathematics and mathematicians is both motivating and enlightening. Careers and mathematics are a natural team.

One way to increase students' awareness of careers is to ask them to keep a running Taxonomy of Careers (see Figure 9.1). Encourage students to add to the Taxonomy as they learn about mathematics-related careers through discussion and research. Another way to further students' interest in careers is to encourage them to use the Career Profile (Figure 9.2) for recording detailed information about specific mathematical careers.

Researching and Writing About Mathematicians

It is also important that students research and write about mathematicians as they study mathematics. One way to increase students' awareness of mathematicians is to have them to keep a running Taxonomy of Mathematicians of Magnitude (Figures 9.3 to 9.6). You may also want to post a Taxonomy of mathematicians in your classroom. Encourage students to add to the Taxonomy any time they learn about a mathematician. They can also use Profiles or Frames to record biographic information about Mathematicians of Magnitude (see Mathematics the Write Way, below).

Some teachers have expressed the concern that the mathematical ideas of great mathematicians are too difficult for their students, and certainly that is likely to be true. What students learn from this study, however, is that mathematics is a dynamic subject that has evolved from the work of mathematicians and that what we study in school is related to their discoveries (e.g., zero, triangles, algebra, and much more) and often to our everyday lives. For those of you who work with upper grade levels, the activities adapted from Euler, Ulam, and Fermat (Figures 9.12, 9.13, 9.14) may be of interest to students who like a challenge. Studying about mathematicians leads to interesting research, and the Internet is a valuable tool for finding out about contributions of mathematicians from diverse backgrounds and time periods.

Mathematics the Write Way

Writing Activities Related to Who's Who

(Intermediate and Up)

Because this chapter focuses more on people and careers than the mathematical content areas, these content areas will not be covered in this section. Instead, the writing activities in this section focus on learning about mathematical careers and notable mathematicians. The activities in this section can be used to develop an exciting project in your classroom and can be integrated with language arts, science, and even social studies.

■ ACTIVITY 1

Discovering Mathematical Careers

The following activity introduces students to careers in or related to mathematics. You may duplicate the list in Figure 9.1 as a starter to which you add careers, or you can have your students build their own Taxonomy without this starter.

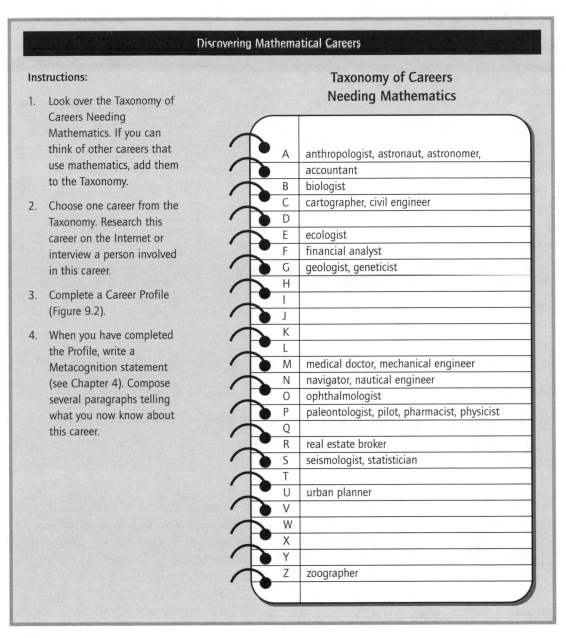

Discovering Mathematical Careers

Instructions:

1. Look over the Taxonomy of Careers Needing Mathematics. If you can think of other careers that use mathematics, add them to the Taxonomy.

2. Choose one career from the Taxonomy. Research this career on the Internet or interview a person involved in this career.

3. Complete a Career Profile (Figure 9.2).

4. When you have completed the Profile, write a Metacognition statement (see Chapter 4). Compose several paragraphs telling what you now know about this career.

Taxonomy of Careers Needing Mathematics

A	anthropologist, astronaut, astronomer, accountant
B	biologist
C	cartographer, civil engineer
D	
E	ecologist
F	financial analyst
G	geologist, geneticist
H	
I	
J	
K	
L	
M	medical doctor, mechanical engineer
N	navigator, nautical engineer
O	ophthalmologist
P	paleontologist, pilot, pharmacist, physicist
Q	
R	real estate broker
S	seismologist, statistician
T	
U	urban planner
V	
W	
X	
Y	
Z	zoographer

Figure 9.1

Career Profile—Knowledge of Mathematics Required

Name of career: _____

Salary range:

Major duties or tasks:

Education needed or required:

Personal abilities needed:

Likely places of work (indoors, foreign countries, etc.):

Reason(s) that mathematical knowledge is needed in this career:

Other information about this career:

Figure 9.2

■ ACTIVITY 2
Meeting Mathematicians of Magnitude

The four Taxonomies included in this activity highlight Mathematicians of Magnitude (Figures 9.3 to 9.6). The first Taxonomy, Mathematicians of Worldwide Magnitude (Figure 9.3), includes the names of mathematicians who are often cited in school mathematics textbooks; they are names that students may have heard over the course of their secondary school studies. (Most of the names on this Taxonomy come from Wells, 1995.)

The second Taxonomy, Women Mathematicians (Figure 9.4), contains a sampling of names of women who, because of gender bias and historic neglect, have been omitted from most school and other textbooks. The third Taxonomy, Mathematicians of the African Diaspora (Figure 9.5), contains a sampling of names of people of African descent who, like women, may not have received recognition in school textbooks. The last Taxonomy is Mathematicians of Latino/a Heritage, which includes women and men of Hispanic heritage (Figure 9.6). Students can add more names to each Taxonomy as they discover mathematicians in their research. The Web sites are listed at the end of this chapter.

Taxonomies of Mathematicians

Taxonomy of Mathematicians of Worldwide Magnitude*

A	Archimedes, Al-Khwarizmi
B	Bernoulli, Banneker, Babbage
C	Cauchy
D	Descartes, Dirichlet
E	Euclid, Euler, Einstein
F	Fermat, Fibonacci, Fuller, Feynman
G	Galileo, Galois, Grothendieck, Gauss
H	Hypatia, Hilbert
I	Ibn Sinan
J	Jacobi
K	Kepler, Koch, Kelvin, Kowalewska, Koenigsberg, Khayyam
L	Legendre, Leibniz, Lagrange
M	Möbius, Meitner, Mumford, Mahavira, MacLane, Mitchell
N	Noether, Newton, Nash
O	Olber, Orezme, Ozanam
P	Pythagoras, Poincare, Pascal
Q	
R	Ramanjun, Richardson, Reimann,
S	Sylvester, Steinhaus, Steinmetz, Steiner
T	Tamura, Torricelli
U	Ulam
V	
W	Wallis, Watson, Wagner, Wiles, Wolfskehl
X	
Y	
Z	Zworykin

*Most of the names are cited in Wells (1995).

Figure 9.3

Taxonomy of Women Mathematicians

A	Agnesi, Andrews
B	Bacon, Bernstein
C	Cartwright, Chang
D	Daubechies, Dickerman
E	
F	Falconer, MacKinnon-Fitch
G	Germain, Granville
H	Hjagood, Herschel
I	
J	Janovskaja
K	Karp, Kupferberg
L	Lassar, Litivinova
M	Macintyre, Moufang
N	Nightingale, Noether
O	Oleinik, Owens
P	Pierce, Pless
Q	
R	Ragsdale, Robinson
S	Sodosky, Srinivasan
T	Theano, Turner
U	Uhlenbeck
V	Velez-Rodriguez, Vivian
W	Weiss, Wheeler
X	
Y	Young (Anna Irwin), Young (Lai-Sang)
Z	

Figure 9.4

Taxonomy of Mathematicians of the African Diaspora*

A	Agboola, Assani
B	Blackwell
C	Chukwu
D	
E	Ekhaguerre
F	Farley
G	Gangbo, Graham
H	Hunt
I	
J	
K	
L	
M	Massey
N	
O	Okikiolu
P	Petters
Q	
R	Richards
S	
T	
U	
V	
W	Wilkins
X	
Y	
Z	

*The term African Diaspora and the names listed are from http://www.math.buffalo.edu/mad/index.html. African Diaspora refers to people of African birth or descent who live in various parts of the world.

Figure 9.5

Taxonomy of Mathematicians of Latino/a Heritage

A	Adem-Diaz de Leon, Alarcon, Alvarez, Argaez
B	Banuelos, Beriozalba, Bustoz
C	Calderon (Alberto), Calderon (Calixto), Cafarelli. Carraminana, Castillo-Chavez, Castro, Cordero-Epperson, Cordero-Brana, Cortez, Corto
D	
E	Epperson
F	Flores
G	Gatica, Gonzalez, Gutierrez
H	Hernandez
I	Iovino
J	
K	
L	
M	Martinez (Cleopatria), Martinez-Gamba, Medina, Mendez (Celestino), Mendoza, Moll, Morales
N	
O	Otero
P	
Q	
R	Rodriguez-Villega, Rubio-Canabel
S	Saavedra, Sadosky
T	Tapia, Torchinsky, Torrejon
U	Uribe-Ahumada
V	Valdes (Linda), Valdez (Luis), Valezquez, Velez
W	
X	
Y	
Z	

Figure 9.6

After students have completed one or more Taxonomies of Mathematicians of Magnitude, they can do the following research and writing.

- Do research on one mathematician.
- Complete a Profile of a Mathematician (Figure 9.7).
- Write a Framed Sentence as a summary for that mathematician (Figure 9.8).
- Complete a Frame of Accomplishment (Figure 9.9).
- Complete a Personal Essay Frame (Figure 9.10).

Profile of a Mathematician

• PROFILE •

Profile of a Mathematician

Directions: Select a mathematician who interests you and complete the Profile below.

Name of mathematician:

Years of mathematician's life:

Nationality:

Major mathematical interests:

Major contributions to mathematics:

Publications:

Special recognition and awards:

Other information:

Figure 9.7

Framed Sentences for Mathematicians of Magnitude

• FRAME •

Framed Sentences for Mathematicians of Magnitude

Directions: Use the following form to write one sentence about each of the mathematicians you have studied:

_____ was/is a _____ who _____

Here are some examples:

Mohammed Al-Khwarizmi was a Muslim scholar living in the 10th century who coined the words *algorithm* and *algebra* and contributed the idea of polynomials with an infinite number of terms.

Charles Babbage, living in nineteenth-century England, was a scientist and mathematician who designed a machine that could automatically perform calculations based on a program of instructions. This machine became the basis in the twentieth century for the development of computers.

Leonard Euler was a Swiss mathematician living from 1707 to 1783 who, among his many mathematical discoveries, showed the patterns that are formed by different polyhedra (dimensional shapes). He established what is known as Euler's relationship.

Pierre de Fermat (1601–1665) was a French-born lawyer, parliamentarian, and mathematician who invented coordinate geometry, explained how light is refracted when it passes from air to water, and investigated the properties of numbers and their squares.

Omar Khayyam was a twelfth-century Persian poet and mathematician who studied the Hindu decimal system of arithmetic and discovered methods for extracting cube roots to include fourth, fifth, and higher roots.

Ilse Meitner (1878–1968) was an Austrian-born nuclear physicist and mathematician who contributed numerous papers related to quantum theory and was a member of the Swedish Nobel Institute and the Atomic Energy Laboratory.

Katherine Okikiolu, born in Nigeria and living in the United States, is a scientist and mathematician who has done innovative research in geometric analysis and has also developed curricula in mathematics for children in urban schools.

Arlie Petters, born in Belize, is an American mathematician who works in the area of the mathematical theory of gravitational lensing and has published 26 scholarly papers and two on this topic.

Stanislaw Ulam was a twentieth-century Swedish mathematician who worked on the first atomic bomb and early computers and whose interest was showing how simple structures such as squares and triangles could become extremely complex.

Lai-Sang Young, born in Hong Kong in 1952 and living in the United States, is a professor of mathematics doing research on the mathematical theory of dynamical systems and a winner of a Guggenheim Fellowship that is given for "unusually distinguished achievement and exceptional promise for future accomplishments."

Figure 9.8

Frame of Mathematician's Accomplishments

• FRAME •

Frame of Mathematician's Accomplishments

_____ is/was a mathematician who is famous or known for

_____ .

She or he studied mathematics during the years _____ in _____ and was especially interested in

We celebrate/honor this mathematician for several reasons.

First,

In addition,

Above all/Finally,

Figure 9.9

Personal Essay Frame on a Mathematician of Magnitude

• FRAME •

Personal Essay on a Mathematician of Magnitude

As I read about the life and accomplishments of _____, I was especially inspired/touched/moved by three aspects of this person's life.

First,

Furthermore,

Last,

If I had the opportunity to meet _____, I would want to know (or I would like to tell him or her)

Figure 9.10

■ ACTIVITY 3

Learning About Mathematics From Mathematicians

Following are three tasks that combine learning about mathematicians with learning about mathematics. The mathematicians featured are Leonard Euler, Stanislaw Ulam, and Pierre de Fermat. The works of these mathematicians are highly complicated and are normally studied by advanced students. However, you can introduce these great scholars and the nature of their work so that students can gain a sense of the inventiveness, curiosity, and dedication of mathematicians. For detailed explanations of these activities, see Wells (1995).

Give students the Frame for Mathematicians and Their Ideas (Figure 9.11). Tell students to use the Frame as they study each of the three mathematicians and their ideas. Hand out the worksheets for each mathematician and tell students to complete each worksheet.

Frame for Mathematicians and Their Ideas

• FRAME •

Frame for Mathematicians and Their Ideas

Many mathematicians are interested in patterns. Here is a pattern from a mathematician named
_____. This is what I learned from studying this pattern.

First,

Second,

In addition,

Figure 9.11

Euler's Relationships

• FRAME •

Euler's Relationships

Leonard Euler (1707–1783) was a Swiss mathematician who showed the patterns that are formed by different polyhedra (dimensional shapes). He established what is known as Euler's Relationships. This discovery led to extensive mathematical developments. Study the information below. Then answer the questions. When you are finished, you will have an introductory understanding to Euler's Relationships.

	Faces	Vertices	Edges	Faces + Vertices − Edges
Tetrahedron	4	4	6	2
Octahedron	8	6	12	2
Cube	6	8	12	2
Dodecahedron	12	20	30	2
Square Pyramid	5	5	8	2
Cube + Pyramid	9	9	16	2

Note to Teacher: The answer to question 2 in Figure 9.12 is $F + V = E + 2$. The answer to question 3 is complicated. According to Wells (1995, p. 61), this pattern allows us to "make many deductions. . . . For example, we can deduce that there are only five regular polyhedra (a polyhedron is regular if all its faces and all its vertices are identical). Another consequence is that, in a very large but finite plane in which at most three countries meet at any point, the average number of countries neighboring a country will be slightly under six."

1. What pattern do you see?

2. Write the patterns as an algebraic formula.

3. What importance does this relationship have?

Figure 9.12

Ulam's Cellular Automata

• FRAME •

Ulam's.Cellular Automata

Stanislaw Ulam, a twentieth-century Swedish mathematician, was interested in showing how simple structures such as squares and triangles could become extremely complex. Wells (1995) explains that Ulam wanted to show how "simple rules can create structures which are astonishingly complex" (p. 146). For example, very complex patterns, such as snowflakes observed under a microscope, may look complicated but may be "quite simple too."

"To get some understanding of Ulam's structures you will need to make patterns with squares and triangles. Follow these instructions:

1. Re-create the following pattern using squares:

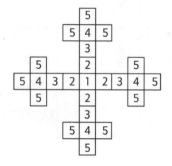

2. Explain how you re-created the pattern. List your steps in order.

3. What other patterns can you find in the pattern you re-created?

Figure 9.13

Pierre de Fermat's Patterns

• FRAME •

Pierre de Fermat's Patterns

Pierre de Fermat (1601–1665) was a French-born mathematician who, like other mathematicians, was interested in patterns of numbers (Wells 1995, pp. 42–44). Today we can find many more number patterns because we can use computers to find them. Fermat held that studying simple patterns could lead to the discovery of more complicated patterns.

Here is an example:

| 1 | 16 | 81 | 256 | 625 | 1296 | 2401 | 4096 |

To figure out this pattern, you need to know the mathematical concept of powers. Each of these numbers comes from other numbers to the fourth power. For example, 1 to the fourth power is 1, 2 to the fourth power is 16, 3 to the fourth power is 81, and so forth.

1. Use a calculator to continue the pattern.

2. What is the pattern for all or most of the last digits in each number?

3. What is the exception to this pattern?

4. What is the next exception?

5. Write your findings for this problem by stating the pattern, the first exception, and the next exception.

Figure 9.14

INTERNET LINKS

Mathematicians of the African Diaspora

http://www.math.buffalo.edu/mad/index.html

Mathematicians of Hispanic Heritage

http://mathpost.asu.edu/~dtello/mentors.html

Women Mathematicians

http://www.agnesscott.edu/lriddle/women/women.htm

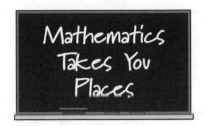

10

Where in the World for Relating Geography to Mathematics

Did the Indians really sell Manhattan for $24?

> —*Don't Know Much About History* (Davis, 1995, p. 2)

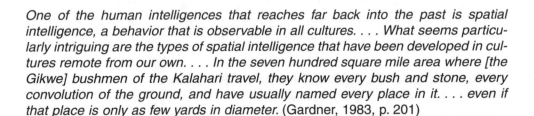

One of the human intelligences that reaches far back into the past is spatial intelligence, a behavior that is observable in all cultures. . . . What seems particularly intriguing are the types of spatial intelligence that have been developed in cultures remote from our own. . . . In the seven hundred square mile area where [the Gikwe] bushmen of the Kalahari travel, they know every bush and stone, every convolution of the ground, and have usually named every place in it. . . . even if that place is only as few yards in diameter. (Gardner, 1983, p. 201)

WHAT IS WHERE IN THE WORLD?

Where in the World focuses on the inseparable relationship between geography and space and mathematics. We can't go anywhere without knowing the distance or how long "it" will take to get there or what size "it" is or how far "it" is from other places. The whole field of geography and outer space is inextricably tied to mathematics, yet many students can have years of "math" barely touching the mathematics of our world and universe. Kenneth Davis (1995), in his lively (and profound) book on geography, refers to geography as the "mother lode of sciences" from which "other sciences radiate: meteorology and climatology, ecology, geology, oceanography, demographics, cartography," and so forth (p. 17). And, in our study of outer space we enter the far reaches of mathematics with light years, relativity, gravitational force, and so forth. Can we, indeed, separate mathematics (as we do) from these giant topics of geography and space?

WRITING STRATEGIES AS UNIFIER

Perhaps you are thinking, I teach third grade (or first grade or sixth grade) and my students are just getting to understand the basic operations and are still struggling to solve simple word problems. How can I even think of introducing the type of "high level" mathematics that relate to geography and the universe? One answer is to begin by helping students become aware of these relationships as early as possible. Students can think about and find answers to questions such as

- How far is the school from my house if I measure the distance in feet, meters, miles, kilometers?
- What is the population of my town (city)?
- How many acres of land is my housing development, how many people live in this development, and what is the population density?
- What is my weight on Earth and what would my weight be on other planets?

Hope Martin, in her excellent book *Integrating Mathematics Across the Curriculum* (1996), integrates learning mathematics with weather, rivers, travel, land, and rockets, among other applications and aligns all of these topics with NCTM standards of communication. In addition, by integrating mathematics with geography, students are involved in every aspect of mathematics—number and operations, algebra, geometry, measurement, data and probability, and money.

To help your students understand the relationship of mathematics to geography, we recommend that you integrate all the previously introduced strategies: Taxonomies; Composing With Keywords; Metacognition; Defining Format; Morphology and Etymology; Profiles and Frames; Reasons, Procedures, Results; and Who's Who. By adding the strategy of Where in the World, students will be involved in an exciting and meaningful application of mathematics.

Taxonomies and Defining Formats Relating Where in the World to Mathematics

Early in school life students become aware that they need mathematics to "know where they are" and the distances and sizes related to where they are. How far do you live from the school? How long will it take to get home by car? By bus? Which is bigger, a lake or an ocean? How do I know that I'm not in New Jersey anymore? How many people live in my town? From these basic questions, students build a mathematical/ geographic vocabulary and *apply past knowledge to new situations* (Costa & Kallick, 2000). So, once again, we present a Taxonomy collected by sixth-grade students that represents many of the terms that mathematicians and geographers share.

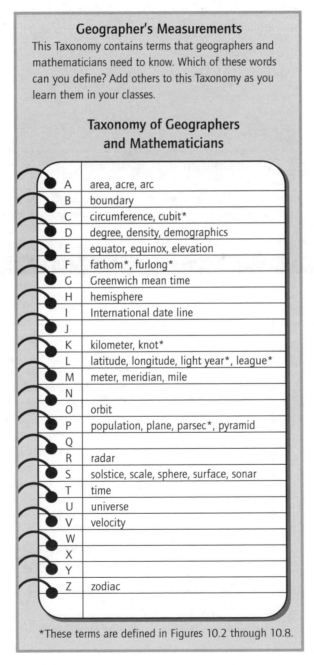

Geographer's Measurements

This Taxonomy contains terms that geographers and mathematicians need to know. Which of these words can you define? Add others to this Taxonomy as you learn them in your classes.

Taxonomy of Geographers and Mathematicians

A	area, acre, arc
B	boundary
C	circumference, cubit*
D	degree, density, demographics
E	equator, equinox, elevation
F	fathom*, furlong*
G	Greenwich mean time
H	hemisphere
I	International date line
J	
K	kilometer, knot*
L	latitude, longitude, light year*, league*
M	meter, meridian, mile
N	
O	orbit
P	population, plane, parsec*, pyramid
Q	
R	radar
S	solstice, scale, sphere, surface, sonar
T	time
U	universe
V	velocity
W	
X	
Y	
Z	zodiac

*These terms are defined in Figures 10.2 through 10.8.

Figure 10.1

Defining Formats for Geographical and Space Terms

Ever since humans first needed to measure time, distance, speed, or space they have searched for different types of measurement systems. Some of the systems were based on body measurements (hand, foot, elbow). Others were based on objects such as rods and furlongs. In modern times, many measurements are based on metrics that, compared to the previous measurements, are standardized. The following are terms that students are less likely to know and that also have a "history" or story. These words are likely to appear in literature (e.g., cubit in Noah's ark, fathoms in Shakespeare, furlongs in Medieval history as well as in stories of the sea or agriculture).

Measurement

• DEFINING FORMAT •

And thus you shall make it [the ark]; three hundred cubits the length, fifty cubits its breadth, and thirty cubits its height. (God's instructions to Noah for building the ark, Genesis 6:15)

Question	Category	Characteristics
What is a cubit?*		
A cubit	is a type of measurement that	1. was used in several early civilizations. 2. was based on the distance between the elbow and the tip of the middle finger. 3. was about 20.3 inches or 53 centimeters in Egypt, 17.1 inches or 44 centimeters in Rome, and 25.1 inches or 64 centimeters among the Israelites in King Solomon's time. 4. was the measurement used for Noah's ark. 5. comes from the Latin word *cubitum*, which means elbow.

*Davis, 2005.

Figure 10.2

Measurement

• DEFINING FORMAT •

Full fathom five thy father lies,
Of his bones are coral made.

From Ariel's song in *The Tempest* by William Shakespeare

Question	Category	Characteristics
What is a fathom?		
A fathom is a	unit of measurement that	1. is a unit of length equal to six feet (1.8 meters). 2. is based on the span of outstretched arms. 3. is used chiefly in nautical measurements. 4. measures the depth of water by means of a sounding line.

Figure 10.3

Measurement

• DEFINING FORMAT •

Furlong is a unit of length in the inch-pound system of measurement that is customarily used in the United States. Furlong originally meant the length of a furrow in a plowed field. However, this meaning was indefinite because farmers plowed furrows of many different lengths. Gradually, the furlong became a standard length. Today, the furlong is used mainly to measure distances in horse races.

Question	Category	Characteristics
What is a furlong?*		
A furlong is a	unit of distance that	1. is equal to 220 yards (201 m) or 1/8 mile (0.2 km). 2. is equal to a furrow (in farming). 3. is based on the rod, which is a square that measures 30 1/4 square yards (25.29 sq. m). 4. is still used in horse races.

*Davis, 2005.

Figure 10.4

Measurement

• DEFINING FORMAT •

Speed played a major part in the story of the Titanic. *Her maximum speed was 21 knots. Instead, she was traveling at the dangerous speed of 26 knots* (Titanic's Mistakes, http://www.euronet.nl/users/keesree/mistakes.htm).

Question	Category	Characteristics
What is a knot?		
A knot	is a measure of speed that	1. is equal to one nautical mile per hour,* and is used for measuring the speed of ships. 2. comes from a sailor's practice of throwing a knotted rope over the side of a ship to determine the ship's speed. 3. gets it name from the knotted rope with a piece of wood called the "ship's log." *A nautical mile is 6,076 feet compared to a statute or land mile, which is 5,280 feet.

Figure 10.5

Measurement

• DEFINING FORMAT •

Half a league, half a league,
Half a league onward,
All in the valley of Death
Rode the six hundred.

"Charge of the Light Brigade," Alfred Lord Tennyson

Question	Category	Characteristics
What is a league?		
A league	is a measure of distance that	1. is approximately three statute miles or 4.8 kilometers. 2. comes from the Latin word *leuga*, which means a "measure of distance." 3. is used only in English-speaking countries.

Note to Teacher: An excellent Web site for junior high and high school students is "Converting to Nautical Measurements" at http://pao.cnmoc.navy.mil/educate/neptune/lesson/math/nautical.htm.

Figure 10.6

Defining Formats for Astronomy and Space Travel

Most students are fascinated by astronomy and space both from fictional and nonfictional perspectives. Students are likely to easily learn the names of the planets and their order in relation to the sun. Many will be able to rank the planets in order of size and know many mathematical details about them. The activities here can be a starting point for integrating mathematics with the universe (see Figure 10.21 for Planet Profile).

Measurement

• DEFINING FORMAT •

Question	Category	Characteristics
What is a light year?		
A light year	is a measure of distance that	1. is used for measurements in interstellar space. 2. is 5,880,000,000,000 miles or approximately 6 trillion miles. 3. is the distance that light travels in a vacuum in a year. 4. travels at the rate of 186,281.7 miles (299.792 kilometers) per second.

Figure 10.7

Measurement

• DEFINING FORMAT •

Question	Category	Characteristics
What is a parsec?		
A parsec	is a unit of distance that	1 is used in measuring interstellar space. 2. is approximately 3.26 light years. 3. is a combination of two words: *parallax** and *second*. *In astronomy, the apparent angular displacement of a celestial body due to its being observed from the surface instead of from the center of the Earth (diurnal parallax or geocentric parallax) or due to its being observed from the Earth instead of from the sun (annual parallax or heliocentric parallax).

Figure 10.8

Taxonomy of Careers Relating to Both Geography and Mathematics

This Taxonomy contains terms that require study of both geography and mathematics. Select three or four careers and write a definition for each of them. Then try to locate a person in one of these careers. Write a letter or send an e-mail asking that person to tell you something about her or his work. (You can add other careers that relate to this Taxonomy.)

Taxonomy of Careers Needing Mathematics

A	archaeologist, astronomer, agriculturist, agronomist, anthropologist, architect
B	botanist, builder
C	cartographer, climatologist
D	demographer*
E	economist, explorer, ecologist
F	financial analyst
G	geologist, geometer
H	horticulturist
I	
J	
K	
L	landscaper
M	meteorologist, mountain climber
N	navigator
O	oceanographer
P	political scientist, paleontologist*
Q	
R	radiologist
S	seismologist,* sociologist
T	
U	urban planner
V	
W	
X	
Y	
Z	zoologist

*Careers defined in this chapter.

Figure 10.9

Defining Formats for Careers
Related to Geography, Space, and Mathematics

The careers defined below offer opportunities for travel, creativity, and prestige. They also build an interest in and knowledge of mathematics. Suggest that your students check out these careers on the Internet or in books and relate what they find to mathematics.

Careers

• DEFINING FORMAT •

Question	Category	Characteristics
What is a demographer?		
A demographer	is a professional (or person) who	1. studies the science of vital and social statistics, such as the births, deaths, diseases, marriages, etc., of populations (related to the Greek word *demos* for "people"). 2. specializes in the area of mathematics called statistics. 3. writes about the economic, environmental, and social effects of population growth and decline on different areas of the world.

Figure 10.10

Careers

• DEFINING FORMAT •

Question	Category	Characteristics
What is a paleontologist?		
A paleontologist	is a professional (or person) who	1. studies the science of the forms of life existing in former geologic periods, as represented by their fossils (e.g., dinosaurs). 2. studies the mathematics related to growth and change of organisms and also mathematics related to ancient (paleo-) periods of time.

Figure 10.11

Careers

• DEFINING FORMAT •

Question	Category	Characteristics
What is a seismologist?		
A seismologist	is a professional (or person) who	1. studies the science of earthquakes or *seisms,* from the Greek "to shake or quake." 2. studies the mathematics related to instruments such as the Richter scale, a scale ranging from 1 to 10 to measure the intensity of an earthquake (named after Charles F. Richter, an American seismologist). 3. also studies mathematics related to geologic changes in the Earth.

Figure 10.12

Mathematics the Write Way

Profiles and Frames for Geography and Outer Space

Profiles and Frames related to geography and outer space will naturally combine mathematical information with writing about these areas. Below are Profiles for continents, countries, and cities that require information on area, distance, population, food production, and so forth, offering the student opportunities for creating and solving mathematical problems. Planet Profile includes mathematical information for a specific planet, which can then be compared with other planets. Adapt these Profiles to your mathematical course of study and your students' levels and needs. After the students have completed the Profiles, ask them to create as many word problems as they can from the data they have researched.

Completed Continent Profile

After the students have completed a Profile, they should work in small cooperative groups and create as many questions and problems as they can based on the information researched. For example, they might ask:

- How many times larger is Africa compared to Australia?
- What is the approximate ratio of square kilometers to square miles?
- If Asia has a yearly population growth of 10 percent and Europe has a yearly population growth of 1 percent, what will be the difference in numbers of people in one year? In two years?

• PROFILE •

Continent Profile

Definition of a Continent (use Defining Format): _____

_____

_____

Names of Continents:

_____   _____   _____

_____   _____   _____

_____

Size of Continents by Square Miles and Kilometers:

Continent   *Square Miles*   *Square Kilometers*

_____

_____

_____

_____

_____

_____

Population of Continents:

Continent   *Population*

_____

_____

_____

_____

_____

_____

_____

Highest Mountain of Each Continent: **Height of Mountain**

_____

_____

_____

_____

_____

_____

Longest River in Each Continent:

Name of River   *Continent(s)*   *Miles Long*   *Kilometers Long*

_____

_____

_____

_____

_____

_____

Figure 10.13

• PROFILE •

Continent Profile

A continent is a large land mass that (1) is separated from other continents by water and/or mountains, (2) was formed millions of years ago by movements of the Earth known as global plate tectonics, and (3) in modern times may be divided into political divisions called countries.

Name of Continents

Africa	Asia	Australia
Antarctica	North America	South America
Europe		

Size of Continents by	Square Kilometers and	Square Miles
Africa	30,355,000	11,709,000
Asia	44,908,000	17,300,000
Australia*	7, 682,000	2,966,000
Antarctica	14,000,000	5,400,000
North America	24,700,000	9,500,000
South America	17,800,000	6, 900,000
Europe	9,900,000	3,800,000

Population of Continents

Continent	Population (Estimated)
Africa	1,170,000,000
Asia	4,568,000,000
North America	319,000,000
South America	647,000,000
Europe	615,000,000
Australia*	8,000,000
Antarctica	0

*Includes Australia and surrounding Pacific Islands

Highest Mountain of Each Continent	Height of Mountain
Aconcagua, South America	22,834 feet/6,960 meters
Kilimanjaro, Africa	19,340 feet/5,895 meters
Mont Blanc, Europe	15,770 feet/4,808 meters
Mt. Everest, Asia	29,028 feet/8,848 meters
Mt. Cook, Australia	12,349 feet/3,764 meters
Mt. McKinley, North America	20,320 feet/6,194 meters
Vincent Massif, Antarctica	16,860 feet/5,140 meters

Longest River in Each Continent

Name of River	Continent(s)	Miles Long	Kilometers Long
Nile	Africa	4,160	6,695
Amazon	South America	4,050	6,515
Yangtze	Asia	3,965	6,380
Mississippi/Missouri	North America	3,740	6,019
Murray-Darling	Australia	2,330	3,750
Volga	Europe	2,290	3,688
None in Antarctica			

*Data taken from *Rand McNally Classroom Atlas,* 2004.

Figure 10.14

Profile of a Capital City

Figure 10.15 is a Capital City Profile and provides the students with an excellent integration of social studies and mathematics. After the students have completed the Capital City Profile, they should work in small cooperative groups and create as many questions and problems as they can based on the information researched. For example, they might ask

- What effect does density of population have on the quality of life?
- What are the advantages of having a city on a river?
- What is life like in a city with high rainfall compared to a city with little rainfall?
- What are the distances from this city to other capital cities?

• PROFILE •

Capital City Profile

Complete the information on a capital city that interests you. You can get this information from the Internet or your social studies textbook. When you have finished the Profile, write as many questions as you can that would require further research.

Name of Capital City: _____

Country Location: _____

Population of City: _____

Population Density: _____

River(s) or Waterway(s) of City: _____

Length of River(s): _____

Elevation (Height) of City: _____

Area: _____

Average Precipitation by Month:

Measurements of Tallest or Largest Structure (if applicable)

Figure 10.15

• PROFILE •

Completed Capital City Profile

Complete the information on a capital city that interests you. You can get this information from the Internet or your social studies textbook. When you have finished the Profile, write as many questions as you can that would require further research.

Name of Capital City: _____ Paris _____

Country Location: _____ France _____

Population of City: _____ 2,175,000 people _____

Population Density: _____ 53,000 people per square mile or 20,700 per square kilometer _____

River(s) or Waterway(s) of City: _____ The Seine River _____

Length of River(s): _____ curves through Paris for about 8 miles or 13 kilometers _____

Elevation (Height) of City: _____ Paris lies in a lowland called the Paris Basin _____

Area: _____ approximately 41 square miles or 50 square kilometers _____

Average Precipitation by Month:

	January	2.1 in.	5 cm
	February	1.8 in.	5 cm
	March	2.1 in.	5 cm
	April	1.8 in.	5 cm
	May	2.5 in.	6 cm
	June	2.3 in.	6 cm
	July	2.1 in.	5 cm
	August	2.0 in.	5 cm
	September	2.1 in.	5 cm
	October	2.2 in.	6 cm
	November	2.2 in.	6 cm
	December	2.2 in.	6 cm

Measurements of Tallest or Largest Structure (if applicable)

The Eiffel Tower: Made up of 18,038 pieces, 2,500,000 rivets

    Weight of Metal Structure: 7,300 tons

    Total Weight: 10,100 tons

    Height: 324 meters with flagpole

    Number of Steps: 1,665

Figure 10.16

Profile of North America Using a Map

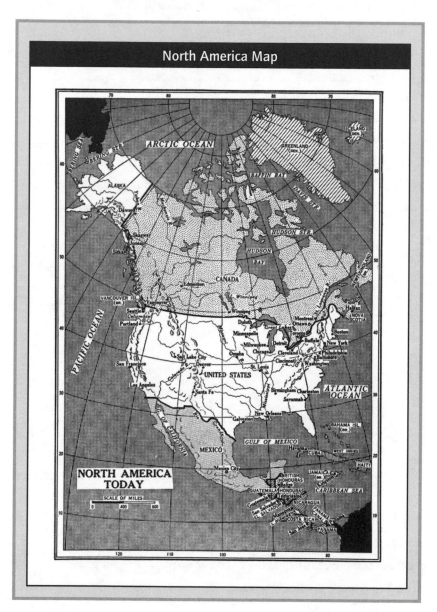

Figure 10.17

• PROFILE •

Profile of North America Using a Map

Continent Map Illustrates: _____

Range of Latitude Degrees from Southern Border to Northern Border: _____

Range of Longitude Degrees from Eastern Border to Western Border: _____

Range of Latitude from the Tropic of Cancer to the Arctic Circle: _____

Scale in Kilometers: _____

Scale in Miles: _____

Approximate Air Distance from New York to Los Angeles in Kilometers: _____

in Miles: _____

Approximate Air Distance from Mexico City, Mexico to Fargo, ND in Kilometers: _____

in Miles: _____

Approximate Air Distance from Panama City, Panama to Whitehorse, Yukon Territory,

Canada in Kilometers: _____ in Miles: _____

Nearest Latitude and Longitude of Seattle: Latitude _____ Longitude _____

Two Cities in North America That Have Approximately the Same Latitude: _____

Two Cities in North America That Have Approximately the Same Longitude: _____

Figure 10.17

After the students have completed the Profile, working in groups they can again create questions such as

- How long would it take to get from (city) to (city) by car going at an average rate of 60 miles per hour?
- How would two cities in the same latitude be similar? How would two cities in the same longitude be similar?
- If the distance from Tijuana, Mexico to Mazatlan, Mexico is 90 nautical miles, how long would it take to get from one city to the other by ship at the rate of 12 knots per hour?

The Frame in Figure 10.19 integrates map study with mathematics and provides an opportunity for broad-based research. Again, we suggest that students (Grades 5 and up) work together with globes and atlases to guide them. Although the Frame and its geography will be the same for all groups, responses will vary and will make a good lesson on the reasons for the variations.

• PROFILE •

Completed Profile of North America Using a Map*

Continent Map Illustrates: _North America_

Approximate Range of Latitude Degrees from Southern Border to Northern Border: _10 degrees north to 80 degrees north_

Approximate Range of Longitude Degrees from Eastern Border to Western Border: _50 degrees west to 130 degrees west_

Range of Latitude from the Tropic of Cancer to the Arctic Circle: _20° N to 75° N_

Scale in Kilometers on Your Map: _5 cm = 1,500 kilometers_

Scale in Miles on Your Map: _2 inches = 1,000 miles_

Approximate Air Distance from New York to Los Angeles in Kilometers: _3,903_ in Miles: _2,426_

Approximate Air Distance from Mexico City, Mexico to Fargo, ND in Kilometers: _3,048_ in Miles: _1,894_

Approximate Air Distance from Panama City, Panama to Whitehorse, Yukon Territory, Canada in Kilometers _7,314_ in Miles _4,545_

Nearest Latitude and Longitude of Seattle: Latitude _47" 36' N_ Longitude _122" 20' W_

Two Cities in North America That Have Approximately the Same Latitude: _Bangor, ME and St. Paul, MN_

Two Cities in North America That Have Approximately the Same Longitude: _Cheyenne, WY and Colorado Springs, CO_

*You can also use the Internet by searching for a gazetteer.

Figure 10.18

• FRAME •

Traveler in Need of a "Mathematical Geographer"

A person who travels needs mathematical information. The Frame below is an imaginary letter from a traveler asking a "mathematical geographer" for information. Complete the Frame with the correct information. You will need to check dictionaries, encyclopedias, and the Internet.

To: Y.B. Geographer-Mathematician:

I am a traveler in need of information that is mathematically related to geography. I would appreciate your filling in the spaces I have left so that I can proceed with my project of circumnavigating the Earth by water and ground transportation. I plan to follow the circumference of the Earth around the equator, which is _____ miles or _____ kilometers. I would like to visit at least two cities that are close to the equator, one of which is _____ and another is _____. The latitude of the first city I will visit is _____ and its longitude is _____. The latitude of the second city is _____ and its longitude is _____. The distance between the two cities is _____ miles or _____ kilometers. I would also like to visit the _____ that flows near the equator and is _____ miles long or _____ kilometers. In addition, I can travel on the _____ river, which is about _____ miles or _____ kilometers. I am also a mountain climber. I have heard that in South America I could climb elevations of _____ meters in the _____ mountains and elevations of _____ meters in Africa.

I will not burden you with the mathematics related to the rest of my voyage and will try to figure everything out myself. However, thank you for all this mathematical help so far.

Respectfully,
J.P. Traveler, III

Figure 10.19

• FRAME •

Completed Letter to a "Mathematical Geographer"

Dear Traveler:

Here is the information you requested, which I was able to get by checking maps and atlases. You can follow the circumference of the Earth around the equator, which is 24,901 miles or 40,075 kilometers. You might want to visit Nairobi in Kenya and Bangkok in Thailand. The latitude of Nairobi is between 0 and 15 degrees south of the equator and its longitude is between 30 and 45 degrees east of Greenwich, England. The latitude of Bangkok is between 0 and 15 degrees north of the equator and its longitude is between 90 and 105 degrees east of Greenwich. The distance between the two cities is approximately 5,000 miles or 8,500 kilometers. You should also visit the Nile River that flows near the equator and is 4,160 miles long or 6,695 kilometers. In addition, you can travel on the Amazon River, which is about 4,050 miles or 6,615 kilometers long. Since you are a mountain climber, you could go to South America and climb elevations of 6,960 meters in the Andes and then travel back to Africa for elevations of 5,895 meters at Mount Kilimanjaro.

I do hope that you will try to figure out everything for yourself, but you are always welcome to ask me.

Respectfully,
Y.B. Geographer-Mathematician

Figure 10.20

Planet Profile

Select a planet in our solar system. Use the Profile to collect information about that planet. An easy way to search on the Internet is to type in keywords such as World Book Encyclopedia or Encarta; then type in the name of the planet. After you have completed the Profile, write a factual or science fiction story using the information from the Profile.

After the students have completed the Profile, have them work in groups and create questions such as

- How much farther is (planet) than (planet) from the sun?
- What is the distance between (planet) and (planet)?
- How many times larger is (planet) than (planet)?
- How many times larger is the sun compared to (planet)?

• PROFILE •

Planet Profile

Name of Planet: _____

Origin of Planet's Name: _____

Distance from the Sun: Miles _____ Kilometers _____

Distance from the Earth: Miles _____ Kilometers _____

Number of Days or Earth Years to Orbit the Sun (Revolution): _____

Hours to Rotate on Its Axis (Rotation): _____

Number of Satellites (Moons): _____

Temperature Range(s) of Planet: _____

Mass (Quantity of Matter) Compared to Earth: _____

Density Compared to Earth: _____

Force of Gravity at the Surface Compared to Earth: _____

Your Own Weight on Earth: _____ Your Weight on Planet (of Profile): _____

Magnetic Field Compared to Earth: _____

Composition of Planet (e.g., gas, minerals): _____

Special Features of Planet (e.g., rings, volcanoes, radio waves):

Figure 10.21

• PROFILE •

Example of Completed Planet Profile

Name of Planet: *Jupiter*

Origin of Planet's Name: *Named after the ruler of the Roman gods*

Distance from the Sun: Miles: *483,600,000*   Kilometers: *778,300,000*

Diameter: Miles: *88,846*   Kilometers: *142,984*

Distance from the Earth: Miles: *370,600,000*   Kilometers: *650,300,000*

Number of Days or Earth Years to Orbit the Sun: (Revolution): *4,333 Earth days or 12 Earth years*

Hours to Rotate on Its Axis (Rotation): *9 hours 55 minutes*

Number of Satellites (Moons): *28 known satellites*

Temperature Range(s) of Planet: *At the top of Jupiter's clouds it is about −220° Fahrenheit or −140° Celsius; in the center or core it is about 43,000° F or 24,000° C (hotter than the sun); between the top of the clouds and the center it is about 70° F or 21° C, like a nice summer day on Earth*

Mass (Quantity of Matter) Compared to Earth: *318 times larger than Earth*

Density Compared to Earth: *1.33 grams per cubic centimeter, slightly more than the density of water, and about 1/4 that of Earth*

Force of Gravity at the Surface Compared to Earth: *2.4 times stronger than Earth*

Your Own Weight on Earth: *100 pounds*

Your Weight on Planet (of Profile): *240 pounds*

Magnetic Field Compared to Earth: *14 times stronger than Earth (the strongest in the solar system)*

Composition of Planet (e.g., gas, minerals): *about 86 percent hydrogen, 14 percent helium, and very small amounts of methane, ammonia, phosphorus, water, acetylene, ethane, germanium, and carbon monoxide*

Special Features of Planet (e.g., rings, volcanoes, radio waves): *dense red, brown, yellow, and white clouds; a Great Red Spot three times the size of Earth whirling like a hurricane; radio waves and continuous radiation; powerful magnetic field that traps electrons, protons, and other particles in radiation belts around the planet*

Figure 10.22

Profiles for Comparing the Mathematics in Two Field Sports Played in Different Countries

Sports are popular all over the world. Some sports, such as soccer, are played in many countries. American football is played mainly in the United States and also in Canada, where it is called Canadian football. Complete one Profile for American football and one for soccer. You may also work with a partner, in which case each of you complete a different Profile. Then, together or separately, write a comparison of these two sports based on the information from the two Profiles. Information on these sports can be found using the Internet. You can use the name of the sport as a keyword (e.g., soccer). These examples may include more detail and be of greater length than you might like to spend on these topics, so feel free to limit fields as needed.

• PROFILE •

Profile for American Football

Sport (Soccer or American Football): _____

Countries Where Popular: _____

Shape of Field: _____

Size of Field: _____

Names of the Lines on the Field: _____

Description and Measurements Related to Goal Area(s): _____

Description and Measurements of the Ball: _____

Number of Players: _____

Names and Roles of Different Players (e.g., linemen for blocking and catching passes):

- _____

- _____

- _____

Playing Time: _____

Other Time Periods (e.g., time out, overtime): _____

Scoring System: _____

Figure 10.23

• PROFILE •

Completed Profile for American Football

Sport: *American Football*

Countries Where Popular: *United States, Canada, Germany*

Shape of Field: *Rectangle*

Size of Field: *120 Yards × 50 Yards*

Names of the Lines on the Field: *yard markers, hash marks, goal lines, boundary lines, line of scrimmage (where each play begins)*

Description and Measurements Related to Goal Area(s): *End zones are 10 yards deep × 50 yards wide. They are placed at the far ends of the rectangular playing field. There are no yard markers in the end zones. The name of the home team often appears in the end zone.*

Description and Measurements of the Ball: *Oval with pointed ends, laces to place fingers, often made of leather. The football is about 13 inches long and 19 inches in circumference at the center.*

Number of Players: *Each side of a football team has 11 players. However, most teams use different players on offense, defense, and special teams. Plus, teams like to have back-up players for most positions. Therefore, the entire football team roster may have 45 players.*

Names and Roles of Different Players (e.g., linemen for blocking and catching passes): *Every position player on a football team has a title and role. The titles correspond to either the location the players assume on the field or the key function they serve. Below are some examples.*

- *Quarterbacks line up just behind the offensive line. Quarterbacks serve several functions, the most important being distributing the ball to other offensive players who run or catch it. The quarterbacks distribute the ball by either handing it off or throwing it. Quarterbacks can also run with the ball themselves.*
- *Fullbacks usually line up behind the quarterback. They can either run with the ball, catch the ball, or block against defensive players.*
- *In defiance of measurement rules, halfbacks may line up behind quarterbacks and fullbacks instead of between them. When halfbacks line up that way, they are called tailbacks.*
- *The offense has three receivers whose main job is catching passes (throws) from the quarterback. Receivers sometimes block defensive players or run with the ball. The three receivers are designated by how close they get to the offensive linemen. The receiver closest to the offensive linemen is the tight end. The furthest is the split end or wide receiver.*
- *There are five offensive linemen: the center; two guards (left and right); and two tackles (left and right). The main job for offensive linemen is to block defensive players. The center also hikes (snaps) the ball to the quarterback to start each play.*
- *Defensive players who start on the line of scrimmage are called down linemen. There are always two ends (left and right). Usually there are two tackles (left and right). Down linemen try to stop running backs carrying the ball or rush (charge) the quarterback to keep him from passing the ball.*
- *Most teams use three or four linebackers. Linebackers cover the middle of the defense. They tackle offensive players with the ball. Sometimes they charge the quarterback or cover receivers.*
- *Defenses have cornerbacks and safeties. These players primarily cover the offensive receivers, prevent the completion of passes, and tackle offensive players with the ball.*
- *Some football players have very specialized roles—kickers, for example. Kickers, as the title suggests, are the only players in American football who actually use their feet to move the ball. Place kickers kick the ball off the ground. Sometimes they kick it to score points for their team. Some kicks are worth three points, some worth one point. Other times, kickers kick the ball for no points. They do this when their team is deliberately giving the ball to the other team.*

Playing Time: *Football games are divided into quarters. Depending on the league, quarters can run from 12 to 15 minutes in length. However, playing time in football is often interrupted. Reasons for stopping the clock can be time outs, incomplete passes, out of bounds plays, scores, first downs (not in professional football), injuries, changes of possession of the ball, commercials, and measurements. Therefore, an entire football game can take a couple of hours to play.*

Other Time Periods (e.g., time out, overtime): *Besides quarters, there are time outs, two-minute warnings (professional only), overtime, and referee time outs.*

Scoring System: *Touchdowns are worth six points, kicked points after touchdowns are worth one point, conversions after touchdowns are worth two points, field goals are worth three points, and safeties are worth two points.*

Figure 10.24

• PROFILE •

Profile for Soccer

Sport: _____

Countries Where Popular: _____

Shape of Field: _____

Size of Field: _____

Names of the Lines on the Field: _____

Description and Measurements Related to Goal Area(s): _____

Description and Measurements of the Ball: _____

Number of Players: _____

Names and Roles of Different Players (e.g., linemen for blocking and catching passes):

- _____

- _____

- _____

Playing Time: _____

Other Time Periods (e.g., time out, overtime): _____

Scoring System: _____

Figure 10.25

• PROFILE •

Completed Profile for Soccer

Sport: *Soccer*

Countries Where Popular: *Approximately 200 countries throughout Europe, South America, Africa, North America, and most of Asia.*

Shape of Field: *Rectangle*

Size of Field: *90–120 meters long × 45–90 meters wide*

Names of the Lines on the Field: *penalty areas (2), center line, sidelines, end lines, and corner kick quarter-circles*

Description and Measurements Related to Goal Area(s): *Rectangular goals at each end of the field 7.32 m (24 ft) wide and 2.44 m (8 ft) high. Penalty area 40.32 m (44 yd) wide and extending 16.5 m (18 yd) in front of the goal.*

Description and Measurements of the Ball: *Round leather ball between 68 and 71 cm (27 and 28 in) in circumference and weighing between 396 to 453 g (14 and 16 oz).*

Number of Players: *11*

Names and Roles of Different Players (e.g., linemen for blocking and catching passes):

Offense: *Attacker (Forwards)*

Defense: *Goalkeeper, Defender (Fullbacks)*

Offense and Defense: *Midfielder (Halfbacks)*

Playing Time: *Two 45-minute halves.*

Other Time Periods (e.g., time out, overtime): *The only time that play stops is when a player commits a foul, a player is injured, or a goal is scored.*

Scoring System: *Goal (1 point each)*

Figure 10.26

Setting Up Other Profiles

Students can also create their own Profiles for other sports, following the above models, tailoring them to the mathematical information of the sport. They can set up Profile comparisons for

- badminton and tennis
- lacrosse and jai alai (or squash)
- baseball and cricket

• PROFILE •

Comparison Between Soccer and Football

American football and soccer have mathematical similarities and differences. Both are popular in the United States, Canada, and Germany. However, soccer is much more popular in Germany than in America. American football is a much more popular spectator sport in the United States than soccer, though soccer is a very popular participatory sport in the U.S.

Football and soccer are both played on rectangular fields with goals at both of the long ends. The size of the two fields is similar, but football has a much larger end zone for goals than soccer. The football field is measured in yards and is 120 yds. × 50 yds. A soccer field will vary in size, but is usually 100 m × 50 m. Football's goal zone has goal posts while soccer's has a net. Football fields are marked by the yard while soccer fields have center lines and penalty areas. Football uses chains to mark off ten-yard distances and to help place the ball for each play. Soccer is a sport of continuous play, and the lines serve to locate the ball for certain situations, such as where to place it when it has gone out of bounds. Both fields have boundary lines and confine play to the interior of the rectangular playing fields.

Footballs are oval spheres with pointed ends, usually with leather exteriors. There are laces for placing the fingers when throwing the ball. Footballs are usually 13 inches long by 19 inches in circumference at the center. Soccer balls are round spheres of interconnected hexagons or pentagons. Soccer balls are approximately 25 inches in circumference.

Football teams and soccer teams have eleven players on a side. Since football players change with each possession of the ball, they have larger rosters than soccer teams. Soccer players are responsible for both offense and defense. Soccer teams designate one player as a goal tender. The rest are designated by their general position on the field (center forward, wing, tackle, etc.). Football players are also designated by their location (quarterback, fullback, end, linebacker, etc.) as well as their function (kicker, receiver, punter).

Both football and soccer games are divided into halves, with football games being further divided into quarters. Soccer halves are 45 minutes long (running time). They are interrupted for time outs, injuries, substitutions, penalties, and goals. Both football and soccer games have 15-minute breaks at the half. Football games have 24- to 30-minute halves, broken into quarters. The clock can be stopped for changes of possession, time outs, injury, scores, out of bounds, incomplete passes, penalties, and commercials.

Each goal in soccer is worth one point. Football has several values for different types of scores. Touchdowns are worth six points. A successful kick immediately following a touchdown is worth one point. Running or passing the ball into the end zone immediately following a touchdown is worth two points. Field goals are worth three points and safeties are worth two points. Both games can end in ties.

Figure 10.27

INTERNET LINKS

Converting to Nautical Measurements

http://pao.cnmoc.navy.mil/educate/neptune/lesson/math/nautical.htm

Geographic Dictionary

http://www.netcore.ca/gibsonjs/dict1g.htm

Mayan Mathematics

http://www.civilization.ca/civil/maya/mmc05eng.html

Titanic's Mistakes

http://www.euronet.nl/users/keesree/mistakes.htm

United States Gazetteer

http://www.census.gov/cgi-bin/gazetteer

Know Thyself

11

Personifications and Interactions for Knowledge and Humor

Pooh asked, "Is [a Knight] as Grand as a King and Factors . . . ?"

"Well, it's not as Grand as a King," said Christopher Robin, . . . "But it's grander than Factors."

—The House at Pooh Corner
(Milne, 1956, p. 311)

Mathematics . . . a fine and wonderful refuge of the divine spirit—almost an amphibian between being and non-being.

—Gottfried Wilhelm Leibniz

WHAT ARE PERSONIFICATIONS AND INTERACTIONS?

In the opening quotation for this chapter, Pooh and Christopher Robin refer to numbers as living entities, personified with human attributes. Both A. A. Milne, the esteemed creator of Winnie the Pooh, and Gottfried Wilhelm Leibniz, the great mathematician and philosopher of the seventeenth century, give a life force to numbers even though others usually think of numbers only in mathematical or abstract terms.

Through Personifications and Interactions, students give life to mathematical terms and ideas by assuming the "role" of a term or idea and writing to another personified term or idea. As students interact, they exchange information and ideas about mathematical terms and ideas that involve "creating, imagining, and innovating," another of the essential habits of the mind cited by Costa and Kallick (2000).

Personifications and Interactions are especially helpful when learning about two ideas that are connected or related. For example, the right triangle is inextricably tied to the rectangle. Yet in most classrooms, these two polygons may rarely meet (at least in the eyes of the students). However, when students assume the roles of a triangle and a rectangle (Personifications) and interact with one another (Interactions), the relationship between these polygons assumes greater clarity and provides the student with greater mathematical understanding.

THE PURPOSE AND VALUE OF PERSONIFICATIONS AND INTERACTIONS

This strategy, like Metacognition, Defining Format, and Reasons, Procedures, Results, helps students expand their knowledge and gain greater insight into mathematical concepts and ideas. By using imagination and role-playing in their writing, students are able to

- assume the point of view of mathematical terms or concepts (I am a numeral. I can take many forms.);
- explain the attributes or characteristics of mathematical terms or concepts (I am the diameter. Look for me in a circle or globe. Without me, the radius is meaningless.);
- tell about the history of mathematical terms or concepts (I am zero, the symbol that shows place value. But for a long time, no one understood me, except some astute mathematicians in India.);
- describe the cultural background of mathematical terms or concepts (I am the Hebrew symbol called *chai*. When I am thought of simply as letters, I mean life. However, I can also represent the number 18, so the number 18 symbolizes life.).

Personifications and Interactions allow students to merge writing creativity with mathematical knowledge. They start to understand and value the relationship between language and numbers. In addition, and most significantly, students begin to think of the larger picture into which mathematics fits, another aspect of the metacognitive thinking that helps build successful problem solving (Carr & Biddlecomb, 1998).

Skuy and Mentis (1999) advocate strategies that enhance students' "cognitive development in general and thinking skills in particular" (p. iii). Their work is based on Feuerstein's Instrumental Enrichment (IE), a learning mediation program that builds students' cognitive skills. Many of the skills mediated through IE are especially pertinent to mathematics—organization, comparison, orientation in space, analytic perception, categorization, and numerical progressions (among others). All of the writing strategies presented in this book—and most especially Personifications and Interactions—are designed to further students' cognitive skills in mathematics and beyond.

Following are examples and activities for Personifications and Interactions for all five of the NCTM standards for mathematics (NCTM, 2000).

Mathematics the Write Way

Writing Activities Related to Personifications and Interactions

This strategy can be used by students in all grades and with different abilities because, like the strategy of Metacognition (see Chapter 4), it allows the students to write what they already know. For example, a primary grade student can assume the "persona" of the number four and write to the "persona" of number seven. A student of any age can "be" a triangle or a calculator or a coin or an algorithm and explain "itself" to another mathematical entity. The following Personifications provide students with lively writing topics that can give them deeper understanding of the mathematics they need to know.

- An addition algorithm (e.g., 42 + 25) writes to the subtraction algorithm 42 − 25.
- A Fahrenheit thermometer describes itself to a Celsius thermometer.
- The number 5 explains to the number 2 its sequence and asks for a reply from the number 2.
- A dollar bill tells a child the many ways to use coins to equal a dollar.

As you introduce new concepts to your students, have them write at least one Personification about that concept or topic. After they are familiar with this process, have two students work together to set up an "interaction" (e.g., A scale and a tape measure exchange letters). Brainstorm with your students other Personifications and Interactions and post them on the wall for continuous reference.

Personifications and Interactions for Number and Operations

Following are activities involving numbers and numerals. In the first example, an odd number writes to an even number (Figure 11.1). From this model, you can have your students assume the persona of an even number and write a reply to the odd number.

Number and Operations

• PERSONIFICATIONS AND INTERACTIONS •

An Odd Number Writes to an Even Number

Tri Septo
379 Odd Drive
Five Towns, ID 97531

Four Ward
2684 Even Lane
Eightville, UT 86428

Dear Four:

You have asked me to explain what it means to be an odd number. Here are some important ideas to know. First, I start off the numbers by being 1, which is an odd number. That means I can't be divided into two equal numbers like you can, such as 2 plus 2 equals 4. The next odd number is 3, so you notice that I skip 2. I can't be 4 like you, because you are even. So I have to be 5. You will notice now that I skip the next number and go on to 7 and then to 9. There is a lot more I can tell you about being an odd number, but I would like to hear from you now so I can learn more about your being even. If we continue writing, we will learn a lot about each other.

A pal,

Tri Septo

P.S. In case you don't know, my first name, Tri, means three and my last name, Septo, means seven.

> **Note to Teacher**: This activity (as in the subsequent examples) can be written at virtually any grade level—the student writes as much as she or he knows. That knowledge can range from basic to complex, once again allowing for differences and differentiation.

Figure 11.1

In Figure 11.2, a person who uses Arabic numerals describes the Arabic system to a person who uses Roman numerals. The letter focuses on the history of Arabic numerals and the concept of zero. In the follow-up activity (Figure 11.3), students are asked to personify a Roman numeral who feels that he or she is being "pushed out" by Arabic numerals. These Personifications and Interactions require students to research the story or history of zero (see Internet Links) and can be written from both simple and complex perspectives, again depending on student interest and ability. We recognize that some of the models may be lengthy, but we would like you to see the possibilities for in-depth learning and writing (with a touch of humor). Your students will gain great insights about mathematics as a living and growing subject from the research that this writing requires.

• PERSONIFICATIONS AND INTERACTIONS •

An Arabic Numeral Writing to a Roman Numeral

Omar Hasim Singh
Indian-Arabic Council of Mathematicians
123 Zero Place
Desert Road, India 67890

November 10, 1502
Portia Cassius
Director of Roman Mathematical Academy
VI Roman Way
Appia, Rome IXMCD

Dear Portia:

Note to Teacher: This letter is an example of an Arabic numeral writing to a Roman numeral. For an excellent account of the development of zero, see *Number Words and Number Symbols* (Menninger, 1992). You may ask students to do a similar activity or adapt the activity to students' needs.

I was delighted to get your letter of January 7, 1502 or, as you wrote, January VII, MDII. Your people want to change over from Roman numerals to (as you say) Arabic numerals and need information on how our system works.

First, I would like to give you a short history of our numbers. The direct ancestors of the numerals we use today come from India but were spread to other parts of the world by Arab traders. At first, we did not have a zero, but we understood that we could place numerals in columns and that, depending on the column, the numerals would have different magnitudes or "sizes." For example, we could write 456 and mean four hundreds, five tens, and six ones. But without the symbol of a zero, we had to figure out a different system. The system came from the Arabs who used dots in their alphabet to show vowel sounds. So a few years ago, with the idea of dots, the Indians placed dots over the numerals to show a missing place. This is how 450 looked with dots:

$$\overset{..}{4}\overset{.}{5}$$

This is how 406 looked with dots:

$$\overset{..}{4}6$$

Can you figure out the system of dots?

Then the Arabs came up with the idea of a zero. Of course, having a zero makes reading these numbers much easier, and with the invention of zero, the numerals we use became known as Arabic numerals.

The zero, however, was not easily understood, so many people, like yourself, continued to use Roman numerals or a counting board called an abacus. They asked, "What kind of crazy symbol is this, which means nothing at all?" But as the traders and merchants gradually realized that they had an easier system for

Figure 11.2

Algebra

• PERSONIFICATIONS AND INTERACTIONS •

Create Your Own Number Patterns

The great Italian mathematician known as Fibonacci became famous for discovering a number pattern that looks like this:

1, 1, 2, 3, 5, 8, 13, 21, 34, 55, 89, 144, 233, 377, 610 . . . and so forth.

Can you figure out what this pattern is?

Now write a letter to Fibonacci. Follow these steps:

1. Address the letter to Fibonacci. (His original name was Leonardo, son of Bonacci.) Use this address:
   Signore Leonardo di Pisa
   Figlio de G. Bonacci
   Via Fibonacci
   Pisa, Italy
2. Give Fibonacci some information about yourself that includes numbers (your age, street address, grade in school, etc.).
3. Show him a number pattern you know or you have created. You can use the following example or develop your own:

1	2	3	4	5	6	7	8	9
3	5	7	9	11	13	15	17	19
4	7	10	13	16	19	22	25	28

4. Explain how the pattern works.
5. Ask Fibonacci some questions about his work.

Note to Teacher: In this activity, students write back to Fibonacci about number patterns that they have created or learned from another source.

Figure 11.5

Personifications and Interactions for Geometry

For many students, learning geometry means grappling with vocabulary. Learning the definitions for words such as *volume, area, plane, circumference, radius,* and *diameter* is not easy. Often the meaning of such words seems even more obtuse when measurements and calculations are included.

Following are two Personifications and Interactions activities featuring geometric terms. In the first example (Figure 11.6), a rectangle writes to a brick and, in turn, receives a response from the brick. Each describes his or her own vocabulary. In the second activity (Figure 11.7), students are asked to personify a globe and write a monologue

---

Number and Operations

• PERSONIFICATIONS AND INTERACTIONS •

An Arabic Numeral Writing to a Roman Numeral

counting, they saw the importance of this symbol that meant "nothing" but soon meant everything. Now that we understand zero, we can easily add (or subtract, multiply, and divide), which we can't do with Roman numerals. Look at the difference.

$$\text{XX compared with } 20$$
$$\underline{\text{XIII}} \qquad \underline{-13}$$

In the Roman numeral system, you have to do the computation in your head. In the Arabic system, you can regroup. Because zero represents no ones and the 2 represents two tens, you can move one of the tens to the ones place. Now 10 take away 3 equals 7. In the tens the 2 has become 1, so, when I take away 1, I have 0. I hope this explanation is clear.

If you need help in changing over to the Arabic system, please let me know. We have numerous excellent mathematicians, well-versed in their knowledge of numerals and numeration systems, who will be delighted to work with your people. Your children will easily learn this system and will be able to do an infinite number of computations and eventually learn whole areas of mathematics.

Please respond at your convenience, and we look forward to serving your people accurately in every way.

Very sincerely,
Omar Hasim Singh
Chief Mathematician

Figure 11.2

Number and Operations

• PERSONIFICATIONS AND INTERACTIONS •

A Roman Numeral Defends Itself

Imagine that you are a Roman numeral who feels that you are being "pushed out" by Arabic numerals. Write a letter to an Arabic numeral. Be sure to do the following:

1. Make up your address using Roman numerals for the street.
2. Write the Arabic numeral's address with Arabic numbers.
3. Describe which letters represent which numbers.
4. Tell how you can be used for adding and subtracting.
5. Explain how you were used in the past and how you are used today.
6. Tell why you believe you have lasted since the days of the Roman empire.

Note to Teacher: Because Roman numerals are still in use today and are part of our numbering system, students must learn how to read and write them. This activity uses Personification and Interaction to help students learn about Roman numerals.

Use Nova Roma (http://www.novaroma.org/via_romana/numbers.html) to get information to help you write your letter.

Figure 11.3

Personifications and Interactions for Algebra

In Chapter 9, students were introduced to Mathematicians of Magnitude. The goal of the chapter was to help students realize that our knowledge and understanding of mathematics comes from the minds of humans who had curiosity, wonderment, and insight about numbers, patterns, computations, equations, problem solving, and all the other aspects of mathematics. As students become familiar with mathematicians and the world of mathematics, they can follow—in basic or advanced ways—the steps that led mathematicians to great discoveries. Using Personifications and Interactions makes this task creative and lively. Students can begin to sense the curiosity that impelled mathematicians to "play" with mathematics and change the way we see the world.

> For added fun and appreciation, be sure your students read *Math Curse,* in which the character of the teacher is Mrs. Fibonacci (Scieszka & Smith, 1995).

Following are two Personifications and Interactions focusing on the great mathematician of the Middle Ages, Leonardo of Pisa, also know as Fibonacci. In Figure 11.4, the student role-plays Fibonacci and describes Fibonacci's mathematical discoveries about number patterns to today's students. In Figure 11.5, students write back to Fibonacci about other number patterns that they have created or learned from another source.

Algebra

• PERSONIFICATIONS AND INTERACTIONS •

Fibonacci Explains His Patterns

Fibonacci
15th January, 1210

Pisa, Italy

I am writing this letter to students of the future, students who will be living in the twenty-first century or almost a thousand years from now. I have had the good fortune of living in the city of Pisa, Italy, a center of learning, and my father, Signor Bonaccio, has allowed me to travel widely to learn the art of computation. I believe that this art of computation will have a lasting effect upon the world of mathematics. This is why I am writing to those of you who will be living long after I am gone, but maybe not forgotten.

> **Note to Teacher:** In this example, the student role-plays the great mathematician of the Middle Ages, Fibonacci. The mathematician introduces himself and describes his patterns to twenty-first century students.

In addition to having the wisdom of my father, I was introduced in the city of Bugia to magnificent teachers (perhaps Arabs) who showed me the art of computing with the nine Indian numerals—9, 8, 7, 6, 5, 4, 3, 2, 1. These teachers also introduced me to the zero sign (0), which the Arabs called *cephirum.*

I was so excited about learning these numbers that I began to experiment with different computations, which I had not been able to do before. I was especially interested in patterns and began by playing with numbers. I started with the number 1 and added 1 to get 2—that was easy. So I added 1 and 2 to get 3—still easy. So I added 2 and 3 to get 5.

I now wanted to see how the numbers would progress by doing these sequences. This is how it began to look:

1, 1, 2, 3, 5, 8, 13, 21, 34, 55, 89, 144, 233, 377, 610 . . .

I knew I could go on, but the calculations were getting harder. I wished that there could be some magic calculating machine that would do the job for me. Well, maybe one day in the future there would be such a machine. I don't know whether there is any special use for this sequence I discovered, but maybe future students like yourself will find a use.

Because I had so much fun playing with numbers, I would suggest that you do the same. What sequences can you discover or create? Can you do a sequence with multiplication?

Or maybe you can create some geometric patterns? Keep a record of your mathematical play in a journal. Some day, the patterns you create may lead to great ideas and discoveries.

With my best to all of you,
Leonardo, son of Bonaccio
(also known as Fibonacci, from the Italian "Figlio de Bonacci")

Figure 11.4

about themselves to a cube, using three terms in the monologue. You can modify and adapt these models for your own students. First, you might want to read our models "as is." Then discuss with your students what geometric figure they would like to be and which figure they would like to write to. Students can pair up for this activity, write their letters, and then share them with classmates.

Geometry

• PERSONIFICATIONS AND INTERACTIONS •

Plane and Dimension

To: R.U. Brick
6 Mortar Place
Mason, AZ 66666

Dear Ms. Brick:

When we last met, you wanted to know more about me and also what relationship we have to each other. First, we come from a common ancestry—you are always part of me and I am always part of you. The most common thing we share is our right angles (each equaling 90 degrees).

However, there are some significant differences. First, I am a plane figure or polygon. Now don't get confused with the word *plain*, meaning simple or unadorned. The word *plane* that describes me means that I am two-dimensional. As a result of being a plane figure, it is easy to find my area or my surface space.

You will find this area by simply multiplying the vertical edge (let's call it *a*) times the horizontal edge (call it *b*). Write a simple formula: $A = a \times b$. Presto! You have my area.

Let's look at this formula in numbers: $A = 3 \times 4$. The answer is 12, but the question is 12 what? When you do the multiplication, you get 12 equal squares or square units. The units may be centimeters, inches, feet, or whatever units you are using.

I hope this information helps, and I look forward to hearing from you. I have enclosed a picture to help you recognize me.

Sincerely,
Y.B.A. Rectangle

To: Y.B.A. Rectangle
4 Plane Road
Quadrangle, CO 90909

Dear Mr. Rectangle:

I was pleased to learn of our common ancestry and the fact that we both contain right angles. However, we have some significant differences. You are a plane surface. (Yes, I understand the difference between plane and plain.) I am dimensional, in fact three-dimensional. This means that I have six faces (unadorned with eyes, nose, or mouth) and twelve edges.

I have both area and volume. If you were to measure each of my faces, you would use the same formula for measuring yourself: $A = a \times b$. Since I have six faces, and should you want my total area, the formula would be $A = 2ab + 2ac + 2bc$.

However, I also have volume, which means that I take up space. The formula for figuring out my volume is $V = a \times b \times c$ because I am three-dimensional. For example, by converting the formula to numbers, we could have $V = 3 \times 4 \times 2$ or 24. I, too, can be measured in square units similar to you, so in the above example, the answer is 24 units.

I hope I have been clear. I have received your picture and it is very lovely. Enclosed is one of mine that was taken recently. Let's continue this correspondence. In the next letter, let's share how we are used and the places where we can be found.

Kindest regards,
R.U. Brick

Figure 11.6

Geometry

• PERSONIFICATIONS AND INTERACTIONS •

Globe Monologue

Below are the definitions of three terms related to a globe: circumference, radius, and diameter. Read the definitions, imagine that you are a globe, and then write a monologue (personal statement) about yourself. Be sure to explain what these terms mean and to describe what you look like. Imagine that your audience is a cube.

circum·fer·ence, *n.*
1. the outer boundary, esp. of a circular area; perimeter: *the circumference of a circle.*
2. the length of such a boundary: *a one-mile circumference.*
3. the area within a bounding line: *the vast circumference of his mind.*
    Syn. 1. periphery, circuit.

ra·di·us, *n., pl.,* -di·us·es.
1. a straight line extending from the center of a circle or sphere to the circumference or surface: *The radius of a circle is half the diameter.*
2. the length of such a line.
3. any radial or radiating part.
4. a circular area having an extent determined by the length of the radius from a given or specified central point: *every house within a radius of 50 miles.*

di·am·e·ter, *n.*
1. *Geom.*
    a. a straight line passing through the center of a circle or sphere and meeting the circumference or surface at each end.
    b. a straight line passing from side to side of any figure or body, through its center.
2. the length of such a line.
3. the width of a circular or cylindrical object.

Figure 11.7

Personifications and Interactions for Measurement

In the English measuring system, the measurement using the word *foot* comes from the length of the human foot. Even though humans have different-sized feet, this form of measurement has been used for hundreds of years and is still in use in the United States. The hand and parts of the hand are also used for measurement.

Following are two activities featuring foot and hand measurements. In Figure 11.8, a foot and a hand correspond with each other, describing their uses as measurements. The letters illustrate a combination of measurement, research, and writing. You may adapt this activity to your students or ask them to write correspondence between two other units of measurement. These activities will also require research, and the Internet will be a good source. In Figure 11.9, students are asked to measure their feet and hands to learn more about our measurement systems.

Measurement

• PERSONIFICATIONS AND INTERACTIONS •

Correspondence Between a Hand and a Foot

Dr. Footloose B. Foot, Podiatrist
12 Feet Lane
Foot Pedal, AZ 341216

Dr. C.A. Hand, Chiropractor
10 Finger Circle
Palm Acres, CA 510510

Dear Dr. Hand:

You have recently asked me the history of my life related to measurement and I am most happy to respond. I am indeed based on the part of the body known in the Anglo-Saxon languages as the foot. Because people's feet (the plural of foot) are likely to be of different sizes, I have had many different measurements over the years of my existence. For example, in early Roman days, when I was called *ped* or *pes,* I was about 9.8 inches long or 25 centimeters in a modern measuring system. Over time, however, men's feet became longer, so a foot came to be 30 centimeters. This measurement is still used in the Roman measurement system. (Women's feet were not used because, I think, women didn't want to think of themselves as having large feet. That's just my guess.)

Before the metric system was invented, however, the measurement of a foot was also measured in comparison to hands, palms, thumb widths, and finger widths.

>   1 foot = 3 hands or
>   4 palms or
>   12 inches (thumb widths) or
>   16 digits (finger widths)

If we get to meet, we can see whether my foot relates to these hand measurements. My measurement today comes from the English foot rather than the Roman foot, and is about 30.5 centimeters or 1/3 of a yard (another English measurement). I think this was the size of King Henry I's foot. He was King of England from 1100 to 1135 and probably wanted to be remembered for something important.

Just in case you're interested, my name, Foot, is used in many expressions such as swift of foot, foot of the bed, footnote, best foot forward, and many others. I am proud of my contribution to measurement and hope I will not be replaced by the metric system, even though I recognize its greater accuracy.

I hope I haven't gotten off on the wrong foot telling you all this information. Please write back and tell me about yourself.

Your friend,
Footloose B. Foot

Dr. C. A. Hand, Chiropractor
10 Finger Circle
Palm Acres, CA 510510

Dr. Footloose B. Foot, Podiatrist
12 Feet Lane
Foot Pedal, AZ 341216

Dear Dr. Foot:

I too am a measurement although I am used mainly, if not solely, for measuring horses. I do not know whose hands I represent, and I might guess that I, too, got my measurement from King Henry I. After all, if King Henry's foot was equal to 3 hands, it would have to be his hands that were used. On the other hand, while not as famous as you for measuring, parts of my hand have become popular. The inch represents my thumb and 12 of them are equal to your foot. And four of my palms can also equal a foot. The tip of my thumb to the edge of my pinky is a span and is a handy measure of approximation.

Like you, I also am used in many expressions. In fact, in one unabridged dictionary there are at least 80 entries for using me. You may know some of these, such as all hands on deck, lend a hand, eat out of one's hand, hands down, hands up, hands off, and hands full.

Maybe you and I can visit a classroom and suggest some measurement activities using us. Please keep in touch.

With my sincerest handshake,
C. A. Hand

Figure 11.8

Measurement

• PERSONIFICATIONS AND INTERACTIONS •

Measurement: Hands and Feet

In this activity, you will measure your foot and your hand. Follow these instructions:

1. Trace your foot on a centimeter grid.

2. Measure the length of your foot from your middle toe to your heel. The length tells you what your adult shoe size should be.

3. Measure the width of your foot at its widest points. Estimate whether you wear an A (narrow) or EEE (very wide) or something in between.

4. Trace your hand on another centimeter grid. Spread your fingers as far apart as you can when you trace your hand.

5. Measure the length of your hand from your middle finger to your wrist.

6. Measure the width of your hand from the side of your hand to the V point between your pointer finger and your thumb.

7. Measure the span of your hand diagonally from the tip of your pinky finger to the tip of your thumb.

8. To measure the approximate area or space that your foot takes up, count the full centimeter squares first. Then estimate the total of all the pieces or fragments of squares.

9. To measure the approximate area or space that your hand takes up, count the full centimeter squares first. Then estimate the total of all the pieces or fragments of squares.

10. If you wish, compare the measurements of your hand and foot. See if you can discover why you might need three hands to equal one foot.

Figure 11.9

Personifications and Interactions for Data Analysis and Probability

Every student should make (or have) a "hundred chart" for doing quick calculations and also for discovering the many number patterns in this chart.

Following are two activities based on the hundred chart. In Figure 11.10, a Martian describes several patterns she has discovered in the hundred chart. In Figure 11.11, students are asked to answer a Martian's questions about patterns in the hundred chart. You may use this activity as written or adapt it to your students' needs.

Data Analysis and Probability

• PERSONIFICATIONS AND INTERACTIONS •

A Martian Discovers the Hundred Chart

1	2	3	4	5	6	7	8	9	10
11	12	13	14	15	16	17	18	19	20
21	22	23	24	25	26	27	28	29	30
31	32	33	34	35	36	37	38	39	40
41	42	43	44	45	46	47	48	49	50
51	52	53	54	55	56	57	58	59	60
61	62	63	64	65	66	67	68	69	70
71	72	73	74	75	76	77	78	79	80
81	82	83	84	85	86	87	88	89	90
91	92	93	94	95	96	97	98	99	100

Dear Earthlings:

You are truly amazing mathematicians. I just received your hundred chart via rocket ship, and I have been studying it for weeks, searching out its numerous patterns. I would like to tell you the patterns I have noticed and would appreciate your writing back to me with others that you on Earth can see because of your experience.

First, I notice the obvious. The horizontal numbers increase by ones, but the vertical numbers increase by tens. Yet there is a difference in each vertical column, so that the first column goes from 1 to 91, but the last column goes from 10 to 100. How fascinating!

In addition, I discovered that there is a diagonal system. If I start with 1 and move diagonally, each number increases by 11. On the other hand, if I start with number 10 on the opposite side and go diagonally, each number increases by 9. How did you manage to do that?

Then I also realized that I could count by 11's and go all the way to 99. I also saw that I could do the 9 times table and go to 81. If I ever have to memorize the 11 and 9 times tables, I can just check my answers by using the hundred chart.

This chart is a brilliant invention, and when I come to visit you on Earth, I hope you will show me some of your other mathematical inventions. In the meantime, please write to me and tell me whether there are any patterns I missed on the hundred chart.

With my thanks,

Figure 11.10

Data Analysis and Probability

• PERSONIFICATIONS AND INTERACTIONS •

E-Mail to a Martian About the Hundred Chart

1	2	3	4	5	6	7	8	9	10
11	12	13	14	15	16	17	18	19	20
21	22	23	24	25	26	27	28	29	30
31	32	33	34	35	36	37	38	39	40
41	42	43	44	45	46	47	48	49	50
51	52	53	54	55	56	57	58	59	60
61	62	63	64	65	66	67	68	69	70
71	72	73	74	75	76	77	78	79	80
81	82	83	84	85	86	87	88	89	90
91	92	93	94	95	96	97	98	99	100

A Martian has been studying the hundred chart for a while and has been trying to figure out how it works. In an e-mail from Mars to Earth, the Martian has sent the following questions to an Earthling:

1. Why do all the columns on the left side have the number 1?
2. Why do all the columns on the right side have a 0?
3. Why do the numbers that go diagonally from 1 to 100 increase by 11?
4. Why do the numbers that go diagonally from 10 to 91 increase by 9?

Send an e-mail to the Martian answering the Martian's questions. Ask the Martian three questions about mathematics on Mars.

Figure 11.11

INTERNET LINKS

Fibonacci

http://www.mcs.surrey.ac.uk/Personal/R.Knott/Fibonacci/fib.html

Origins of Measurements

http://www.iofm.net/community/kidscorner/maths/origin.htm

Roman Numerals

http:// www.novaroma.org/via_romana/numbers.html

Mathematically Literate

Knowing, Applying, and Communicating Mathematics

It's fine to get the right answer, but what good is that answer if you can't explain it to anyone?

—*Writing to Learn Mathematics* (Countryman, 1992, p. 2)

Quite possibly, the most central, least replaceable feature of the mathematician's gift is the ability to handle skillfully long chains of reasoning. (Gardner, 1983, p. 139)

All reasoning begins somewhere and ends somewhere else. (Van Tassel-Baska, 1996, p. 363)

Thinking with what you learn is one of the goals of education. (Perkins, 1992, p. 28)

If you can't compute accurately, explain your ideas, discover solutions, and apply math in the real world, you don't know math. (Strong et al., 2001, p. 79)

We are concluding this book by restating the communication standard of the National Council of Teachers of Mathematics (NCTM, 2000, p. 402) and then recapitulating the 10 strategies of this book (illustrated in Figure 12.1) using the topic of "zero" as the centerpiece of learning. Under each standard we have listed the strategies that are most likely to target that standard, although all the strategies are interrelated and bring the best results when used regularly and cohesively.

Instructional programs from prekindergarten through Grade 12 should enable all students to

- *organize and consolidate their mathematical thinking through communication;*

  Metacognition; Profiles and Frames; Reasons, Procedures, Results; Personifications and Interactions

- *communicate their mathematical thinking coherently and clearly to peers, teachers, and others;*

  Defining Format; Reasons, Procedures, Results; Personifications and Interactions; Metacognition

- *communicate and evaluate the mathematical thinking and strategies of others;*

  Who's Who; Reasons, Procedures, Results; Personifications and Interactions

- *use the language of mathematics to express ideas precisely.*

  Taxonomies; Defining Format; Morphology and Etymology; Where in the World; Profiles and Frames

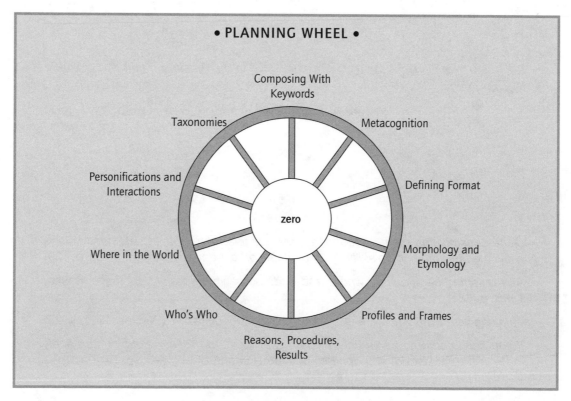

Figure 12.1

Imagine that your students already know that the numbers one to nine exist and can be used for counting. Your students also recognize the symbols 1, 2, 3, 4, 5, 6, 7, 8, 9 and can match objects to these symbols. Your focus now (and all mathematics teachers' focus henceforth) is explaining the unique number called zero. Zero is the number that is no number, yet without which we cannot have a viable number system. As stated by Wells, zero is "a mysterious number, which started life as a space on a counting board, turned into a written notice that a space was present, . . . then confused medieval mathematicians who could not decide whether it was really a number or not" (Wells, 1995, pp. 6–7).

We have chosen to use zero as the centerpiece of uniting the writing strategies with mathematics because zero is so mysterious, yet it enters students' lives the moment they encounter the numeral 10. The numeral 10 is a combination of two symbols that looks to be less than 9, yet it is not. In fact, understanding 10 requires students to know about place value, regrouping, multiplying and dividing by zero, positive and negative numbers, infinity, and all the other nearly unexplainable mathematical ideas. Seife (2000), in his brilliant (and humorous) book, *Zero*, explains that zero is an "innocent-looking number" that rattled "even this century's brightest minds . . . threatening to unravel the whole framework of scientific thought" (p. 12). He quotes the great mathematician Danzig: "In the history of culture the discovery of zero will always stand out as one of the greatest single achievements of the human race" (cited in Seife, 2000, p. 12).

> Charles Seife's book *Zero* (2000) includes a complete history of this amazing number.

So we use zero as our centerpiece as we review each of the 10 writing strategies outlined in this book to show how students can use writing activities to build in-depth knowledge about a concept or topic. Adapt this model to teach the mathematics content that is appropriate for your curriculum and grade level.

TAXONOMIES

Zero underlies the whole basis of our counting system as well as the understanding of all modern mathematics (Seife, 2000). Therefore, it is important to begin your teaching about zero by assessing students' prior knowledge of this amazing number. Begin with a Taxonomy and ask students to supply words that they associate with the word *zero* (Figure 12.2). Students' responses will depend upon their grade level and previous curriculum coverage of the topic.

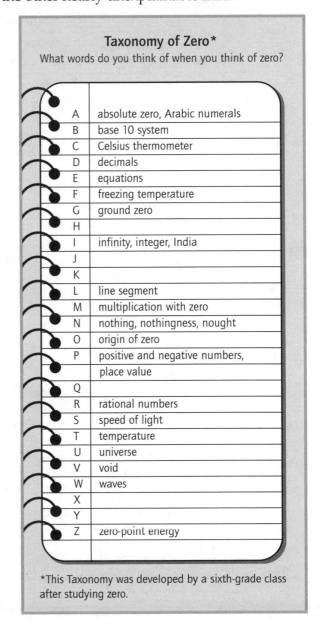

Taxonomy of Zero*
What words do you think of when you think of zero?

A	absolute zero, Arabic numerals
B	base 10 system
C	Celsius thermometer
D	decimals
E	equations
F	freezing temperature
G	ground zero
H	
I	infinity, integer, India
J	
K	
L	line segment
M	multiplication with zero
N	nothing, nothingness, nought
O	origin of zero
P	positive and negative numbers, place value
Q	
R	rational numbers
S	speed of light
T	temperature
U	universe
V	void
W	waves
X	
Y	
Z	zero-point energy

*This Taxonomy was developed by a sixth-grade class after studying zero.

Figure 12.2

COMPOSING WITH KEYWORDS

Using the words on the Taxonomy as a foundation of knowledge about zero, encourage students to take the next step—Composing With Keywords. This strategy requires students to select three words from the Taxonomy and compose one sentence mathematically relating the words. Figure 12.3 includes examples of sentences using words that can communicate ideas about zero.

• COMPOSING WITH KEYWORDS FOR ZERO •

Words	Sentence
Celsius, zero, freezing	A Celsius thermometer uses zero degrees as the freezing point compared to a Fahrenheit thermometer, which uses 32 degrees for freezing.
positive and negative numbers, zero	To show positive and negative numbers on a number line, we need zero as the divider between −1 and +1.
base 10 system, place value, integer	Zero is an integer that allows us to have a base 10 system for counting and is the integer that allows us to have place value. Without zero we would have to count with stones or an abacus.

Figure 12.3

METACOGNITION

Metacognition statements allow students to expand upon their existing and growing knowledge and focus on the topic they are studying. Students practice telling what they know about the subject, using the Metacognition template, as in Figure 12.4.

• METACOGNITION •

Metacognition Statements About Zero

I know that I now know many things about zero. *First, I know* that in space travel we count backwards from ten, nine, eight, seven, six, five, four, three, two, one, and wait for zero for the blast-off. *I also know* that when something very important happens it's called the zero hour, making what happened very important. *Finally, I know* that the place where a bomb goes off is called ground zero, like in the World Trade Center. So zero is a very important word in my vocabulary.

I know that sometimes I don't understand zero. I have to think hard why multiplying with zero always gives me zero. It seems that if I have three and multiply it with zero I should still have three. But then I know I have to remember that I am multiplying zero three times. I am not multiplying the number three. The teacher said that zero is a mysterious number and she's right.

Figure 12.4

DEFINING FORMAT

When students begin to define the term *zero,* they have to think deeply about a concept that eluded humans from the beginning of counting. As Seife (2000) points out, the Egyptians, the Greeks, and the Romans did not have zero, yet today we assume that all children can readily grasp this elusive number. Figure 12.5 is an example of a definition of zero based on a fourth-grade class collaboration. As you will notice, students can continue to add more concepts about zero as they discover them.

• DEFINING FORMAT FOR ZERO •

Question	Category	Characteristics
What is zero?		
Zero is a	number that	1. can mean there is nothing. 2. comes before one. 3. is used to show the sum of 9 + 1 is 10. 4. holds the place, like in 100, which means there are no ones and no tens, but just one hundred. 5. is even. 6. can go on to infinity like 1,000,000,000,000,000 . . . 7. always stays zero when multiplied or divided. 8. helps us to add and subtract in our heads instead of counting with stones or on an abacus.

Figure 12.5

MORPHOLOGY AND ETYMOLOGY

Throughout this book, you have discovered that students can better understand mathematical words if they know the morphology (formations) and etymology (origins) of those words. For your information and for your students' research, we include a Taxonomy of Mathematical Terms With Fascinating Etymologies (Figure 12.6). The Taxonomy contains words that we have discussed in this book as well as other words that can be used for further study. All of the words in the Taxonomy are linked to the concept of zero. We believe your students will enjoy learning the stories of these words and hope that these vocabulary activities will enrich your students' understanding of mathematics.

Taxonomy of Mathematical Terms With Fascinating Etymologies

A	abacus, algebra, algorithm, arithmetic
B	
C	Celsius, cipher, calculate
D	digit
E	eight
F	fraction, four, five
G	geometry
H	harmonic
I	integer
J	
K	Kelvin
L	logarithm
M	mathematics, measurement
N	number, nine
O	one
P	
Q	quantum
R	radius
S	six, seven
T	two, three, ten
U	
V	volts
W	watts
X	
Y	
Z	zero

Figure 12.6

PROFILES AND FRAMES

As students continue to learn about zero, they should collaborate to develop their own Profiles and Frames to explain zero to others. The Profile is an organizing outline for placing information taken from text or research. The Frame is a syntactic outline that provides the student with the sentence structure for placing information. Use the examples in Figures 12.7 and 12.8 as starters. Modify or expand the examples to meet your students' needs.

• PROFILE •

Profile of Zero

Instructions: Complete this Profile and write your discoveries about zero.

$0 + 0 =$

$1 + 0 =$

$0 - 0 =$

$1 - 0 =$

$0 - 1 =$

$2 \times 0 =$

$0 = 2x$

$2 + 0 =$

$0 + 2 =$

$2 + 0 =$

$(1 - 1) + (1 - 1) + (1 - 1) + (1 - 1) + \ldots =$

$\frac{1}{2} + \frac{1}{3} + \frac{1}{4} + \frac{1}{5} + \frac{1}{6} \ldots$ eventually equals:

1 million zeros plus 1 million zeros =

Time a stopwatch starts ticking:

Freezing point on a Celsius thermometer:

The first hour of the day starts at _____ seconds.

Before a baby is one year old, the baby is _____ year(s) old.

Figure 12.7

• FRAME •

Frame for Zero

Instructions: Complete this Frame for a better understanding of zero and how we count our birthdays and years.

A child is born in the first second of the first day of the year: January 1, in the year 1 A.D. (or C.E.). In the year 2, the child is _____ year old. In the year 3 the child is _____ years old. In the year 4 the child is _____ years old, and so forth. In the year 100, the child (now grown into old age) is _____ years old. On January 1, 101 this older person celebrates (his/her) _____ birthday. This birthday on January 1, 101 is also the beginning of the _____ century.

Now you realize that because of zero, the twenty-first century began with the year _____.

Adapted from Seife (2000, p. 57).

Figure 12.8

REASONS, PROCEDURES, RESULTS

After students have completed Profiles and Frames, they are ready to move on to using the Reasons, Procedures, Results strategy. This strategy encourages students to write personal, persuasive, and explanatory essays. Figure 12.9 gives an example of an explanatory essay. You can also have your students write a personal essay such as "There Are Three Ways That I Use Zero," or a persuasive essay such as "There Are Three Reasons Why We Need to Study the History of Zero."

• EXPLANATORY ESSAY •

Reasons, Procedures, Results for Zero

A visiting Martian was told that he can only subtract a smaller number from a larger number. However, when the Martian visited a classroom, he noticed this equation on the chalkboard: $5 + (-9) = 5 - 9$. The Martian was puzzled and asked an Earthling to explain the equation. Write an explanation that the Earthling could give to the Martian. Follow these instructions:

1. Draw a horizontal line that has room for 19 numbers.

2. Place 0 in the center of the line.

3. Write the numerals 1 to 9 to the right of the zero. Evenly space the numbers on the line.

4. Write −1 immediately to the left of the zero. Continue numbering to the left: −2, −3, etc., until you reach −9. (See example below.)

   −9 −8 −7 −6 −5 −4 −3 −2 −1 0 1 2 3 4 5 6 7 8 9

5. Begin writing your explanation of the equation: $5 + (-9) = 5 - 9$. Use the following Frame.

   Follow along with me and you will understand this equation.

   First, start with zero and move _____ numbers. You will be at number _____.

   Then move _____ steps to the left. You will be at number _____.

   Third, ask the Martian to tell you the answer, which is _____.

6. If the Martian doesn't understand, tell the Martian to move nine steps to the left, then five steps to the right. Explain why you could get the same answer both ways.

7. Suppose that the Martian asks why you needed zero to get the answer. Write an explanation about why you needed zero.

Figure 12.9

WHO'S WHO

The story of zero begins with Babylonians around 300 B.C.E. Zero was brought into India through the invasions of Alexander the Great. It remained unknown or unaccepted by the Greeks and Romans. Then Arab traders brought it into the Western world from India. The history of zero is fascinating and makes for excellent student research projects. Ask your students to select any of the names from the Taxonomy of Mathematicians and write a brief report of their chosen mathematician's role in the history of zero (see Figure 12.10).

• TAXONOMY •

Mathematicians Who Contributed to the Concept of Zero

Who's Who in the History of Zero*

Instructions: Choose one mathematician from the Taxonomy of Mathematicians. Do some research about the mathematician and then write a brief report about his or her role in history of zero.

	Mathematicians	Nationality or Place of Origin
A	Al-Khwarizmi	Baghdad (Iraq)
	Antoine de l'Hôpital	French
B	Brunelleschi	Italian
	Bernouli	Swiss
	Berkeley	Irish
C	Copernicus	Polish
	Cavalieri	Italian
	Cantor	Russian
	Casimir	Dutch
	Chandrasekhar	Indian
D	Descartes	French
	D'Alembert	French
E	Einstein	German/American
F	Fibonacci	Italian
	Feynman	American
G	Galileo	Italian
	Gauss	German
	Geller	German/American

Figure 12.10

(Continued on page 236)

• TAXONOMY •

Mathematicians Who Contributed to the Concept of Zero

	Mathematicians	Nationality or Place of Origin
H	Heisenberg	German
	Hubble	American
K	Kepler	German
	Kronecker	German
	Kelvin	English
L	Leibniz	German
M	Maimonides	Jewish (Spain)
	Maclaurin	English
	Michelson	American
	Morley	American
	Millis	American
N	Nicholas of Cusa	Italian
	Newton	English
O	Oresme	French
P	Pascal	French
	Planck	German
	Polder	Dutch
	Pauli	German
	Puthoff	American
Q		
R	Riemann	German
S		
T	Tempier	French
	Taylor	English
	U V W X Y Z	

*Names in this Taxonomy are adapted from Seife, 2000. This Taxonomy does not include the countless African American, Arab, Asian, and women mathematicians who have contributed to our mathematical knowledge. For a more complete listing of mathematicians, see Chapter 9.

Figure 12.10 *(Continued from page 235)*

WHERE IN THE WORLD

All peoples have experienced the need to count or keep track of amounts. This need arose at the dawn of humanity. Humans have always asked, How many? How much? How big? How small? How much more? How much less? Humans began counting and calculating by using stones and tally sticks. (The word *calculus* comes from the Latin term for stone or pebble.) Later humans used the abacus, and today we have calculators and computers to count, calculate, and tally.

Teachers are often under serious time constraints to teach calculation and its related ideas. Finding time to teach the history and geography of calculation can be difficult. Yet the history and geography of mathematics is important and can be of great interest to students. We offer Figure 12.11 as a small sample that can lead students to further exploration and understanding.

PERSONIFICATIONS AND INTERACTIONS

For this strategy, ask students to imagine themselves to be the number zero. Tell students to write a letter to one of the other numbers explaining (or boasting) about zero's history and importance in the world of mathematics. Figure 12.12 is a sample letter that you can use as a model for your students.

ᴇMATICS

• WHERE IN THE WORLD •

Follow the Geographic Path of Zero

ıde your students with a map of trade routes used during Medieval times. (You may download
s from A Medieval Atlas at http://historymedren.about.com/library/weekly/aa071000a.htm.)

2. Ask students to locate these geographic names: Europe, Africa, Arabia, and India. Tell them to also
   locate Rome (in modern Italy), Lyons (in modern France), and Cologne (in modern Germany).

3. Notice the languages and the region where the language was used in relation to the history of zero.

Language	Region
Sanskrit	India
Arabic	Arabia
Latin*	Rome
French	Lyons
German	Cologne

   *Although Latin was no longer spoken in the Middle Ages, it was used for scholarly writing.

4. Present the following tree to the students. (The tree is adapted from Seife, 2000, p. 401.)

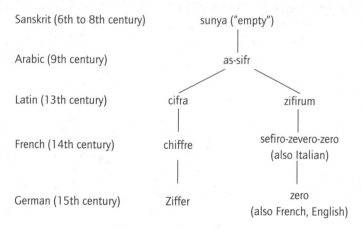

5. Ask the students this question: How do you think the word *zero* and the idea of zero traveled from
   India to Europe? Tell students to use the map and the tree to help them make their speculations.
   List students' ideas on a large chart.

6. Have students check their speculations by searching the Internet.

Figure 12.11

• PERSONIFICATIONS AND INTERACTIONS •

A Number Boasting About Zero

Cipher B. Zero, PhD
000 Naught Circle
New Delhi, India
Phone: 000-000-0000
e-mail: zero@placevalue.com

1/0/2020
Dr. Twyla R. Two
222 Twilight Lane
Twin Falls, TN 222222

Dear Dr. Two:

Your letter was hand delivered to me yesterday at 0:00:00 o'clock, and as a fast reader, I had read it by 0:01:00, or, as we say, in barely a split second. I will attempt to answer two of your most important questions out of the 20 you asked me.

In your second question, you asked why I took so long to be accepted when you had already achieved success for hundreds of years before me. It's at least a two-hour story, but I'll tell it to you briefly here, and then we can continue to correspond. Around 400 C.E., our Indian mathematicians realized that the Greek system of numbering was good enough for studying geometry (which the Greeks, as you know, loved). However, we Indians were merchants and traders and needed a better system. Some of our well-traveled mathematicians were familiar with Babylonian counting. The Babylonians had already invented a wonderful device that you call an abacus. The abacus helped them understand that after counting from 1 to 9 they needed to move to another "place," and they made a symbol called a *wedge* to hold that place. The symbol looked like this: ◁

The Indian mathematicians moved to the next idea, called place value. First, the wedge was replaced with a dot and then the dot was enlarged to a circle.

Another question you asked was how the idea of zero traveled to Europe and, of course, America. That is a very long story—more than two hours I am sure. But to sum it up, around the years 800 to 900 C.E. Arab traders came to India for our beautiful silks and spices and noticed that our merchants were great calculators because they had zero. The Arabs were impressed with the power of zero and adopted it for themselves. Their numbers soon looked liked this:

(Menninger, 1969, p. 418)

When they traveled west back home, they traded with Europeans who began to realize that their Roman numerals were rather clumsy and not good for adding and subtracting, never mind multiplying and dividing. So after a lot of discussion and even fights among themselves, the Europeans took the "Arabic" number (which should be called an "Indian" number) and put it at the beginning of their number symbols. Many years later, zero would be put at the end on the telephone and the computer. But that's a different story.

I hope you have enough information from my answers to these two questions to move ahead and do your own research. However, if you have any difficulty, please write or e-mail me.

Sincerely,
Cipher B. Zero

Figure 12.12

INTERNET LINKS

Ask Dr. Math About Zero

http://mathforum.org/library/drmath/sets/select/dm_about_zero.html
http://forum.swarthmore.edu/dr.math/

Medieval Atlas

http://historymedren.about.com/library/weekly/aa071000a.htm

Resource A

Rubrics for Writing for Mathematics

With the emphasis on combining writing with mathematics, teachers are likely to feel a "double load." Many have asked us, "How am I supposed to grade the writing when my focus is on the mathematics?" The question is fair and certainly important and we hope our suggestions below can provide guidance for you and fairness to the students.

We recognize, first, that your major goal is for your students to "know" the mathematics you are teaching them. To assess the mathematical knowledge, we refer you to the Table of Standards and Expectations in the NCTM publication *Principles and Standards* (NCTM, 2000, pp. 392–401). There are also numerous Web sites with rubrics based on NCTM standards, two of which are http://www.exemplars.com and http://math.about.com, which follow the NCTM guidelines as well as guidelines from the various states. The Oregon Department of Education (among other state departments) offers a specific rubric for communication which states, "in assessing the student's ability to communicate, particular attention should be paid to both the meanings he/she attaches to the concepts and procedures and also to his/her fluency in explaining, understanding, and evaluating the ideas expressed" (see "Overview of the Mathematics Assessment" at http://www.ode.state.or.us/search/results/?id=239).

However, because this book emphasizes writing for mathematics using specific strategies, we have created rubrics that relate to the relationship of each writing strategy to the mathematical concepts that a student is learning or practicing. These writing strategies are Taxonomies; Composing With Keywords; Metacognition; Defining Format; Morphology and Etymology; Profiles and Frames; Reasons, Procedures, Results; Who's Who in Mathematics; Where in the World; and Personifications and Interactions. Also included is a rubric for "writing conventions," which means that the students

- communicate their thinking effectively to their audience,
- use details that fit the concept or problem,
- use transitions so that one step flows to the next and shows organization, and
- add strong supporting arguments in their presentation.

In addition, we would like the students to use clear sentence structure, capitals and punctuation, and spelling to allow the reader to recognize the mathematical terms. We strongly believe that if students are taught writing strategies for mathematics (and other subjects), they have a much better chance of meeting the above rubrics of good writing.

We have used a scale from 1 to 4, but you may want to use words such as distinguished, proficient, apprentice, or novice (or synonyms), which many schools have adopted. In addition to the rubrics related to the strategies, we have also included assessments from *Writing as Learning* (Rothstein & Lauber, 2000) you may find helpful in guiding your students to becoming expert writers (as well as mathematicians), which means they show "a deep understanding of the problem by writing a clear effective explanation . . . so that the reader does not need to infer how and why decisions were made" (Exemplars, 2004).

RUBRICS FOR WRITE FOR MATHEMATICS STRATEGIES

Strategy	4 (high)	3	2	1
Taxonomies	Consistently keeps track of mathematical terms in notebook; refers to them frequently and accurately in writing and use.	Maintains mathematical terms in notebook with occasional lapses; refers to them sporadically with some accuracy in writing and use.	Needs prodding to maintain in notebook; may use the terms from time to time in writing and use, with occasional inaccuracies of meaning.	Rarely enters terms; shows little reference to them in writing and use.
Composing With Keywords	Creates mathematically accurate sentences using selected mathematical terms and includes appropriate illustrations and diagrams related to the sentence(s).	Creates mathematical sentences with some relationship of selected terms and nearly accurate or complete illustrations or diagrams.	Creates sentences using the targeted words but shows little mathematical relationship of the words to each other.	Omits one or two of the targeted words and/or has little sense of mathematical relationship.
Metacognition	Follows Metacognition template; includes three significant, accurate pieces of information on a mathematical topic, concept, theorem, etc.; adds several supporting details to each stated piece of information.	Follows template; includes three pieces of information, with possible overlap or redundancy; adds limited amount of details as support.	Follows template, but information is insignificant or redundant; few or no details.	Barely follows template with little mathematical information or details.
Defining Format	Writes appropriate category; lists five or more significant characteristics; gives examples or details; can write detailed dialogue on mathematical topic or problem.	Writes appropriate category; lists fewer than five characteristics; provides few examples or details; writes simple dialogue on topic or problem with some details.	Writes vague or general category; gives one or two characteristics with few details; writes bare dialogue with little mathematical information.	Omits category; gives one or two characteristics; limited dialogue.

Strategy	4 (high)	3	2	1
Morphology and Etymology	Organizer specific mathematical terms and places them correctly in the morphology template; researches mathematical terms and provides historic details related to current mathematics.	Finds limited number of mathematical terms; some inaccuracies in placement in template; provides small number of historic details with limited relationship to current mathematics.	Finds few expansions of terms with limited historic and mathematical relationship.	Shows limited knowledge of morphological extensions; finds few historic relationships.
Profiles and Frames	Researches and completes mathematical information for a Profile; completes frame with accuracy and details.	Completes most of information; completes frame with accuracy, but misses details.	Shows limited information in Profile; puts limited information in Frame.	Very little information in both Profile and Frame.
Reasons, Procedures, Results	Writes detailed reasons, procedures, or results following the template requiring three paragraphs with accurate supporting information; writes opening statement and conclusion.	Follows the template but puts in limited, but accurate, details; has opening and closing.	Writes fewer than three reasons, procedures, or results. Misses opening and/or closing.	Doesn't follow the template; has inaccuracies.
Who's Who	Writes an opening sentence or statement that focuses on the significant contribution of the mathematician; provides three major ideas of the mathematician; illustrates in simplified form one of the ideas or states how this idea added to our knowledge of mathematics.	Writes opening statement but has fewer than three ideas; shows limited details in illustration or in contribution of mathematician to mathematics.	Shows limited use of template for opening statement and little detail related to accomplishment.	Shows very limited information beyond name and statement of accomplishment.
Where in the World	Completes Profiles and Frames related to geography and mathematics with many details; creates an explanation of the relationship by incorporating the mathematical information into text; uses transitions to move from one idea to the next.	Uses limited details and text; uses some, but not all, of the transitions from the Profiles.	Very limited use of mathematics and geographic details in connected text; limited use of transitions.	Barely any connected text or transitions.
Personifications and Interactions	Sets up letter-style format with addresses that show mathematical and historic knowledge of the "correspondents"; writes a detailed informative letter indicating significant knowledge of the mathematical topic or proof.	Sets up letter-style format with addresses that show some mathematical knowledge of "correspondents"; writes informative letter with small amount of mathematical knowledge related to the topics.	Is missing some of the letter-style information and shows limited knowledge of topic.	Is missing most of the letter-style format and has very little mathematical information in the letter.

RUBRICS FOR ASSESSING WRITING GENERICALLY AND FOR MATHEMATICS

The following rubrics have been adapted from *Writing as Learning* (Rothstein & Lauber, 2000) and offer teachers and students a simple, yet clear, way to assess writing that focuses on a specific subject area (e.g., mathematics). We suggest that you review these rubrics with your students before they begin to write and then after they have written. Taking this extra time on "what is good writing" will provide a guide to your students concerning your expectations and will let you "grade" your students objectively and fairly.

Begin with making your students aware of the "Rubrics of Good Writing." Post them on the wall and have the students copy them into their mathematics notebooks. (Be sure they enter this topic into the Table of Contents for easy retrieval.)

Rubrics of Good Writing

- Think of your audience and write to that audience (e.g., teacher, friend, younger student).
- Keep to the topic throughout the whole piece.
- Organize ideas in sequence (e.g., First, After that, Finally) so that the reader can follow your ideas.
- Give the reader details or information so that the reader can visualize or understand what you are saying.
- Illustrate (draw) your ideas and label as much as you can.
- Remember to use capitalization and punctuation and spell the words as correctly as possible so that the reader understands them.
- Write in the best English you know, which means writing sentences that "sound" like the sentences in your school books.

Making Good Writing Better

The first writing on any topic is always a draft. Students must understand this idea so that they develop the habit of rereading their writing. However, rereading is not enough if the students do not know why they are rereading. Therefore, we urge that you tell your students about the following four improvers of writing, and have them practice using them in as many pieces of writing as possible. Again, post these "improvers," have your students enter them in their notebooks, and guide your students through practicing them. The time and effort spent on this activity will pay off in better writing and communication, not only in mathematics but in every subject area that requires writing.

The Four Improvers of Writing

You can make your writing better by knowing and following these editing procedures after you have written your piece.

As you read over your first draft, whether it is written by hand or on the computer, ask yourself these questions and make the changes that are needed. If you are not writing for a test, you can ask a classmate or friend to read your writing as you ask them to think of the same questions.

1. Is there any information I need to **ADD** so that my reader knows what I know? Is there any punctuation I need to **ADD**?

2. Are there any words I need to **SUBSTITUTE** with more accurate words or with words that will make my writing clearer to my reader? Is there any punctuation I need to **SUBSTITUTE** (e.g., a period instead of a comma)?

3. Are there any words I need to **DELETE** or take away because I have repeated them too many times or they don't help my reader understand what I want to say? Is there any punctuation I need to **DELETE** (e.g., a comma that is not needed)?

4. Do I need to **MOVE** or **REARRANGE** any sentences or paragraphs so that my reader can follow what I am writing? Is there any punctuation I need to **MOVE** (e.g., a comma in the wrong place)?

Checklist for Evaluating Writing

The checklist below is a rubric for evaluating writing. We have ranked the assessment scale from high to low so that the writing is seen from a "positive" perspective, or what we call V.G. (very good). When the first draft is already *very good*, improvements will make the writing excellent. A good plan is to give the students a copy of this evaluation form so they understand the rubric and have them evaluate one of their own written pieces. This activity will provide them with insight about their writing. You can also use this form for peer editing and, of course, as a guide for your evaluations.

Rubric for Evaluating My Writing

Scores: 4 (high) 3, 2, 1 (low)

Name _____

Title or Subject of Writing _____

Date _____

RUBRIC	4	3	2	1
Wrote on the topic				
Organized so the reader can follow				
Used topic sentence(s)				
Added support sentences				
Included important details				
Used illustrations or examples				
Had a variety of words or terms				
Contained several ideas on the topic				
Used capital letters where needed				
Used punctuation where needed				
Spelled carefully				
Other comments				

Resource B

Reproducible Templates for Students

Below are templates related to specific strategies that you may wish to duplicate and use with your students. While we strongly suggest that your students create these templates in their notebooks, we realize that there are times you may want to have them separately so that you can post them or have your students hand them in (completed) for evaluation.

Taxonomy

Name: _____

Topic: _____

A	
B	
C	
D	
E	
F	
G	
H	
I	
J	
K	
L	
M	
N	
O	
P	
Q	
R	
S	
T	
U	
V	
W	
X	
Y	
Z	

Name: _____

Topic: _____

Metacognition for Stating Knowledge

I know that I know *something* about _____

First, _____

In addition, _____

Finally, _____

Now, you know something that I know about _____

Name: _____

Topic: _____

Metacognition for Knowing How

I know that I know *how to* _____

First, I _____

After that, _____

Then, _____

Finally, _____

When I have completed these steps, I have shown or proved that I _____

Name: _____

Topic: _____

Metacognition for Knowing Why

I know why _____

One reason is _____

A second reason is _____

Last, _____

For these three reasons, I know why _____

Name: _____

Topic: _____

Metacognition for Knowing Steps and Procedures

I know several ways to (use, represent, solve) _____

I begin _____

I then _____

After that, _____

FInally, _____

By doing these steps or procedures, _____

Name: _____

Topic: _____

Metacognition for Solving a Problem

I read the problem and this is what I know: _____

This is what I don't know: _____

This is what I need to know: _____

Here is how I solved the problem: _____

For these three reasons, I know why _____

- _____

- _____

- _____

Name: _____

Topic: _____

Defining Format

QUESTION	CATEGORY	CHARACTERISTICS
		(1)
		(2)
		(3)
		(4)
		(5)

Name: _____

Topic: _____

Morphology

Include all words related morphologically.

NOUN *(include plural when applicable; include all related nouns)*	VERB *(4 forms— base, -s, -ing, past)*	ADJECTIVE	-ly ADVERB
	(1)		
	(2)		
	(3)		
	(4)		
	Add any other related verbs. Show all four forms.		

Profiles and Frames

We have included several representative Profiles and Frames as models. In many cases, you will have to create your own because of the specific mathematics you are teaching. We hope, however, that these models can be a good starting point for your students.

Name: _____

Topic: _____

Profile of a Number

Fill in as much information on the Profile as you know or can understand. You can put D/K if you don't know. Then write a story or article about the number you have selected including as much information as you have. Be sure to follow the organization of the Profile. You can also use this Profile to write about other numbers.

Select any number from 1 to 9: _____

Tell if the number is odd or even: _____

Write the word for the cardinal name: _____

Write the word for the ordinal name: _____

Write the Roman numeral: _____

Add a zero to the number: _____ Write this number in words: _____

Add two zeros to the number: _____ Write it in words: _____

Write the number with six zeros added: _____

Write this number in words: _____

Write if this number is prime or composite: _____

What are the factors of this number? _____

Use this number in a fraction: _____

Write the fraction as a decimal: _____

Does this number have a square root that is a whole number? _____

If yes, what is the number? _____

What is the negative of this number? _____

Add the negative of this number to any positive number: _____

What is the answer: _____

Write the negative of your number again: _____.

Add it to another negative number: _____ What is the answer? _____

Is there any geometric figure associated with your number? _____

If yes, what is the figure? _____

Is there any other information on your number that you can add to your Profile?

Name: _____

Topic: _____

Profile of a Polygon

An excellent way to learn about polygons is to observe them and write about their characteristics. Complete the Profile to deepen your understanding about a polygon. You can use any reference you need (dictionary, encyclopedia, Internet) to get the information. You may wish to cite your source(s). Write D/K if you don't know the information and ask someone to help you get it. Then write a description of this polygon to someone who may need to know about it, but doesn't have all the information you have.

Name of polygon: _____

Number of sides: _____ Number of angles: _____

Number of degrees in each angle: _____ Total number of degrees: _____

Points at which angles meet are called: _____

Formula or procedure for finding the perimeter: _____

Formula or procedure for finding the area: _____

Places and/or objects where you see this polygon: _____

_____

Origin of the name of the polygon: _____

Illustrate this polygon:

Name: _____

Topic: _____

Profile of a Coin

There are six types of United States coins: penny, nickel, dime, quarter, half dollar, and dollar. Each coin is made of metal and has a different value. There is also a lot of information on a coin. Complete the Profile and then write a letter to someone in another country describing the coin you have "profiled." You can get some of this information from the Internet.

Coin: _____

Value of coin in cents: _____

Metal used for coin: _____

Number needed to equal one dollar: _____

Number needed to equal ten dollars: _____

Number needed to equal one hundred dollars: _____

Year coin was minted: _____

Person represented on the coin: _____

Other symbols on the coin: _____

Words or phrases written on the face and reverse side and their meaning:

word(s) _____ meaning _____

word(s) _____ meaning _____

word(s) _____ meaning _____

(add others)

Other Information:

_____

_____

Name: _____

Topic: _____

Profile of a Mathematician

Read about a mathematician of accomplishment and complete the Profile. Then meet with a classmate and compare the mathematician you have researched with the one your classmate has written about. You might suggest to your teacher that the class put together a book of Profiles of Mathematicians.

Name of mathematician: _____

Years of mathematician's life: _____

Nationality of mathematician: _____

Major mathematical interests:

- _____
- _____
- _____

Major contributions to mathematics:

- _____
- _____
- _____

Publications: _____

_____

_____

Special recognition and awards: _____

_____

Other information: _____

_____

Name: _____

Topic: _____

Frames for Mathematical Essays

The Personal Essay—In a personal essay, you write about a topic or problem from a personal viewpoint. You frequently use the word "I" to express your own views and ideas. The Frame below is a simple outline for you to follow. Leave lots of space between the three sections. After you have completed the outline, go back to these three sections and add at least three important details to each section.

Select one of these starters or compose your own using a similar format.

There are three reasons why I

There are three ways that I

I obtained the following results by

I solved the problem using the following steps or procedures.

First,

In addition,

Then (or Finally or Last)

Write your own ending or conclusion. Refer to your opening statement.

Name: _____

Topic: _____

Frames for Mathematical Essays

The Persuasive Essay—In the persuasive essay, you have to convince others of an idea or procedure. Below are several persuasive starters. Select one of them. Then follow the transitions with three persuasive statements. Then go back to each persuasive sentence and add three or more sentences that support your persuasive idea. Finally, write your own concluding sentence.

Select one of these starters or compose your own using a similar format.

There are three reasons why we should (or have to)

We need to consider three ways

In order to solve _____, we must do the following.

We must understanding the following three concepts (in order to)

To achieve the correct results, we should

First, or Begin

After (or Second)

When you have (or Last, Then,)

Write your own conclusion. Refer to your opening statement.

Name: _____

Topic: _____

Frames for Mathematical Essays

The Explanatory Essay—In the explanatory essay, you have to write like a textbook writer. You normally do not use the words "I" or "we should," but this is not an absolute rule. Here are several explanatory starters you can use, or you can create your own. After you have written your three ways or steps, go back to each one and add supporting statements and details. Then write your own conclusion.

There are three (or several) reasons why

Here are three (or more) ways to

We can solve for x using the following steps.

To understand decimals, we need to know

A___ and a ____ are similar (different) in these ways.

To convert ____ to ____, follow these procedures.

First,

A second step or procedure

Complete the process (problem) by

Write your own conclusion.

Bibliography

Adams, D., & Hamm, M. (1998). *Collaborative inquiry in science, math, and technology.* Portsmouth, NH: Heinemann.

Ainsworth, L., & Christianson, J. (2004). *Five easy steps to a balanced math program.* Englewood, CO: Advanced Learning Centers.

Andrews, A. G. (2002). *Little kids—Powerful problem solvers: Math stories from a kindergarten classroom.* Portsmouth, NH: Heinemann.

Ayto, J. (1990). *Dictionary of word origins.* New York: Arcade.

Barker, P. L., et al. (1996). *Learning standards for mathematics, science, and technology* (Rev. ed.). Albany: New York State Education Department. (ERIC Document Reproduction Service No. ED401141)

Bass, H. (1993). *Measuring what counts: A conceptual guide for mathematics assessment.* Washington, DC: National Academy.

Berlitz, C. (1982). *Native tongues.* New York: Grosset & Dunlap.

Blanton, M. L., & Kaput. J. J. (2003). Developing elementary teachers' algebra eyes and ears. *Teaching Children Mathematics, 10*(2).

Bomer, R. (1995). *Time for meaning: Crafting literate lives in middle and high school.* Portsmouth, NH: Heinemann.

Bracey, G. W. (2000). The TIMSS final year: Study and report: A critique. *Educational Researcher, 29*(4), 4–10.

Braselton, S., & Decker, B. C. (1994). Using graphic organizers to improve the reading of mathematics. *Reading Teacher, 48*(3), 276–281.

Brewster, G., Fleron, J. F., Giuliano, F., Hoagland, B., & Rothermel, B. (2000). *Writing in mathematics. Westfield State College writer's guide.* Westfield, MA: Westfield State College. Retrieved April 7, 2006, from http://biology.wsc.ma.edu/wscwg/mathematics

Brumbaugh, L. (1994). *Scratch your brain where it itches B-1: Math games, tricks, and quick activities.* Pacific Grove, CA: Critical Thinking Books & Software.

Burns, M. (1992). *About teaching mathematics.* Sausalito, CA: Math Solutions.

Burns, M. (2004, October). Writing in math. *Educational Leadership, 62*(2), 30–38.

Caine, R. N., & Caine, G. (1991). *Teaching and the human brain.* Alexandria, VA: Association for Supervision and Curriculum Development.

Carpenter, T.C., Franke, M. L., & Levi, L. (2003). *Thinking mathematically: Integrating arithmetic and mathematics in elementary school.* Portsmouth, NH: Heinemann.

Carr, M., & Biddlecomb, B. D. (1998). Metacognition in mathematics. In D. J. Hacker, J. Dunlosky, & A. C. Graesser (Eds.), *Metacognition in educational theory and practice* (pp. 69–92). Mahwah, NJ: Lawrence Erlbaum Associates.

Carroll, L. (1965a). *Alice's adventures in wonderland.* New York: Random House.

Carroll, L. (1965b). *Through the looking glass.* New York: Random House.

Clawson, C. C. (1991). *Conquering math phobia.* New York: Wiley.

Clements, D. H. (1991). Enhancements of creativity in computer environments. *American Educational Research Journal, 28*(1), 173–187.

Cobb, P. (1994). Where is the mind? Constructivist and sociocultural perspectives on mathematical development. *Educational Researcher, 23*(7), 13–20.

Cobb, P., Wood, T., Yackel, E., & McNeal, B. (1992). Characteristics of classroom mathematics traditions: An interactional analysis. *American Educational Research Journal, 29*(3), 573–604.

Coffland, J. A., & Coffland, D. A. (1995). *Football math: Touchdown activities and projects for grades 4–8.* Glenview, IL: Scott Foresman.

Costa, A. L., & Kallick, B. (2000). *Habits of mind: Discovering and exploring.* Alexandria, VA: Association for Supervision and Curriculum Development.

Countryman, J. (1992). *Writing to learn mathematics.* Portsmouth, NH: Heinemann.

Crannell, A. (1994). *A guide to writing in mathematics classes.* Retrieved April 7, 2006, from http://server1.fandm.edu/departments/Mathematics/writing_in_math/guide.html

Crawford, D. B., & Snider, V. E. (2000). Effective mathematics instruction: The importance of curriculum. *Education and Treatment of Children, 23*(2), 122–142.

Crowe, R. (2000). *Strategies for success in mathematics.* Austin: Steck-Vaughn/Berrent.

Davenport, E. C., Jr., Davison, M. L., Kuang, H., Ding, S., Kim, S. & Kwak, N. (1998). High school mathematics course-taking by gender and ethnicity. *American Educational Research Journal, 35*(3), 497–514.

Davis, K. C. (1995). *Don't know much about history.* New York: Avon.

Davis, R. (2005). Cubit. *World Book Online Reference Center.* Retrieved October 12, 2005, from http://www.aolsvc.worldbook.aol.com/wb/Article?id=ar142960

Dial, M., & Baines, L. (1998). The language of words and numbers. In J. S. Simmons & L. Baines (Eds.), *Language study in middle school, high school, and beyond: Views on enhancing the study of language* (pp. 79–109). Newark, DE: International Reading Association.

Einstein, A. (1954). *Ideas and opinions.* New York: Bonanza.

Exemplars: Standards-Based Assessment and Instruction. (2004). *Revised NCTM-based math rubric.* Retrieved April 7, 2006, from www.exemplars.com/media/pdf/rubrics/nctm.pdf

Fairley, J. (1998). *Money talks.* New York: Wiley.

Fennema, E., & Carpenter, T. P. (1998). New perspectives on gender differences in mathematics: An introduction. *Educational Researcher, 27*(5), 4–5.

Fennema, E., Carpenter, T. P., Jacobs, V. R., Franke, M. L., & Levi, L. W. (1998). A longitudinal study of gender differences in young children's mathematical thinking. *Educational Researcher, 27*(5), 6–11.

Fennema, E., Franke, M. L., Carpenter, T. P., & Carey, D. A. (1993). Using children's mathematical knowledge in instruction. *American Educational Research Journal, 30*(3), 555–583.

Freeman, M., & Murphy, M. (1992). History, mathematics, and writing: An experience in which the whole is greater than the sum of its parts. *Mathematics and Computer Education, 26*(1), 15–20.

Fuchs, L. S., Fuchs, D., Hamlett, C. L., & Karns, K. (1998). High-achieving students' interactions and performance on complex mathematical tasks as a function of homogeneous and heterogeneous pairings. *American Educational Research Journal, 35*(2), 227–267.

Fuchs, L. S., Fuchs, D., Karns, K., Hamlett, C. L., & Katzaroff, M. (1999). Mathematics performance assessment in the classroom: Effects on teaching, planning, and student problem solving. *American Educational Research Journal, 36*(3), 609–646.

Funk, W. (1989). *Word origins and their romantic meanings.* New York: Grosset & Dunlap.

Gardner, H. (1983). *Frames of mind.* New York: Basic.

Gardner, H. (1993). *Multiple intelligences.* New York: Basic.

Gopen, G. D., & Smith, D. A. (1990). What's an assignment like you doing in a course like this? Writing to learn mathematics. *College Mathematics Journal, 21*(1), 2–19.

Harmon, M. E., Smith, T. A., Martin, M. O., Kelly, D. L., Beaton, A. E., Mullis, I. V. S., et al. (1997). *Performance assessment in IEA's Third International Mathematics and Science Study.* Boston, MA: Boston College, Center for the Study of Testing, Evaluation, and Educational Policy. Retrieved April 7, 2006, from http:// timss.bc.edu/timss1995i/PAreport.html

Harnadek, A. (1989). *Math mind benders book A-1: Deductive reasoning in mathematics.* Pacific Grove, CA: Critical Thinking Press and Software.

Hart, L. A. (1993). *Human brain and human learning.* Oak Creek, AZ: Books for Educators.

Hirsch, E. D., Jr. (1996). *The schools we need.* New York: Doubleday.

Hoffer, T. B. (1992). Middle school ability grouping and student achievement in science and mathematics. *Educational Evaluation and Policy Analysis, 14*(3), 205–227.

Jennison, C. (1995). *Baseball math: Grand slam activities and projects for grades 4–8.* Glenview, IL: Scott Foresman.

Jensen, E. (1998). *Teaching with the brain in mind.* Alexandria, VA: Association for Supervision and Curriculum Development.

Johnson, M. L. (1983). Writing in mathematics classes: A valuable tool for learning. *Mathematics Teacher, 76*(2), 117–119.

Juster, N. (1964). *The phantom tollbooth.* New York: Random House.

Kennedy, B. (1980, February). Writing letters to learn math. *Learning,* 59–61.

Kline, M. (1985). *Mathematics for the nonmathematician.* New York: Dover.

Laufer, G., Belsky, W., & Belsky, T. (1997). *Discovering the magic of math.* Sparta, IL: Prism Educational Services.

Locher, J. L. (1971). *The world of M. C. Escher.* New York: Harry N. Abrams.

Ma, X., & Willms, J. D. (1999). Dropping out of advanced mathematics: How much do students and schools contribute to the problem? *Educational Evaluation and Policy Analysis, 21*(4), 365–383.

Maple, S. A., & Stage, F. K. (1991). Influences of the choice of math/science major by gender and ethnicity. *American Educational Research Journal, 28*(1), 37–60.

Martin, H. (1996). *Integrating mathematics across the curriculum.* Thousand Oaks, CA: Corwin Press.

Marzano, R. J. (2004). *Building background knowledge for academic achievement.* Alexandria, VA: Association for Supervision and Curriculum Development.

Marzano, R. J., Pickering, D. J., & Pollock, J. (2001). *Classroom instruction that works.* Alexandria, VA: Association for Supervision and Curriculum Development.

Mathematical Sciences Education Board, National Research Council. (1989). *Everybody counts: A report to the nation on the future of mathematics education.* Washington, DC: National Academy Press.

McArthur, T. (Ed.). (1992). *The Oxford companion to the English language.* New York: Oxford University Press.

Meier, J., & Rishel, T. (1998). *Writing in the teaching and learning of mathematics.* MAA Notes Number 8. Washington, DC: Mathematical Association of America. (ERIC Document Reproduction Service No. ED421362)

Menninger, K. (1969). *Number words and number symbols: A cultural history of numbers.* Cambridge, MA: MIT Press.

Menninger, K. (1992). *Number words and number symbols: A cultural history of numbers.* New York: Dover.

Miller, L. D. (1991). Writing to learn mathematics. *Mathematics Teacher, 84*(7), 516–521.

Milne, A. A. (1956). *The house at Pooh Corner.* New York: Penguin Books.

Mokros, J. (1995). *Beyond arithmetic: Changing mathematics in the elementary classroom.* Palo Alto, CA: Dale Seymour.

Motz, L., & Weaver, J. H. (1991). *Conquering mathematics.* New York: Plenum.

National Center on Education and the Economy. (1995). *Performance standards: English, language arts, mathematics, science, applied learning.* Consultation draft (3 vols.) Washington, DC: Author.

National Council of Teachers of Mathematics. (2000). *Principles and standards for school mathematics* [Electronic version]. Reston, VA: Author. Retrieved April 7, 2006, from http://standards.nctm.org/

National Council of Teachers of Mathematics. (2004). *Standards and curriculum: A view from the nation.* Reston, VA: Author.

Office of Superintendent of Public Instruction. (2004). *K–12 grade level expectations: A new level of specificity.* Olympia, WA: Author.

Oregon State Department of Education. (n.d.). *Mathematics skill test knowledge and overview.* Retrieved April 7, 2006, from http://www.ode.state.or.us/teachlearn/subjects/mathematics/assessment/mathasmtoverview.pdf

Pappas, T. (1995). *The music of reason.* San Carlos, CA: Wide World.

Paulos, J. A. (1988). *Innumeracy: Mathematical illiteracy and its consequences.* New York: Hill and Wang.

Payne, K. J., & Biddle, B. J. (1999). Poor school funding, child poverty, and mathematics achievement. *Educational Researcher, 28*(6), 4–13.

Perkins, D. N. (1992). *Smart schools: From training memories to educating minds.* New York: Free Press.

Perkins, D. N., & Simmons, R. (1988). Patterns of misunderstanding: An integrative model for science, math, and programming. *Review of Educational Research, 58*(3), 303–326.

Piccirilli, R. (1996). *Write about math.* New York: Scholastic.

Pinker, S. (1994). *The language instinct: How the mind creates language.* New York: Perennial Classics.

Pinker, S. (2002). *Words and rules: The ingredients of language.* New York: Perennial Classics.

Potter, B. (1997). *The complete tales.* London: Frederick Warne.

Pugalee, D. K. (2001, May). Writing, mathematics, and metacognition: Looking for connections through students' work in mathematical problem solving. *School Science and Mathematics, 101*(5), 236–245.

Random House Webster's unabridged dictionary (2nd ed.). (2001). New York: Random House.

Reeves, D. R. (2002). *Reason to write.* New York: Kaplan Publishing.

Ring, R., Pape, S. J., & Tittle, C. K. (2000). *Student attitudes in a reformed mathematics classroom.* Paper presented at the annual meeting of the Association of Mathematics Teacher Educators, Charlotte, NC. (ERIC Document Reproduction Service No. ED437288)

Rishel, T. W. (1991). The geometric metaphor: Writing and mathematics in the classroom. *Primus, 1*(2), 113–128.

Rishel, T. W. (1993). *The well-tempered mathematics assignment.* Paper presented at the 44th Annual Meeting of the Conference on College Composition and Communication, San Diego, CA (March 31–April 3). (ERIC Document Reproduction Service No. ED359561)

Rizzo, J. A., et al. (1998). *Performance standards New York City—Mathematics.* New York: Board of Education of the City of New York.

Ronis, D. L. (1999). *Brain-compatible mathematics.* Thousand Oaks, CA: Corwin Press.

Rothstein, E., & Lauber, G. (2000). *Writing as learning.*Thousand Oaks, CA: Corwin Press.

Saltzman, J. (1993). *If you can talk, you can write.* New York: Warner.

Schmidt, W. H., & Prawat, R. S. (1999). What does the Third International Mathematics and Science Study tell us about where to draw the line in the top-down versus bottom-up debate? *Educational Evaluation and Policy Analysis, 21*(1), 85–91.

Scieszka, J., & Smith, L. (1995). *Math curse.* New York: Penguin.

Seife, C. (2000). *Zero.* New York: Penguin.

Skaalvik, E. M., & Rankin, R. J. (1995). A test of the internal/external frame of reference model at different levels of math and verbal self-perception. *American Educational Research Journal, 32*(1), 161–184.

Skuy, M., & Mentis, M. (1999). *Bridging learning in and out of the classroom.* Thousand Oaks, CA: Corwin Press.

Sousa, D. A. (1998). The ramifications of brain research. *School Administrator, 55*(1), 22–25.

Sowder, J. T. (1998). Perspectives from mathematics education. *Educational Researcher, 27*(5), 12–13.

Stahl, S. A., & Fairbanks, M. M. (1986). The effects of vocabulary instruction: A model-based meta-analysis. *Review of Educational Research, 561*(1), 72–110.

Stanish, B., & Eberle, B. (1997). *Be a problem-solver: A resource book for teaching creative problem-solving.* Waco, TX: Prufrock.

Stedman, L. C. (1997). International achievement differences: An assessment of a new perspective. *Educational Researcher, 26*(3), 4–15.

Stenmark, J. K. (1989). *Assessment alternatives in mathematics.* Berkeley: University of California, EQUALS.

Stodolsky, S. S., Salk, S., & Glaessner, B. (1991). Student views about learning math and social studies. *American Educational Research Journal, 28*(1), 89–116.

Strong, R. W., Silver, H. F., & Perini, M. J. (2001). *Teaching what matters most: Standards and strategies for raising student achievement.* Alexandria, VA: Association for Supervision and Curriculum Development.

Stuart, V. B. (2000). Math curse or math anxiety? *Teaching Children Mathematics, 6*(5), 330–335.

Strunk, W., Jr., & White, E. B. (2000). *The elements of style* (4th ed.). New York: Longman.

Tangretti, L., & Liptak, J. (1995). *Making the transition to everyday mathematics.* Chicago: University of Chicago School Mathematics Project.

Tomlinson, C. A. (1999). *The differentiated classroom: Responding to the needs of all learners.* Alexandria, VA: Association of Supervision and Curriculum Development.

University of Chicago School Mathematics Project. (2002). *Everyday mathematics* [Curriculum package]. New York: SRA/McGraw-Hill.

VanTassel-Baska, J. (1996). *Developing verbal talent.* New York: Allyn & Bacon.

Vernooy, S. (1997). *Solving word problems.* Eugene, OR: Garlic Press.

Wahl, M. (1997). *Math for humans: Teaching math through seven intelligences.* Langley, WA: LivnLern.

Wells, D. G. (1995). *You are a mathematician: A wise and witty introduction to the joy of numbers* (Rev. ed.). New York: Wiley.

Wells, D. G. (1997). *The Penguin dictionary of curious and interesting numbers.* New York: Penguin.

West Hartford Public Schools. (2000). *Mathematics curriculum and resource guide.* West Hartford, CT: Author.

Whiteford, T. (1998). Math for moms and dads. *Educational Leadership, 55*(8), 64–66.

Wurtz, E., & Malcolm, S. (1993). *Promises to keep: Creating high standards for American students.* Washington, DC: National Education Goals Panel, Technical Planning Group.

Zinsser, W. (1990). *On writing well.* New York: Harper & Row.

Index

**CORWIN
PRESS**

The Corwin Press logo—a raven striding across an open book—represents the union of courage and learning. Corwin Press is committed to improving education for all learners by publishing books and other professional development resources for those serving the field of PreK–12 education. By providing practical, hands-on materials, Corwin Press continues to carry out the promise of its motto: **"Helping Educators Do Their Work Better."**